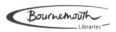

secrets of the red lantern

MURDOCH BOOKS

secrets of the red lantern

STORIES AND VIETNAMESE RECIPES FROM THE HEART

PAULINE NGUYEN

WITH RECIPES BY LUKE NGUYEN AND MARK JENSEN

ACKNOWLEDGEMENTS

I must first thank the team at Murdoch Books whose talent and dedication have made the journey of creating this beautiful book a truly rewarding and enjoyable one. To Kay Scarlett, Paul McNally, Emma Hutchinson, Sarah Odgers, Vivien Valk, Andrew de Sousa, Michelle Noerianto and Alan Benson, my gratitude to you is deep.

To the loyal diners and friends of the restaurant who keep us busy and make it fun. Thank you for appreciating the difference and coming back for it.

To team Red Lantern past and present, thank you for your tireless efforts and for making our lives easier.

To my friend Michelle Bakar, whose sage advice and unceasing encouragement have helped me to believe.

To my dearest brothers Luke, Lewis and Leroy, whose kindness and hilarity keep me laughing and make me strong. You are always there for me. I love you and am proud of all that you do.

To my best friend and sweetheart Mark Jensen, thank you for helping me to become a better person. You are my hero.

Finally to my parents who continue to surprise. This book would not have been possible without the generosity of your knowledge and experience. I am humbled by your humility.

Page 1: My brother Lewis (age 2) and me (age 3), Saigon, October 1976

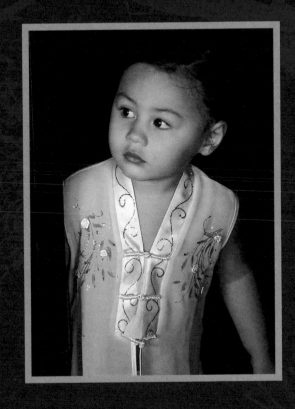

for Mia Angel,
who came to save me in
the nick of time

skin, bones
and the basics

In my family, food is our language. Food enables us to communicate the things we find so hard to say.

We escaped Vietnam not long after the fruitless war and spent a difficult year in a Thai refugee camp before arriving in Australia in the late seventies. My brothers and I grew up in Cabramatta during the bleakest of times. Ruled over by our strict, food-obsessed parents, we ran a busy Vietnamese restaurant on the main street called Pho Cay Du — this is where a significant part of our lives unfolded. Both formally trained chefs, my parents were never relaxed about showing tenderness and understanding with us as children. Whether it was out of disinterest or necessity, they were workaholics who instead poured their knowledge and affection into the food they cooked to feed their children. A strange way to show parental love, but I have grown to accept that this was perhaps the only way they knew how.

A dish of bitter melon soup is a dish of reconciliation. When we quarrel, we cannot speak the words 'I am sorry' — we give this bittersweet soup instead. In another instance, the sharing of a particular meal can offer the sentiment we each crave to hear: 'It's good to see you again — I've missed you'. On rare occasions, too few to forget, I have understood the longed for words, 'Please forgive me'.

I should have known that I was always meant to work with food. After some lacklustre years chasing distant success within a career in film production, I found myself returning to the restaurant life — the life I grew up with, the life I know so well. Along with my brother Luke

Previous page: My maternal grandparents, Lam Sanh Ha and Thi Nguyen Tran, Saigon, 1950. Clockwise from top left: My mother, Cuc Phuong Nguyen, and father, Lap Nguyen, in 1972; my mother's family, she is standing tall in the centre, my grandparents are behind her to the right, first day of spring, 1968.

and my partner Mark, the father of my child, we run Red Lantern, a busy Vietnamese restaurant on the main food strip of Surry Hills, in Sydney.

Many have asked, 'What is Vietnamese food? How is it different to other cuisines?' The first thing I always say is that Vietnamese food is easy — there is no mystery to it. It is simple to prepare, the execution is mostly quick and the cooking methods are straightforward. Another distinction is that ovens don't exist in Vietnam; we prefer to watch our food being cooked — deep fried, steamed, slow braised, chargrilled, barbecued or tossed in a flaming wok. The only oven my family ever utilized was a miniature rotating 'Tiffany' complete with glass-casing, bought second-hand at the local St Vincent de Paul's in Bonnyrigg. We often placed it in the centre of the dinner table so that while eating we could watch the meat brown, the skin crackle and the juices drip. On many occasions, it also served as a distraction to prevent the possibility of any serious conversation arising at dinner.

What most distinguishes Vietnamese food, however, is its emphasis on freshness. We do not use fresh herbs sparingly to flavour or garnish a dish — instead, they play a major role in the food. The herb selection varies according to the meal and there are as many as a dozen commonly-used varieties. Wrapping savoury dishes at the table in lettuce or rice paper with an abundance of the freshest uncooked herbs is very much the signature of Vietnamese cuisine. Several bunches can be consumed during the course of the meal. This combines the raw with the cooked, the cold with the hot and the soft with the crisp. The Vietnamese have a distinct preoccupation with crunch and contrast. Flavours and textures juxtapose for dramatic effect. In Vietnamese cuisine, balance is always at play.

There are a handful of ingredients that are typically Vietnamese. The must haves include spring onion (scallion) oil, crisp-fried onion and garlic, roasted rice powder, crushed peanuts and pickled vegetables. Exciting things can happen with the most simple of produce. But, of course, you can't cook Vietnamese cuisine without understanding the significance of *nuoc mam cham*. It is our condiment of choice. *Nuoc mam* means 'fish sauce', while *cham* means 'to dip'. In its purest form *nuoc mam* is the liquid extraction of fermented anchovies and salt. Like fine wine, the most robust flavour and aroma is in the first pressing — later bottled as the most expensive type. Like fine olive oil, *nuoc mam* can be used in various grades to marinate, season or dress. When used correctly, its sophistication lies in the ability to enhance natural flavours rather than overwhelm. *Nuoc mam cham* is a vital ingredient in salads, wraps, soups and stir-fries — it is the heart of Vietnamese cooking.

Vietnamese food is not overpoweringly hot, the spicing is subtle in the marinades and fresh chilli

My mother (right) with my Uncle Five and grandfather, Saigon, 1957.

From left: My paternal grandfather, Toan Nguyen (age 30), in 1955; my mother (left) with Aunty Eight and Aunty Nine, 1950.

is added at the table, allowing each person to increase the heat as desired. My father prefers plenty of chilli, really only enjoying his meal when the roof of his mouth is burning and sweat is dripping from his brow. The rest of the family prefer a little less fire — appreciating food that knows how to lower its voice.

Because Vietnam is surrounded by bountiful seas and saturated by the Red River Delta in the North and the Mekong Delta in the South, seafood, rice, fresh fruit and vegetables are plentiful and an integral part of the Vietnamese diet. Quality meat, however, is scarce and expensive. Since the mid-nineties, expatriates have taken cases of frozen beef, lamb, pork and goat back to their families. Australian beef in particular is considered a delicacy. Typically in Vietnam, meat dishes are therefore pronounced in flavour so that more rice, fresh herbs and vegetables are consumed. This makes Vietnamese food ideal for the health conscious. The idea is to retain the integrity of the ingredients — raw food is energizing. The combinations that are created aim to retain as much flavour and texture as possible. In Vietnamese cuisine, the physiological and healing effects on the body and soul are always kept in mind.

Goat is a favourite meat in my family. Traditionally my father would use the rib cut of the goat for his famous *ca ri de*. The rib cut retains a large proportion of skin and bone with the meat. Like so many peasant cultures, the 'use everything, waste nothing' approach began as a necessity, later becoming a delicacy. Meat simply tastes better close to the bone and eating good skin done well is such a treat. Sucking on bone and crunching on cartilage is a sensual experience I like to savour.

At my parent's restaurants Pho Cay Du and later Café Cay Du, customers often ordered *ca ri de* for breakfast, with crusty Vietnamese bread and a small dish of chilli salt and fresh lemon to dip the goat pieces into. It is a continuously popular dish. Today, there is a regular customer at Red Lantern who requests that we freeze several portions for her to fly home to her family in Melbourne. At Red Lantern, we changed this recipe after a time to suit a more Western palate. We now use the whole goat, which has more meat, less skin and comparatively fewer bones. My mother still has a difficult time coming to terms with this concept. I love to eat *ca ri de* with a simple serve of jasmine rice or vermicelli, with bean sprouts and fresh herbs for added coolness and crunch. The distinct perfume of rice paddy herb is surprisingly complementary and a little cheeky indeed.

When I think about my father's *ca ri de*, it is inevitable that I am reminded of Thomas and three of the most embarrassing moments of my life. Thomas was an untouchable. I knew little about him, except that he always looked good and didn't move very much. Often expressionless without a hair out of place, he worked at *Loose Threads*, the coolest joint in Cabramatta at the time, selling the latest in street fashion. As an awkward, perpetually frustrated teenager, I fancied Thomas like no other guy.

Every day after school, it was my job to pick up half a goat for my father's curry. My mother would always insist that I use her painfully impractical and superbly indiscreet shopping trolley. Not only was it fluorescent orange, it was also too small to conceal the goat carcass. To top it off, its broken wheel squeaked conspicuously to alert Thomas and his mates of my approach. Every day I had to pass the boy of my dreams wearing my tentlike private girls' school uniform and pushing a malfunctioning orange contraption on wheels with a hairy goat leg sticking out of it. Sure, I could have taken Railway Parade, turned left at Hughes Street, left again at Park Street through Freedom Plaza and back onto John Street, but with the busted wheel and the extra load, it would have taken three times as long and a firm backhand from my father would have ensued.

Back at the restaurant, my father would wait impatiently with his blowtorch at the ready to scorch the dead goat's skin. This idea first came about as a convenient way to remove all traces of hair from the animal. He later discovered that this process actually allowed the skin to maintain a firm, almost crispy texture even when the meat is cooked to tender. It also meant having to wheel the freshly charred creature back past *Loose Threads* so the butcher could then saw the carcass into bite-sized pieces. Other restaurants in Cabramatta quickly adopted my father's ingenious idea. So much so, that most butchers in Cabramatta these days scorch the skin upon request. Sometimes my brother Luke took his turn behind the dreaded goat trolley. He would not have been ten years old at the time. Luke's pint-size allowed the locals freedom to liberally deliver their jeers, 'Your dad got dog on the menu again mate?', 'Fido not good enough for your old man anymore?'

My embarrassment wasn't helped by Thomas' mates' inability to hide their hysteria each time I drove past in our ghastly Toyota Tarago — seemingly every Vietnamese family's vehicle of choice at the time. On this particular day, I was lucky enough to have the Tarago break down again, which meant I could catch a bus home via Thomas' supercool store. The moment is noted in my journal two days before my birthday in 1988. I was feeling pretty confident and proud of myself that day, as we had beaten Our Lady of Rosary in debating at school. After helping my father skim both pork and chicken stocks at Pho Cay Du, I ventured home, stopping only to fix my hair for half an hour before popping into *Loose Threads* for a little 'browsing'.

I packed myself *buon xuon tom* for dinner that night — a delicious dish of vermicelli noodles with juicy clusters of prawn paste in a clear broth slightly tinged yellow with annatto seeds. Less than five minutes after entering Thomas' store, I felt a warm sensation leak out of my school backpack, trickle down my grey, ribbed stockings and onto his shiny white floor. I should have just looked him in the eye and said 'sorry mate', but the stress of the moment caused me to crack an absurd half-smile as I ever so elegantly shuffled cross-legged out the front door — leaving behind a trail of warm, yellow liquid dripping from between my legs. I was so mortified I could hardly breathe. This had to be the least funny thing that had ever happened to me. But then I'm reminded of the time my youngest brother Leroy caught a respiratory tract infection at preschool.

My father demanded that I take Leroy to the doctor once I had completed my chores. First up though, he wanted me to season two new woks he had just bought and my mother needed some onions, ginger and cuttlefish chargrilled for her stock. I could perform all tasks at the same time. I especially enjoy grilling dried cuttlefish; the earthy pungency makes my mouth water every time. The smoke would permeate my school uniform — a smell I secretly devoured at school by constantly sniffing at my sleeves. Somehow, I always managed to burn my hair at the woks — I was never sure if it was because I kept the flame up too high or if it was due to the chemical reaction from all the hairspray used to keep my eighties opera-house fringe upright. Once I had completed my chores, I took Leroy to the doctor and should have known better than to take the fastest route past *Loose Threads*. My poor sick baby brother suddenly lost control and projectile vomited onto Thomas' shiny shopfront window. The horrific coincidence catapulted me into doing the only thing I could — scoop up Leroy mid vomit and run.

As with many moments in my life, I can see the reason for feeling shame back then, but what is hard to see is why I should still feel shame now. ∎

Left: Luke in the early days at Red Lantern nursing his almost completed stock, 2002.
Above: Luke and my father in search of the freshest ingredients in Cabramatta.

CÀ RI DÊ

goat curry

CURRY PASTE
6 cm (2½ in) piece of galangal
3 cm (1¼ in) piece of turmeric
5 cm (2 in) piece of lemon grass,
    white part only
1 onion, chopped
4 coriander (cilantro) roots, skinned
4 garlic cloves
5 dried small red chillies, soaked
    in water
2 tablespoons coriander seeds
1 tablespoon cumin seeds
1 cinnamon stick
2 teaspoons black peppercorns
4 teaspoons salt

2 kg (4 lb 8 oz) goat meat, with skin
    and bone, cut into 4 x 2 cm
    (1½ x ¾ in) pieces
1 tablespoon galangal powder
1½ tablespoons sugar
1 tablespoon olive oil
1 teaspoon butter
10 fresh curry leaves
2 tablespoons plain yoghurt
250 ml (9 fl oz/1 cup) chicken stock
250 ml (9 fl oz/1 cup) milk
540 ml (19 fl oz) tin coconut cream
1 bunch rice paddy herb

Cut the galangal, turmeric and lemon grass into 1 cm (½ in) pieces. In a wok, fry the onion, galangal, turmeric, lemon grass, coriander and garlic until softened, well browned and aromatic. You may need to add some water to stop the ingredients browning too much. Remove from the wok and allow to cool. Add the soaked chilli and pound into a paste in a mortar.

Wet the coriander and cumin seeds, cinnamon and peppercorns slightly with water. Add to a dry wok and fry until well browned and fragrant. Transfer to a spice grinder, add 1 teaspoon salt and grind to a fine powder. Add the powder to the wet paste and mix well. Set aside until ready to use.

Add the goat pieces to a large saucepan with the galangal powder, 1 teaspoon each of the salt and sugar, and cover with water. Bring to the boil over high heat, skimming the surface as the temperature rises. Once boiled, reduce the heat and cover with a lid and cook at a low simmer for 45 minutes. Strain and set the meat aside.

Add the oil and butter to a saucepan and gently fry the curry paste and curry leaves until fragrant, then stir in the yoghurt. Add the meat to the pan and add the stock, milk, coconut cream and the remaining salt and sugar. Bring to the boil, then reduce to a very low simmer and cook for 40–45 minutes, or until the goat is very tender. Serve with rice paddy herb and jasmine rice or baguette.

SERVES 8

22

MARK JENSEN: *The firm texture in the* bi cuon *rolls is due to the pork skin in the* bi *mixture. Pork skin can be bought at any Asian supermarket. It can be found pre-cooked and already cut into strips in the refrigerated section.*

BÌ CUỐN

soft rice paper rolls with pork loin and scented with roasted rice powder

PORK MARINADE
1 tablespoon caster (superfine) sugar
1 tablespoon fish sauce
1 teaspoon salt
1 teaspoon fine white pepper

250 g (9 oz) pork loin
1 tablespoon vegetable oil
150 g (5½ oz) pork skin (da heo),
   cut into thin strips
1 teaspoon salt
2 garlic cloves, pounded

1 teaspoon sugar
2 teaspoons fried garlic (page 39)
1½ teaspoons garlic oil (page 39)
2 tablespoons roasted rice powder
   (page 37)
18 sheets of 22 cm (8½ in) rice paper
80 g (2¾ oz/1 cup firmly packed)
   shredded iceberg lettuce
1 bunch perilla leaf
1 bunch mint
dipping fish sauce (page 33), to serve

Combine all the marinade ingredients in a bowl and mix well to dissolve the sugar. Brush the pork loin with the marinade and leave to stand for 30 minutes. In a wok or frying pan heat the oil and seal the pork well on all sides, add the marinade to the pan and enough water to just cover the pork. Bring to the boil, then reduce the heat to a simmer and cook until the water has evaporated, turning the meat once or twice during cooking. Increase the heat and caramelize the pork on all sides, remove from the pan and allow to cool.

Cut the pork along the grain of the meat into matchstick-sized pieces and mix with the pork skin, salt, garlic, sugar, fried garlic, garlic oil and rice powder.

Roll the pork mixture tightly in rice paper with the lettuce, perilla leaves and mint, following the method for *goi cuon* (page 27). Serve with dipping fish sauce.

SERVES 6

GỎI ĐU ĐỦ

green papaya salad with prawns and pork

180 g (6 oz/2 cups) peeled and finely
   sliced green papaya
60 g (2¼ oz) cooked pork neck,
   finely sliced
10 perilla leaves, finely sliced
10 mint leaves, finely sliced
10 Vietnamese mint leaves, finely sliced
8 cooked king prawns (shrimp), peeled
   and sliced lengthways

3 tablespoons dipping fish sauce
   (page 33), plus extra to taste
2 tablespoons fried red Asian shallots
   (page 38)
1 tablespoon roasted peanuts (page 38)
1 bird's eye chilli, chopped

In a large bowl combine the green papaya, pork and sliced herbs and mix well.
Turn out onto a serving platter and arrange the prawns on top of the salad.
Drizzle with the dipping fish sauce to taste, and garnish with the fried shallots,
peanuts and chilli.

SERVES 2

MARK JENSEN: *When ordering rice paper rolls in a restaurant, it is customary to observe and appreciate (or not) the technique used — it needs to be rolled tight and the flavours should be well balanced. Too much vermicelli will cause the rice paper to burst, too many herbs may overwhelm accompanying ingredients and too much lettuce may appear ungenerous. Rice paper rolls are finger food and should not droop when held at one end. The filling should remain intact after each bite.*

GỎI CUỐN
soft rice paper rolls with prawns and pork

80 g (2³/4 oz) dried rice vermicelli
18 sheets of 22 cm (8¹/2 in) rice paper
18 cooked small prawns (shrimp),
   peeled and sliced in half
120 g (4¹/4 oz) cooked pork neck,
   finely sliced

80 g (2³/4 oz/1 cup firmly packed)
   shredded iceberg lettuce
1 bunch perilla
1 bunch mint
1 bunch garlic chives
hoisin dipping sauce (page 32), to serve

Add the noodles to boiling water and bring back to the boil. Cook for 5 minutes. Turn off the heat and allow the noodles to stand in the water for a further 5 minutes. Strain and rinse under cold water, then leave to dry. For this recipe, it is best to have the vermicelli cooked and strained for at least 30 minutes prior to rolling. This allows the noodles to dry off a little and stick together.

To assemble the rolls, cut 6 sheets of rice paper in half. Fill a large bowl with warm water and dip 1 whole sheet of rice paper in the water until it softens then lay it flat on a plate. Dip a half sheet of rice paper in the water and lay it vertically in the middle of the round sheet. This will strengthen the roll, preventing the filling breaking through. In the middle of the rice paper, place 3 pieces of prawn in a horizontal line approximately 4 cm (1¹/2 in) from the top. Below the prawns add some pork, lettuce, perilla leaves, mint and vermicelli.

To form the *goi cuon*, first fold the sides into the centre over the filling, then the bottom of the paper up and over. Roll from bottom to top to form a tight roll, and just before you complete the roll add 2 pieces of garlic chives so that they stick out at one end. Serve 2 rolls per person with hoisin dipping sauce.

SERVES 6

GỎI GÀ

master stock chicken, shredded cabbage and vietnamese mint salad

1/2 master stock chicken (chicken that has been cooked in the master stock, page 35) or 1/2 bought barbecued chicken
150 g (5 1/2 oz/2 cups) finely sliced white cabbage
12 finely sliced white onion rings
10 perilla leaves
10 mint leaves
1 handful Vietnamese mint leaves
1/2 teaspoon roasted rice powder (page 37)

1 teaspoon fried garlic (page 39)
2 teaspoons garlic oil (page 39)
3–4 tablespoons dipping fish sauce (page 33)
1 tablespoon roasted peanuts (page 38)
1 tablespoon fried red Asian shallots (page 38)
1 red bird's eye chilli, chopped

Remove the skin from the chicken and shred the meat. Mix all of the ingredients except the dipping fish sauce, peanuts, shallots and chilli in a bowl and turn out onto a serving platter. Dress the salad with the dipping fish sauce and garnish with the roasted peanuts, fried shallots and chilli.

SERVES 2

MARK JENSEN: Chao ga *is such a versatile delight. It is eaten mostly for breakfast with a side dish of* trung chien thit bam *(pork and salted radish omelette) or* thit kho trung *(caramelized pork with egg, chilli and black pepper). On its own, it can be consumed to help recover from a stomach upset or the common cold — in this latter instance, a fair amount of ginger can be added to help clear the sinuses and boost the immune system. Pork, fish or beef can be substituted for the chicken, or you can just eat it on its own. If you prefer a more typical rice soup, which is thicker and whiter, do not fry the rice grains before adding water and cook for approximately 1¹/₂ hours. The Chinese have a similar version called* congee.

This recipe calls for the rice to be dry-fried before stock is added — this releases the aromas from the grains. The result is a fragrant soup with rice that has not yet coagulated to a thicker mass. This style of soup is great with goi ga *(opposite) — combining the hot with the cold and the soft with the crisp.*

CHÁO GÀ
chicken rice soup

¹/₂ small onion, sliced
1 tablespoon fish sauce
2 teaspoons sugar
1 teaspoon salt
1 teaspoon cracked black pepper
1 whole chicken (1.8 kg/4 lb)

100 g (3¹/₂ oz/¹/₂ cup) long-grain rice
1 tablespoon sliced spring onions
  (scallions)
1 tablespoon sliced coriander
  (cilantro) leaves

In a large saucepan add 2.5 litres (87 fl oz/10 cups) water, the onion, fish sauce, sugar, salt and pepper. Bring to the boil, then add the chicken, return to a fast simmer for 5 minutes, skimming the impurities from the surface. Cover the saucepan with a lid, turn off the heat and allow to stand for 45 minutes. Remove the chicken and plunge into iced water for 10 minutes, reserving the stock. Put the chicken in a colander and allow to drain. Then, shred the chicken into bite-sized pieces and set aside.

In a clean saucepan, fry the rice over low heat until fragrant but not brown. Add the prepared chicken stock and bring it to the boil. Reduce the heat to a simmer and cook the rice, stirring regularly, for 25–30 minutes. Fold the shredded chicken through the *chao* and pour into a serving bowl. Garnish with the sliced spring onions and coriander.

SERVES 8

29

GỎI MỰC

squid salad with pickled vegetables and fresh herbs

200 g (7 oz) cleaned squid (legs cut
    into individual pieces)
200 g (7 oz) pickled vegetables
    (page 34)
50 g (1³/4 oz) bean sprouts
1 handful mixed herbs (perilla, mint,
    Vietnamese mint)
1 tablespoon chopped lemon grass,
    white part only
1 teaspoon fried garlic (page 39)

2 teaspoons garlic oil (page 39)
2 teaspoons roasted rice powder
    (page 37)
3 tablespoons dipping fish sauce
    (page 33)
1 tablespoon roasted peanuts (page 38)
1 tablespoon fried red Asian shallots
    (page 38)
1 bird's eye chilli, chopped

Lay the cleaned squid on a cutting board, insert your knife into the top edge of the body and run the knife down to the bottom of the squid. Fold it open as you would a book.

Working from the top-right of the squid to the bottom-left, score diagonal slices in the flesh, making sure not to penetrate through. Turn the squid 180 degrees and repeat the diagonal slicing so you now have a crisscross pattern. Cut the squid in half from top to bottom, turn it horizontally and then slice through to make 1 cm (¹/2 in) wide pieces.

To cook the squid, place in boiling water for 30 seconds, then refresh in iced water and reserve for the salad. To make the salad, combine all of the ingredients except the dipping fish sauce, peanuts, shallots and chilli in a bowl and turn out onto a serving platter. Dress the salad with the dipping fish sauce and garnish with the roasted peanuts, fried shallots and chilli.

SERVES 2

30

LUKE NGUYEN: *I have seen a lot of different versions of this hoisin dipping sauce. Many dilute it with water or add cornflour (cornstarch) for thickening. I have also seen peanut butter added to it. This recipe was created by my genius little brother, Leroy. He and mum were messing about with ingredients in the kitchen one day and he had a moment of inspiration to add milk. We now use this recipe at Red Lantern as the dipping sauce for* goi cuon *(page 27).*

NƯỚC TƯƠNG NGỌT
hoisin dipping sauce

125 ml (4 fl oz/1/2 cup) hoisin sauce
1 1/2 tablespoons rice vinegar
125 ml (4 fl oz/1/2 cup) milk

3 teaspoons roasted peanuts (page 38)
1 red bird's eye chilli

In a saucepan combine the hoisin sauce and the rice vinegar, put over medium heat and stir through the milk. Continue to stir just before boiling point is reached, then allow to cool. To serve, chop the roasted peanuts and finely slice the chilli to garnish the sauce.

This dipping sauce will last for up to 1 week stored in the fridge.

MAKES ENOUGH SAUCE FOR 24 GOI CUON

LUKE NGUYEN: *Fish sauce is rated the number one cooking ingredient in Vietnamese cooking. Growing up, when I was sent to the markets by my elders to buy fish sauce, it always had to be the best brand. Mum insisted that the '3 Crab' brand was the finest. Its clear, amber-coloured liquid was by far the most superior. There is always a bottle on our dining table — it never lives in the pantry.*

Eaten with white rice, fish sauce is often poured straight from the bottle and into a small bowl with some chopped fresh chillies. That's it! Rice, fish sauce and chilli — a meal on its own, really.

I have always judged the quality of a Vietnamese cook by their dipping sauce. Each family and restaurant creates its own version. Some like it sweet, salty or tangy. I prefer mine to be a balance of all three of these characteristics.

This nuoc mam cham recipe belongs to my mother. We have used this recipe for as long as I can remember. It can be used as a dipping sauce, in dressings and even in marinades.

NƯỚC MẮM CHẤM
dipping fish sauce

3 tablespoons fish sauce
3 tablespoons rice vinegar
2 tablespoons sugar

2 garlic cloves
1 bird's eye chilli
2 tablespoons lime juice

Combine the fish sauce, rice vinegar, 125 ml (4 fl oz/½ cup) water and sugar in a saucepan and place over medium heat. Stir well and cook until just before boiling point is reached, then allow to cool. To serve, finely chop the garlic and chilli and stir through with the lime juice. To liven it up, add pickled vegetables (page 34).

MAKES 250 ML (9 FL OZ/1 CUP)

ĐỒ CHUA
pickled vegetables

625 ml (21¹/₂ fl oz/2¹/₂ cups)
   rice vinegar
440 g (15¹/₂ oz/2 cups) sugar
1 tablespoon salt
2 Lebanese (short) cucumbers

1 carrot
1 small daikon
1 celery stalk
¹/₂ lemon, cut into thin wedges

In a saucepan combine the rice vinegar, sugar and salt, stir well and bring to the boil. Remove from the heat and allow to cool.

Cut the cucumbers in half lengthways and remove the seeds with a spoon. Cut the cucumber, carrot, daikon and celery into 5 cm x 5 mm (2 x ¹/₄ in) batons.

Combine the lemon wedges with the vegetables and place in a 1 litre (35 fl oz/4 cup) plastic or glass container. Pour the cooled pickling liquid over the vegetables to completely submerge them. Cover with a lid and pickle for 3 days before use.

MAKES ENOUGH FOR 2 SALADS

LUKE NGUYEN: *The master stock is a stock that has been kept alive for a great length of time — the master stock at the Red Lantern is now ten years old and was originally passed down to me by my father. In Vietnamese cooking it is used as a liquid for poaching or braising meat and seafood. The master stock is not to be confused with basic stocks, which are often eaten as a broth or in soups with chicken, pork, beef or fish. Every morning at Red Lantern, the master stock pot is topped up with water and is brought to the boil twice a day. The seasonings are adjusted and the essential herbs and spices are changed regularly. This keeps the stock healthy and the flavours are given depth.*

SÚP CHÁNH
master stock

250 ml (9 fl oz/1 cup) light soy sauce
3 tablespoons dark soy sauce
2 tablespoons salt

4 cinnamon sticks
6 star anise
6 cardamon pods

In a large saucepan combine 6 litres (210 fl oz/24 cups) water, both soy sauces and salt, then place over high heat and bring to the boil. Tie the cinnamon, star anise and cardamom pods in muslin (cheesecloth), then add to the pan. Slowly simmer for 30 minutes to infuse the flavour, then turn off the heat and allow too cool. If not using immediately, the stock can be stored in the fridge for 3 days or frozen until required.

This is how you would use the master stock to cook one whole chicken (1.6 kg/3 lb 8 oz) for use in *goi ga* (page 28) or *ga chien don* (page 303).

To use the stock, bring to a fast boil, then add your chicken, return to the boil, then turn off the heat. The chicken will be cooked in about 45 minutes or once the stock returns to room temperature. Remove the chicken and reserve for use. To maintain the stock, add 1 tablespoon of salt and return to the boil. Skim off the fat and impurities from the surface, strain into another pan and allow to cool, then store as mentioned above.

Each time you use your stock you will need to adjust the water level and seasonings. Top up with water to the 6 litre (210 fl oz) mark, add 1 tablespoon of dark soy sauce and 2 tablespoons of light soy sauce and replace the aromatics about every third use. It is good practice to always taste your stock, this way you will understand if the seasoning and aromatics need adjusting.

MAKES 6 LITRES (210 FL OZ/24 CUPS)

MARK JENSEN: *Stocks in Vietnamese cooking are simple and concise. Essentially, they consist of just the basic meat and water. Different vegetables and aromatics are added to create the desired effect. The strong flavour of grilled dried squid and fish sauce, for example, are added to make the soup for* mi sui cao *(prawn and pork dumplings in pork broth with egg noodles). Chargrilled ginger and star anise are key ingredients for* pho *(page 210).*

The making of basic stocks is the only part of Vietnamese cooking that requires any long period at the stove. Chicken, pork, beef, fish or vegetable stock need some baby-sitting but it is worth it, especially if you were to cook a big batch and freeze it into smaller portions. It takes but a few minutes to defrost a little stock to use instead of water. The difference in flavour is as clear as day. The process of caring for the stock, checking up on it and skimming it of impurities can be a nurturing and meditative experience.

NƯỚC LÈO GÀ
chicken stock

6 garlic cloves
8 spring onions (scallions), white
  part only

1 whole chicken (about 1.6 kg/3 lb 8 oz)
4 cm (1¹/2 in) piece of ginger, sliced

Crush the garlic and spring onions into a paste in a mortar. Wash the chicken thoroughly under cold running water, making sure to remove all traces of blood, guts and fat from the cavity. Place the chicken in a large saucepan with 6 litres (210 fl oz/24 cups) water and bring to the boil. Reduce the heat of the stock to a slow simmer and skim the surface. Continue to skim for 10 minutes until you have removed most of the fat, then add the ginger, garlic and spring onions. Cook for a further 2 hours, then strain and allow the stock to cool. Refrigerate for up to 3 days or freeze until required.

MAKES 5 LITRES (175 FL OZ/20 CUPS)

THÍNH

roasted rice powder

200 g (7 oz/1 cup) jasmine rice

In a dry wok stir-fry the rice over medium heat until it is toasted a soft brown colour. Allow to cool and place in a mortar and pound to a fine powder. This powder will keep indefinitely in an airtight container.

MAKES 200 G (7 OZ/1 CUP)

MỠ HÀNH

spring onion oil

250 ml (9 fl oz/1 cup) vegetable oil
6–8 spring onions (scallions), green
 part only, finely sliced

Put the oil and the spring onions in a saucepan over medium heat. Cook the spring onions until they just start to simmer in the oil, remove from the heat and allow to cool. The spring onion oil will keep for up to 1 week in a covered container in the fridge.

MAKES 250 ML (9 FL OZ/1 CUP)

ĐẬU PHỘNG RANG
roasted peanuts

250 g (9 oz) raw shelled peanuts

In a dry wok, stir-fry the peanuts over a medium heat until the peanuts are cooked to a soft brown colour. Crush the peanuts in a mortar until coarsely ground.
The roasted nuts will keep in an airtight container for up to 2 weeks.

HÀNH PHI
fried red asian shallots

200 g (7 oz) red Asian shallots
1 litre (35 fl oz/4 cups) vegetable oil

Finely slice the shallots and wash under cold water. Dry the shallots with a cloth, then set them aside on some paper towel until they are completely dry.
Put the oil in a wok and heat to 180°C (350°F), or until a cube of bread dropped in the oil browns in 15 seconds. Fry the shallots in small batches until they turn golden brown, then remove with a slotted spoon to paper towel.
The fried shallots are best eaten freshly fried, but will keep for up to 2 days in an airtight container.

TỎI PHI VÀ MỠ TỎI
fried garlic and garlic oil

250 ml (9 fl oz/1 cup) vegetable oil
6 garlic cloves, finely chopped

Put the oil in a wok and heat to 180°C (350°F), or until a cube of bread dropped in the oil browns in 15 seconds. Add the garlic to the oil and fry until it is a golden colour, strain through a metal sieve and then place it on a paper towel to dry. Be careful not to overcook the garlic in the oil, as it continues to cook once it is removed. Reserve the garlic oil to add to salads.

Store the fried garlic in an airtight container for up to 4 days. The garlic oil will last for up to 2 weeks if stored in a cool place.

my mother
and her mother

Fruit and vegetables have been the livelihood of my mother's family for generations.

Dua 23 Choi Cau Ong Lanh (market stall number 23 near Mr Lanh's Bridge) is where my brother Lewis and I were born — the same place my mother and her siblings were born. For as long as anyone can remember, *Choi Cau Ong Lanh* stood as the largest fruit and vegetable market in Saigon. The family business survived there for over fifty years before tragically burning to the ground in 1999. It is unfortunate that the source of the fire came from number 54; the stall belonging to my father's family — the blaze was rumoured to be the consequence of some electrical thievery. Today, both sides of the family still sell fruit and vegetables, though at different markets. Aunty Nine also runs a busy street stand selling handmade noodles and sweets. Aunty Eight, a notoriously masculine woman who has never worn a dress or used female toilets, has a wholesale business selling fresh corn.

My parent's fastidious obsession with all things fresh started back in Vietnam, a long time before they discovered cooking. With two family businesses in Saigon dependent on fresh product for their success, they were obsessed because they had to be. When the restaurant in Cabramatta grew hectic, my mother sent us kids out to buy emergency supplies. I lost count of the amount of times we returned to proudly present our mother with the fresh produce bought, only to be berated by a click of the tongue and a shake of the head, 'Where on earth did you buy this?' With our reply, she would march back to the vendor shooting them a piece of her mind, 'How dare you sell this crap to my children!'

Previous page: My maternal grandmother with my Aunty Two and Uncle Five, Saigon, 1950.
Left: My grandmother (left) with her neighbour going to a wedding, Saigon, 1964.

On her return, she would proudly present the replacement goods to my father who would click his tongue and shake his head and off my mother marched to replace her replacements.

We arrived in Australia as immigrants on 7 July, 1978. Vietnamese food was completely unknown at the time. During those early years, we frequently journeyed to Chinatown for our fix of roast duck, chicken feet and crackling pork. Asian rice and sauces were readily available at the time, but the essential fresh herbs that we love so much were nowhere to be found. Wanting a taste of home, my parents decided to try their hand at growing Vietnamese herbs and vegetables in our yard. It only took a short time before their attempts proved successful — coriander grew in abundance, as did Vietnamese mint, perilla leaf, spring onions (scallions), elephant ear stems and lemon grass. Fish mint and pennywort sprawled across the ground like a carpet of weed. In the backyard, a giant banana tree bore plentiful small, sticky bananas that were perfect for creating our favourite Asian desserts. A guava tree also thrived, giving us wild, crunchy fruit throughout most of the year. A lemon tree stood near the front gate and to the right side of the house three fragrant chilli trees bloomed. The curry tree at the front verandah, where my father would enjoy his evening beer, also helped to keep the mosquitoes away.

This agricultural accomplishment bore a huge significance for my parents — if the herbs of their homeland could flourish on Australia's rich soil, then there was hope that their children could also prosper in this foreign land.

My grandmother was the true keeper of the garden, the rest of us eventually grew too busy to maintain its upkeep. It was due to her efforts that our backyard continued to flourish — our front yard, however, was a different story. To prevent his rottweilers from doing their business on the front lawn, my father used the old trick of strategically placing a few empty milk bottles filled with water on the grass — the theory being that the water bottles marked the territory and the dogs stayed away. My grandmother decided that this trick would work much better if the entire lawn was covered — her theory being that the more bottles there were, the less likely the dogs would poo. So she scattered at least fifty of these stagnant beacons across the length of our yard. Eventually, the tortured dogs had nowhere else to 'do their business' but on top of the milk bottles themselves. Our home was subsequently described as 'the house with the shitty milk bottles' by my high school peers who passed our house by bus every morning and afternoon.

In order to further elevate the aesthetics of the front yard, my grandmother purchased bunches of fake flowers — purple orchards, pink roses, yellow daffodils, glossy water lilies and the occasional Christmas bauble. Her ingenious idea was to tie each plastic flower to an existing bush, making sure that we had a colourful — and, as she believed, 'fragrant' — bloom all year round. Of course, this only added to the schoolyard taunts.

My grandmother was illiterate her entire life and would sign her name with a 'Z'. She raised ten children, my mother being her fifth child, and ran a successful business in Vietnam for almost fifty years. During the summer months in Bonnyrigg, she liked to catch mice with one hand, snapping their necks with the other. She liked to laugh out loud, unaware that her chest and shoulders rose and fell perfectly out of sync with every candid chuckle. I do not know if she was ever happy about being brought to Australia, but it was certain that after a time, all she wanted to do was go back to Vietnam.

Believing it to be for her own good, my parents had sponsored my grandmother to join them in Australia in 1989. She flew alone and arrived in Sydney at the age of 71. Throughout the journey, her first flight ever, she held on tight and did not once let go of her lucky laughing Buddha. It is the size of a butternut pumpkin and today sits on my altar at home. My grandmother desperately missed the animated energy and sensuous smells of her life in Saigon. The market mayhem was all that she had ever known. I cannot begin to imagine the fragmentation and isolation she must have suffered in her new life — a life she did not ask for — a life with no friends and no comprehension of the language or culture. Homesick, she often told me

that it was the noise that she missed most. She hated being left at home alone, waiting all day for someone to return from work or school to keep her company. The lonely silence of suburbia drove her crazy. Sometimes to relieve her boredom she would open the gate and wander off around the block for hours. Our neighbourhood was not a safe one and her disappearance caused my mother much stress. Eventually we chained the gate and locked her in.

In her final years, Leroy was the only one still living at home. Lewis had moved to London, Luke was off travelling through a string of third world countries and I had just returned from several years abroad. Too consumed by my own self-importance, I watched my grandmother's decay into senility from afar. I was not around to help. I did not want to know how hard it was for my mother to care for a dying human being. As a know-it-all young adult, I constantly reminded my mother that she was not 'qualified', did not have enough 'knowledge' or 'professional ability' to deal with the sick and elderly. A sad trait of dementia, my grandmother's paranoid demons attacked the person who loved and cared for her the most. I did not want to be around when my grandmother threw abuse and accused my mother of plotting to throw her out onto the street, 'like common rubbish'. I did not want to be around when my grandmother repeatedly told strangers that she was 'slowly being starved to death'. She refused to eat and would only ever leave the house wearing the most worn and ripped garments, 'she doesn't feed me … look at the rags she makes me wear'. For someone like my mother, who has always lived by the 'what would people think?' mantra, this was a time too difficult to bear. In the middle of the night, when she thought no-one knew, my grandmother would sneak into the kitchen and eat the comfort food my mother left out for her.

~

Unlike the food my mother liked to cook at the restaurant, her home-style cooking centres first on the healing qualities to the body and soul, before appealing to the senses of taste and sight. My grandmother preferred the intense, pungent flavours of food from peasant origins. She liked her meat dishes bold and the smells assertive — this way she could eat more rice, vegetables and herbs. To balance the 'heating' effect that these foods had on my grandmother's body, my mother would cook foods that were 'cooling'. When she was physically and mentally healthy, a typical dinner for my grandmother would consist of a meat dish for iron and protein to keep her strong, a seafood dish to reduce her blood fat level, some vegetables for essential vitamins, a broth or soup for easy digestion and, of course, rice for carbohydrates and energy. It was important for my grandmother to finish her meal with something sweet — my mother would make sure that there was a little ginger in her pudding to boost her immune system and calm her stomach. When she began to lose her mind, my mother would just leave one bowl piled with as many of these elements as she could, instead of having a table spread of many dishes.

My mother's patience and gentle care allowed my grandmother to die at home peacefully in 2001 surrounded by those she loved. She lived eighty-four years. The final years were extremely hard on my mother. With little support from her estranged brothers, she simply accepted that it was her lot in life to endure the burden alone. My mother's selflessness manifests itself in everything that she does. A true Buddhist, my mother believes that what is reaped in this life is the direct result of what she had sown in her past — the good deeds done in this life will surely secure a glorious afterlife for her.

Like me, everyone else sobbed hysterically at my grandmother's funeral, wallowing in our own pathetic guilt, sorrow and frustration. I wish I had been more patient in dealing with my grandmother's senility. I wish I had been more kind. My mother did not shed a tear. She organized the guests, ran around after the children, made sure there was enough incense, thanked the monks and quietly prayed. She had spent the entire morning ironing all the good clothes she wished my grandmother had worn. She placed them gently in her coffin and hoped that she would at least accept them in the next life.

Clockwise from top left: My mother (left) and her sister (my Aunty Nine) enjoying a lunch of seafood wrapped in fresh herbs and rice paper, Saigon, 2005; Aunty Eight, overseeing her wholesale business selling fresh corn; Aunty Nine's street stall selling fresh noodles and sweets; my father enjoying his evening beer on our front verandah, Bonnyrigg, 1985.

Left: My grandmother (left) with a family friend, New Year's Day, 1980. Above: Luke, Lewis, Leroy, Mum and I sharing my grandmother's last day with us, 2001.

LUKE NGUYEN: *Traditionally, vegetables are pickled for the winter months, but of course are eaten all year round. They are combined with many dishes for the added dimension of tart and sour flavours as well as texture.*

ĐU ĐỦ CHUA

pickled green papaya

1 kg (2 lb 4 oz) green papaya
1 teaspoon chilli flakes
500 ml (17 fl oz/2 cups) white vinegar

440 g (15½ oz/2 cups) sugar
250 ml (9 fl oz/1 cup) water
1 teaspoon salt

Peel the papaya, cut in half lengthways and remove the seeds. Continue to halve the papaya lengthways until you have cut it into 8 pieces. Finely cut across the pieces to approximately 2 mm (¹/₁₆ in) wide, then wash under cold water and set aside to dry. Once dry, transfer the green papaya and chilli flakes to a 2 litre (70 fl oz/8 cup) storage container.

In a large saucepan add the vinegar, sugar, water and salt and stir until boiling, then turn off the heat and allow to cool. Once cooled, pour the pickling liquid over the green papaya to completely submerge it, cover with a lid and refrigerate for at least 2 days before use. Use within 2 weeks of preparation.

MAKES 1 KG (2 LB 4 OZ)

DƯA CẢI CHUA
pickled mustard greens

1 kg (2 lb 4 oz) mustard greens
1.5 litres (52 fl oz/6 cups) water
1 tablespoon sugar

2$^{1}/_{2}$ tablespoons salt
8 spring onions (scallions)

Cut the mustard greens in half lengthways, then cut into 5 cm (2 in) long pieces and wash thoroughly. Blanch in boiling water for 30 seconds, then refresh in iced water and place in a colander to drain.

In a saucepan combine the water, sugar and salt and stir until boiling, then turn off the heat and allow to cool. Clean and cut the spring onions into 5 cm (2 in) long pieces, then mix evenly with the mustard greens and place in a 2 litre (70 fl oz/4 cup) storage container. Pour the pickling liquid over the vegetables, making sure they are completely submerged. Cover with a lid and allow to pickle for a least 1 week in the refrigerator before use.

MAKES 1 KG (2 LB 4 OZ)

MARK JENSEN: *This is such a delicate dish. It is the pork fat that gives* Thit Kho *its subtle richness. If you prefer to leave the fat out, substitute the pork leg with more pork neck.*

The length of time given in this recipe should be sufficient for a 'melt in the mouth' result. It is always good practice, however, to continually check for taste and tenderness and adjust the cooking time accordingly.

THỊT KHO TRỨNG

caramelized pork leg and whole egg, with chilli and pepper

500 g (1 lb 2 oz) pork neck
500 g (1 lb 2 oz) pork leg, with skin
   and fat
220 g (7³/4 oz/1 cup) sugar,
   for caramelizing
approximately 2 litres (70 fl oz/8 cups)
   water or pork stock (page 56)
125 ml (4 fl oz/¹/2 cup) fish sauce

75 g (2¹/2 oz/¹/3 cup) sugar, extra
5 spring onions (scallions), white
   part only, bashed
1 teaspoon salt
2 teaspoons fine white pepper
6 hard-boiled eggs, peeled
6 red bird's eye chillies, left whole

Cut the pork neck and leg into 2 x 4 cm (³/4 x 1¹/2 in) pieces and set aside. To make the caramel, put the sugar and 2 tablespoons of water in a large saucepan and place over high heat. Cook until the sugar becomes a rich golden colour, then carefully add the pork pieces to the pan. Stir to coat the pork with the caramel, then add the water or stock. Slowly bring to the boil, skimming off the fat and impurities that rise to the surface.

Reduce the heat to a simmer, then add the fish sauce, extra sugar, spring onions, salt and pepper. Cook for 45 minutes, then add the eggs and cook for a further 30 minutes, adding the chilli in the last 5 minutes of cooking.

SERVES 6

NƯỚC LÈO HEO
pork stock

1 kg (2 lb 4 oz) pork bones
1 chicken carcass
5 cm (2 in) piece of ginger
1 bulb of garlic

1 lemon grass stem
4 spring onions (scallions)
5 litres (175 fl oz/20 cups) water

Wash the bones under cold water, then place them in a large saucepan. Slice the ginger and garlic bulb in half, bash the lemon grass and spring onions with the back of a cleaver or mallet. Put all of the ingredients in the pan and bring to the boil. Skim the impurities from the surface of the stock, reduce the heat to a simmer and continue to cook for 2 hours, skimming constantly. Pour the stock through a fine strainer into another saucepan and allow to cool. Once cooled, portion into smaller amounts and refrigerate or freeze until required. The stock will last in the fridge for 3 days or in the freezer for 3 months.

MAKES 4 LITRES (140 FL OZ/16 CUPS)

MARK JENSEN: *This is my take on a very traditional peasant-style dish. Shrimp paste was originally used to extend the flavour of the pork, compensating for the scarcity of meat in Vietnam. This way, more rice, herbs and vegetables are consumed. The intense flavours of this combination have meant this dish has become comfort food for me. This is eaten with an abundance of raw cabbage, cucumber, bean sprouts, mint, and long stems of coriander (cilantro) and spring onion (scallion).*

THỊT HEO MẮM RUỐC
pork shoulder, slow-cooked with shrimp paste and lemon grass

1 kg (2 lb 4 oz) pork shoulder, with
    skin and fat
1½ tablespoons oil
4 x 8 cm (3¼ in) piece of lemon grass
    (with white part), finely chopped
2 spring onions (scallions), chopped
3 garlic cloves, chopped

1 tablespoon shrimp paste
2 tablespoons fish sauce
1 tablespoon sugar
1 teaspoon salt
2 teaspoons white pepper
approximately 2 litres (70 fl oz/8 cups)
    pork stock (page 56)

Wash the pork under cold water, then pat dry with paper towel. Place onto a cutting board and cut into 4 x 1 cm (1½ x ½ in) pieces. Add the oil to a large saucepan over medium heat, then add the lemon grass, spring onions and garlic. Fry until the lemon grass starts to brown slightly, then add the shrimp paste with 2 tablespoons of water and increase the heat. Add the pork to the pan and stir through well. Seal the pork, then add the remaining ingredients and enough pork stock to cover the meat by about 2 cm (¾ in), then bring it to a slow simmer. Cook for 1½ hours, adding a little extra stock if required. You should be left with enough liquid to sauce the dish.

SERVES 6

MARK JENSEN: *When we ate our way across Vietnam, Pauline, Lewis and I often found ourselves looking for restaurants with a sign reading Com Binh Dan ('home-style cooking'). We tired very easily of the food made fancy in some of the up-market restaurants and craved for more simple and honest food — food that is the true essence of Vietnamese cooking.*

TRỨNG CHIÊN THỊT BẰM

omelette of pork mince, preserved radish and spring onion

4 eggs
1/2 teaspoon salt
1/2 teaspoon cracked black pepper
1 teaspoon fish sauce
2 spring onions (scallions), white part
  only, sliced

1 tablespoon oil
1/2 small red onion, diced
2 garlic cloves, crushed
100 g (3 1/2 oz) minced (ground) pork
1 tablespoon preserved radish
  (available in Asian supermarkets)

In a bowl whisk together the eggs, salt, pepper, fish sauce and sliced spring onions. Place a non-stick frying pan over medium heat, add the oil, then fry the onion and garlic until soft and fragrant. Add the pork and preserved radish and continue to fry until browned. Pour the omelette mixture into the pan and cover with a lid. Cook until the base is golden brown and the top just set. Slide out onto a plate and serve with rice soup or white rice with fish sauce and fresh chilli.

SERVES 2

LUKE NGUYEN: *Mum used to cook this dish at Pho Cay Du. I remember getting excited every time a customer ordered it — it was the most expensive dish on the menu. Mum would send me across to the fresh fish markets to look for the biggest and freshest jumbo king prawn (shrimp) or scampi that I could find.*

I always thought to myself, why don't they just keep a few in the fridge in case we get an order? Sometimes the customer was left waiting for over 20 minutes while I scoured the streets. As I learned later on, the customer never minded waiting as the prawns were so fresh and the flavours so good. The aroma of the sautéed prawns with the tomato has been implanted in my memory. Every time we cook this dish at Red Lantern, I think of the times at Pho Cay Du.

TÔM RIM

king prawns sautéed with tomato, fish sauce and black pepper

2 tablespoons vegetable oil
1 tablespoon minced garlic
2 bird's eye chillies, chopped
1 teaspoon tomato paste
    (concentrated purée)
12 jumbo king prawns (shrimp),
    peeled, deveined, with tails intact
3 tablespoons sugar

1 teaspoon cracked black pepper
4 tablespoons fish sauce
185 ml (6 fl oz/³/4 cup) fish stock
    (page 99) or water
1/2 very ripe tomato, diced
1 spring onion (scallion), finely sliced
1 small handful coriander
    (cilantro) leaves

Add the oil, garlic and chilli to a wok over medium heat and stir until fragrant but not coloured. Add the tomato paste, prawns and sugar. Toss to combine, then add the pepper, fish sauce, fish stock or water and diced tomato.

Increase the heat, bring to a simmer and cook for 3 minutes, or until the prawns are cooked through. Remove the prawns to a serving platter, then reduce the sauce slightly and pour over the prawns. Garnish with the spring onion and coriander.

SERVES 4

LUKE NGUYEN: *In Vietnamese culture and medicine, food is referred to as having 'hot' or 'cold' effects on the body. This doesn't refer to the temperature of the body, but rather the state of wellbeing. Fried food, for example, is 'hot', so you need to eat 'cooling' foods to balance the body. As you can imagine, the 'cooling' foods are all the ones that kids hate to eat. Bitter melon, winter melon and pennywort leaves are all cooling foods and are often used in soups that are particularly nourishing for the body. I always despised these dishes as a child, but now these foods are comforting for me.*

CANH HỦ QUA
bitter melon stuffed with pork and black fungus

50 g (1¾ oz) glass noodles
50 g (1¾ oz) dried black fungus,
    cut into strips
150 g (5½ oz) minced (ground) pork
4 spring onions (scallions), white part
    only, sliced
3 tablespoons fish sauce
½ teaspoon sugar
1½ teaspoons salt

1 teaspoon black pepper
1 egg
2 bitter melons
1.5 litres (52 fl oz/6 cups) chicken
    stock (page 36)
1 spring onion (scallion), green part
    only, sliced
1 tablespoon sliced coriander
    (cilantro) leaves

Soak the glass noodles and black fungus strips separately in boiling water for 10 minutes. Strain, then pat dry with a cloth. Roughly cut the glass noodles into 4 cm (1½ in) pieces and place in a bowl with the pork, black fungus, white part of the spring onions, 1 tablespoon of the fish sauce, sugar, ½ teaspoon of the salt, half the pepper and the egg. Mix well and set aside.

Cut the ends off the bitter melons, then cut into 2 cm (¾ in) wide discs. Remove the soft white flesh and seeds from the melon using a teaspoon and discard. Wash in cold water, drain and pat dry with paper towel. Lay the bitter melon discs flat and fill each one firmly with the pork mixture.

Put the chicken stock in a large saucepan with the remaining fish sauce and salt and bring to the boil. Add the stuffed melon to the soup, return to a simmer and cook for 15 minutes. Ladle into bowls and garnish with the spring onion greens, coriander and remaining black pepper.

SERVES 4

CANH BÍ THỊT BẰM
pork and winter melon soup

200 g (7 oz) minced (ground) pork
4 spring onions (scallions), white part
    only, sliced
2 tablespoons fish sauce
½ teaspoon sugar
1½ teaspoons salt
1 winter melon

1 litre (35 fl oz/4 cups) chicken stock
    (page 36)
1 tablespoon sliced spring onion
    (scallion), green part only
1 tablespoon sliced coriander
    (cilantro) leaves
½ teaspoon cracked black pepper

Put the pork, the white part of the spring onions, half the fish sauce, sugar and ½ teaspoon of the salt in a mortar and pound to a smooth paste. (This can also be done in a food processor.) Put in the fridge to marinate for 30 minutes. Peel the winter melon and slice into 5 x 1 cm (2 x ½ in) batons.

Remove the pork paste from the fridge. Take 1 teaspoon of pork paste in one hand and a teaspoon in the other, then press firmly down on top of the paste with the teaspoon. Using a circular motion, alternate the top spoon to the bottom and the bottom spoon to the top to form a dumpling. Continue in this way until you finish all of the pork paste.

In a large saucepan add the chicken stock, the remaining fish sauce and salt and bring to the boil. Add the dumplings and winter melon to the stock, return to a rapid simmer and cook for 10 minutes, or until all the dumplings float high on the surface of the soup. Ladle into soup bowls and garnish with the green part of the spring onion, coriander and black pepper.

SERVES 4

CANH CẢI XÀ LÁCH SOONG
pork and watercress soup

1 bunch watercress, picked over
1 litre (35 fl oz/4 cups) chicken stock
   (page 36)
200 g (7 oz) minced (ground) pork
2 tablespoons fish sauce
1 teaspoon salt

1 teaspoon cracked black pepper
1 spring onion (scallion), green part
   only, sliced
1 tablespoon sliced coriander
   (cilantro) leaves

Wash the watercress thoroughly in cold water and set aside. In a large saucepan add the chicken stock, pork, fish sauce, salt and pepper. Bring to the boil, stirring occasionally, then reduce to a simmer and skim the impurities from the surface. Cook for 5 minutes, then add the watercress, return to the simmer and cook for a further 5 minutes. Serve in soup bowls and garnish with spring onion and coriander.

SERVES 4

LUKE NGUYEN: *Pennywort leaves have a slightly bitter taste, which the prawns (shrimp) in this soup offset well. The juice of the leaf, when cooked in water, strained and with sugar added, also makes for a refreshing and healthy drink. Pennywort leaves are known to relieve arthritis.*

CANH RAU MÁ TÔM

prawn and pennywort soup

200 g (7 oz) raw prawns (shrimp),
    peeled and deveined
4 spring onions (scallions), white
    part only
1 bunch pennywort
2 tablespoons olive oil
¼ small onion, diced
1 litre (35 fl oz/4 cups) chicken stock
    (page 36)
1 teaspoon salt

1 teaspoon sugar
1 tablespoon fish sauce
1 spring onion (scallion), green part
    only, sliced
1 tablespoon sliced coriander
    (cilantro) leaves
½ teaspoon cracked black pepper

Crush the prawns and the white part of the spring onions into a paste in a mortar. Discard the pennywort stems and set the leaves aside. Heat the oil in a saucepan over medium heat and fry the onion and prawn paste until the paste changes colour, then add the chicken stock, salt, sugar and fish sauce. Bring to the boil, skimming off any impurities, then add the pennywort leaves and cook for 10 minutes. Ladle into soup bowls and garnish with the green part of the spring onion, coriander and black pepper.

SERVES 2

CANH CHUA RAU MUỐNG

tamarind soup with water spinach

150 g (5¹/2 oz) tamarind pulp
1 litre (35 fl oz/4 cups) chicken stock
    (page 36)
4 tablespoons fish sauce
4 tablespoons sugar
200 g (7 oz) water spinach (ong choy),
    leaves and 5 cm (2 in) of stem only
1 tomato, diced
1 elephant ear stem, sliced on the
    diagonal
10 okra, sliced in half on the diagonal

150 g (5¹/2 oz) bean sprouts
250 g (9 oz) beef sirloin steak, sliced
    into 2 mm (¹/16 in) wide pieces
2 teaspoons vegetable oil
1 garlic clove, chopped
1 bunch rice paddy herb, chopped
3 red Asian shallots, finely sliced and
    deep-fried
3 garlic cloves, finely sliced and
    deep-fried
1 bird's eye chilli, chopped

Dissolve the tamarind pulp in 250 ml (9 fl oz/1 cup) warm water. Work the pulp until dissolved and then strain the liquid through a fine sieve, discarding the pulp. Combine the chicken stock, tamarind liquid, fish sauce and sugar in a large clay pot or a saucepan and bring to the boil.

Add the water spinach, tomato, elephant ear stem, okra and bean sprouts and return to the boil. Meanwhile, stir-fry the beef in the vegetable oil with the garlic, then add to the soup. Garnish with the rice paddy herb, fried shallots, fried garlic and chilli. Serve with jasmine rice.

SERVES 6

CHÈ TRÔI NƯỚC

sweet mung bean dumplings in ginger sauce

100 g (3¹/2 oz) ginger, sliced into slivers
750 g (1 lb 10 oz) sugar
175 g (6 oz/1 cup) glutinous rice flour
2 pinches of salt
185 ml (6 fl oz/³/4 cup) warm water
75 g (2¹/2 oz) split yellow mung beans,
 soaked in water overnight, until
 doubled in size

2 tablespoons oil
3 spring onions (scallions), white
 part only
1 tablespoon coconut cream
100 ml (3¹/2 fl oz) coconut cream mixed
 with 1 tablespoon caster (superfine)
 sugar and ¹/4 teaspoon salt
1 tablespoon toasted sesame seeds

To make the ginger sauce, add 1 litre (35 fl oz/4 cups) water, ginger and sugar to a saucepan over high heat. Stir to dissolve the sugar while bringing to the boil, then reduce the heat to a slow simmer and cook for 30 minutes. Strain the ginger from the sauce and reserve for later use, then allow the sauce to cool.

To make the dumpling dough, sieve the rice flour and a pinch of salt into a bowl, then stir through the warm water until combined. Turn out onto a lightly floured bench and gently knead the dough into a ball, then cover with a damp cloth. Allow to rest for 10 minutes, then use your hands to roll it out into a long sausage, about 2 cm (³/4 in) in diameter.

To make the mung bean filling, steam the mung beans until soft and set aside. Add the oil to a saucepan over medium heat and cook the spring onions until fragrant. Stir through the mung beans, then add a pinch of salt and the tablespoon of coconut cream and stir to combine. Put the contents of the saucepan in a mortar and add some of the reserved ginger slivers and work it all into a smooth paste.

To assemble the dumplings, cut the dough into 2 cm (³/4 in) long sections, make an indentation in the centre with your thumb, then spoon ¹/2 teaspoon of the mung bean mixture into the hollow. Draw up all the sides to cover the mung bean, pinch together, then gently roll into a ball in the palm of your hand. Repeat until you have filled all of the dough. Cook the dumplings in boiling water. When they float to the surface, remove and plunge into iced water to cool, then set aside.

To serve, divide the dumplings between the bowls, bring the ginger sauce to the boil and pour over the dumplings, drizzle with the sweetened coconut cream and garnish with the roasted sesame seeds. The dumplings can be made in advance and are best kept refrigerated in the ginger syrup.

SERVES 6

the oceans
of uncertainty

The history of Vietnam is a defiant one.
It is a country made famous by war.

For the last two thousand years, the Vietnamese people have fought and resisted a multitude of foreign invaders to defend what every Vietnamese person is most fiercely protective of — their independence. No matter how many years it took or how many lives were lost on the battlefields, each war resulted in the repeated expulsion of the intruders.

In the early 10th century, the Vietnamese regained their identity following a series of revolts against an era of Chinese rule. The Khmers and Chams were constantly repelled in the Ly Dynasty and the Mongols were destroyed in a well-orchestrated surprise offensive during the Tran Dynasty. Japanese occupation was ferociously resisted during World War II and Vietnamese independence restored when the French surrendered in 1954, ending a century of their reckless colonisation. The poor little peasants in black pyjamas running in and out of the rice paddies eventually defeated even the mighty Americans.

Vietnamese cuisine is essentially an intelligent and sophisticated blend of these ancient and modern influences. The Chinese have made the greatest culinary contribution with noodles and dumplings, as well as cooking techniques and equipment such as the wok, cleaver, chopsticks and steam baskets. It is through the Thai and Khmers that the Vietnamese were introduced to Indian spices and curry powders. The Japanese penchant for raw seafood was acknowledged after World War II, and the Mongols' prevalent use of beef in their diets appreciated. French rule left a culinary legacy of baked bread, pastries, rich desserts and fine

Previous page: Lewis and I before our escape, Saigon, 1977. Clockwise from top left: My father during the war, 1974; two pictures of my parents on their wedding day, 1972.

coffee. French cooking methods also play an important part in some of Vietnam's most traditional dishes such *Pho, Bo Kho* and *Ban Gan*, as well as the making of pâtés and terrines. Intrinsically, the Vietnamese have selected the best of their adversaries' culinary qualities to create a highly evolved cuisine of their own.

Saigon, as my parents knew it, was renamed Ho Chi Minh City after the North Vietnamese founder of the Communist Party. Ho Chi Minh, like many Vietnamese, was well educated, highly cultured and fiercely patriotic. It is interesting that, as well as being fluent in French, German, Mandarin Chinese and English, he was also an accomplished chef formally trained in French cuisine. It is in Ho Chi Minh's famous speeches addressed to the people and his enemies that reflect accurately the Vietnamese determination to regain independence against all odds: 'If they force us into war, we will fight. The struggle will be atrocious but the Vietnamese people will suffer anything rather than renounce their freedom.' 'You can kill ten of my men for every one I kill of yours. But even at those odds you will lose and I will win.'

Ultimately, Ho Chi Minh's communist doctrine was the very ideal that my father and his fellow South Vietnamese vehemently rejected. The Americans joined the South Vietnamese in a decade-long battle against Ho Chi Minh's fanatical regime — a futile war that could not be won. Communism insists upon and receives full commitment from its supporters. Most Southerners had no political agenda; the only ideology we were fanatical about was our freedom — including the freedom from communism. After 25 years on Vietnamese soil, the American government ordered a full withdrawal of their troops. On April 30, 1975, helpless and abandoned, Saigon collapsed completely under communist rule.

There is no greater example of the magnitude of repulsion for the ideals of repression and inherent poverty than the mass exodus from Vietnam in the years to follow. Peace, freedom and democracy could not be attained under communism. In the 15 years following the fall of Saigon, over one million people fled Vietnam. Like my family, most escaped by sea — we became known as 'The Boat People'.

Like many, I have heard countless horrific stories of escape in tiny, unseaworthy vessels, all hopelessly overcrowded with inadequate food and water. When I asked my father how many were crammed into our boat, he snickered and replied, 'We were far more organized than that.'

Foreseeing the inevitable outcome, my father had already begun making plans for our escape long before the fall of Saigon: 'I wanted to die, I was depressed, desperate ... I thought, it is the end, there is no hope for us here.' Having realized the enormity of my father's plan and the dangers that lay ahead, my maternal grandmother begged him not to leave. My father was adamant that he would rather die trying than risk imprisonment or to suffer a fate just as atrocious — the re-education camps: 'It's not enough that they take our freedom they want to take our thoughts as well!' My grandmother pleaded with my father to leave the children behind, but he had made up his mind: 'Without them how can I live? If we die, we will die together.' He had already ticked the items off his checklist including two slings; one for him to carry me and the other for my mother to carry Lewis. I was three years old at the time and Lewis two and, unknown to anyone, my mother was pregnant with Luke.

Originally, my father and three close friends had bought a boat for the hefty sum of fifteen million dong. They soon aborted the escape plan, however, when the corrupt captain they had enlisted boasted in a spy-infested bar of their intentions — it was a deliberate attempt to keep the boat. Fed up, my father and his friends eventually spent twice that amount and built their own boat. It was decided that they would not make the same mistake others had made before them — officials would not be bribed and untrustworthy fishermen would not be relied upon.

My father and his friends built a small but sturdy craft 9 metres (30 feet) long by 2 metres (7 feet) wide. It was made of wood and had a two-cylinder engine with a simple tarpaulin for shelter. The bottom deck was for the women, children and supplies. They kept a second engine just in case. Food and fuel were hoarded in small quantities so as to not arouse suspicion. Their days as

soldiers had taught them how excruciating thirst can be, especially when exacerbated by the blazing sun reflected off the open sea. They packed enough fresh water to drink, cook and bathe with for several weeks. The provisions included bags of rice, fish sauce, soy sauce, fermented beancurd paste, cooking oil, Chinese sausage, eggs, beef jerky, tinned sardines, instant noodles, pickled chilli, dried mushrooms, dried fruit, coconut milk, hard candy for the children, soft drink for the women, cognac for the men and a tape player with their favourite music for morale. My father's companions included three army officers, a government official and a chemistry professor from Saigon University. All up there were six men, six women and twelve children, including Luke in the womb.

Unlike many of our friends who had failed at several attempts to leave Vietnamese shores, our group escaped first go. The men did not risk the surveillance of communist patrol boats by posing as fishermen and leaving from the coast. They wore the uniforms of soldiers and left from the very centre of Saigon. The plan belonged to my father and everyone played their part with precision.

It was October 1977, a bright and simmering morning, hot and humid as usual. The women and children caught the 9.30 bus to *Phu Xuan* wharf where another smaller boat was already waiting. They had to put the plan into action before the afternoon downpour. Good weather was crucial. It was important that we were in clear view of the communist soldiers because, my father explains, 'The suspicious often scan too far in the distance for their enemies and do not see what is blatantly in front of them.' The ruse was that the group of women and children were taking a day trip to visit their husbands at *Thu Thiem* — an island gaol for escapees and political prisoners. In case the communists interrogated them, the women memorized the name, date and circumstance of their counterfeit husband's capture.

In charge of the smaller boat was my father's best friend Truong. My brothers and I call him Bac Truong, *Bac* being the title of respect for anyone who is older than our own parents. Bac Truong had a chubby round face with happy brown eyes; although his beer belly was as round as a giant watermelon, his body stood tall and lanky for an Asian man. Strong and keen, Bac Truong liked to make my father laugh with his unwholesome jokes — his own face turning bright red in hysteria. He and my father had been partners in crime since their teenage years. Like gladiators, loyal to the death, they continued to defend each other's honour and watch each other's backs long after the war.

Bac Truong and his family arrived in Australia six months before we did. Our families lived two blocks away from each other in Bonnyrigg. Bac Truong often stayed at our house to escape his own family pressures. On many occasions we woke to find him slumped and snoring on our sofa — at which time we would jump on top of him and attack the hairs on his head. Bac Truong used to give Lewis, Luke and me fifty cents for every grey hair we picked from his abundant mane. Naturally, we fought one another for the tweezers.

As a child growing up in Australia, I was privy to many stories of escape. Before their lives were committed to the restaurant in Cabramatta, my parents hosted regular social gatherings in our family home. Our dining table was often too small to accommodate all the invited guests, so we had a sort of indoor picnic in the living room. On a long stretch of newspaper, we would spread a feast of traditional Vietnamese dishes across the length of the floor. The men drank Remy Martin on ice mixed with soda water and the women drank Tooheys Draught beer. There was always the sounds of high-pitched laughter and the slow strumming of guitar to silken songs. Each told stories of lives lost or left behind. Most of the time, I sensed that the room pained with much heartache and sorrow. At times, there were long lulls and silent tears. I remember the events clearly because the parties would often continue until late into the night. In the mornings, Lewis, Luke and I would wake up weary-eyed to the smell of old alcohol, dirty dishes and stale cigarettes, and knowing a big job laid waiting for us. We carried out our duties without discussion or protest. Lewis cleared the bowls and chopsticks, Luke swept and mopped the floor and I washed all the dishes.

Clockwise from left: My mother and a cousin in front of Dua 23 (market stall 23), 1968; my mother riding through Cau Ong Lanh markets; my parents in happy times before the collapse of Saigon, 1974.

Back in Vietnam during our families' escape, as Bac Truong steered the boat toward *Thu Thiem* prison, he noticed a communist soldier on the dock with an AK-47 slung adroitly over his left shoulder, his right hand pinching a cigarette between thumb and index finger. He cocked his chin in our direction and narrowed his eyes through the cigarette smoke. The soldier focused hard on Bac Truong, but his glare soon evaporated at the sight of the chatting women and children on board — as expected, he quickly guessed that their destination must be the island gaol.

Bac Truong drove the boat into the mangroves a few kilometres short of the gaol. We hid there until dark. The late afternoon rain came right on cue and the communist soldiers sought shelter away from their posts on the edge of the river. The mothers drugged the children with cough medicine so that we made as little noise as possible. Twelve long hours passed and the surveillance was at its quietest. It was pitch black when my father drove the main boat toward the designated spot. He couldn't see a thing. All he could hear were the vibrating chant of the frogs and the water's rhythmic licking at the side of boat. 'Where are they? They should be here. This is the spot.' As a last resort, he was to make a signal by burning a stack of paper — but that carried the risk of detection. Panic crept its way up the back of his throat. Dread had already settled in his stomach. He was about to light the match when he saw movement at the corner of his eye. From out of the muddy water he immediately recognized his good friend's voice whispering, 'Lap, is that you?'

In silence, they carried the children one-by-one onto the main boat, placing us below deck — the women quickly followed. Bac Truong punctured the small vessel without a sound and watched it completely sink before climbing onboard. No words were spoken until much later when we left the mouth of the river *Cua Can Gio* ('doorway needing time'). Armed with only a rudimentary map and a compass to guide him, my father took us into the South China Sea and set off as far south as possible to the Gulf of Thailand.

The few times I have asked my father about the primordial emotion of fear, he has answered me sternly and without hesitation: 'Fear is the only real oppressor. Fear is the only thing that holds you back. Many doors open when you are without fear.' Anything was better than the Viet Cong. 'We refuse to give up. We cannot be caught. We shall not die. Our will to live is fierce — our will to live a better life is even stronger.' With no knowledge of the sea, but a whole lot of hope, my father steered our sturdy vessel as far away as possible from Vietnamese shores: 'We have our freedom, that is all that matters.'

Good weather, good luck and good spirits kept us alive. In October, there are no typhoons — even the seasonal monsoons are gentle in the Gulf of Thailand. The conditions were near perfect for the 24 boat people who possessed absolutely no sea experience between them. Tensions eased and everyone relaxed a little about 300 kilometres (185 miles) from the coast of Vietnam — we had reached international waters.

We spent our days sun-baking and dreaming of the future. Daybreak always came quickly. We watched in awe at the speed in which the sun rose above the horizon. In the mornings, the children played and danced to the joyful music coming from the tape player. There was not much around except the breathtaking sea and the soothing, cloudless sky. We welcomed the soft wind on our skin when the sun was at its most powerful. The tarpaulin offered the comfort of shade. My mother stayed below deck most of the time — morning sickness amplified by seasickness had weakened her. When she did come on deck, it was with the hope that the change in position would quell her queasiness. She finally discovered that her stomach agreed more with her facing the waves rather than hiding below. She giggled with excitement at the prawns dancing merrily across the surface of the sea. She marvelled at various objects floating in the water; discarded bottles, plastic bags, rubber thongs. All sorts of fish could be seen but were too fast to catch. In the late afternoon, the men stole fish from deep-sea cages left unattended by their masters. They took just enough for the women to cook that night — praise given generously for the fare created for them. When the sun snuck back below the horizon and the moon heaved up to light the sea, we sought comfort in each other's arms, admired the strangeness of the stars and prayed for a better tomorrow.

My parents remember the details of our escape vividly and are able to retell their story with much clarity and emotion. For many of their friends who escaped after them, it is not so easy. Some prefer the memories of the past left untouched. As a family friend said, 'It is better this way ... remembering is too painful.'

At the height of the exodus, during 1978 to 1979, it was estimated that fifty thousand Vietnamese had drowned *each month* in their attempts to escape. Many died due to tropical storms and exposure. Many drowned because passing ships refused to help. Others perished when pushed back into the open sea by supposedly friendly shores. Our group were part of the first wave to leave Vietnam — we were the lucky ones. We left a month before Thai pirates, who maraud the waters of South-East Asia, caught wind of the bountiful opportunities that lay before them. Just once we came across these pirates. 'They were scary looking,' says my mother. All had shaved heads, teeth long ago decayed and the sun-worn skin of cracked, tea-stained leather. Curiosity drove my father to steer our boat toward them. We exchanged words in broken Thai and Vietnamese. Out of pity, they gave us fresh fish and cigarettes. Had they known about the two diamonds my parents had each concealed inside their shirt buttons, they may have acted differently. After the short interlude, we waved goodbye and bade good luck — both pirate and refugee completely ignorant to their future possibilities.

One month later the marauding began. Those who did not drown, fell prey to the wretched vermin of the sea — ruthless pirates who plundered their belongings, killed their men and raped their women.

Already frail and poor in body and morale, a friend of my father's, Tuan Anh, and his fellow refugees were easy targets. Fifty-three of his one hundred and thirty companions had already perished due to lack of food and water when the pirates attacked them. After stripping the refugees of their possessions, the pirates, armed with machetes and hammers, forced the men below deck. Above deck, the women were raped repeatedly in a ten-day orgy crossing the Gulf of Thailand. Those who attempted to save their wives, mothers, sisters and daughters were beaten or simply thrown overboard. They were broken, traumatized and desperate when the first lot of pirates had finished with them. But it was not long until the next boatload came. By the time the last lot arrived, there was nothing left to take. The horrific journey saw Tuan Anh and his companions pillaged seven times and violated in a dozen different ways.

'It is not something I like to think about,' he tells me in perfect English. 'The past must be left in the past — it is our way of surviving.' He tries hard to shut out the horrors but their screams continue in his head. He stops breathing for a moment and casts his eyes to the ground. A gentle breath is released before he softly speaks: 'My sorrow is infinite … It is painful for me to think back … to the evil that man does … and the misery of his randomness.'

*Clockwise from top right: My mother and baby
Lewis, 1974; pictures of Lewis and me, 1977.*

Mark and I in Ha Long Bay, Vietnam, 2003.

LUKE NGUYEN: *This dish is perfect as a light starter — not only is it bursting with fresh flavour, it is also beautiful to look at. The roasted rice powder, thinh, adds texture and a lovely aroma to the dish. Thinh is commonly used in Vietnamese salads. Ensure you slice the salmon and the onion as finely as you can.*

CÁ SỐNG SALMON

salmon sashimi, lemon grass and fresh herbs

600 g (1 lb 5 oz) sashimi-grade salmon
5 basil leaves
5 perilla leaves
5 mint leaves
10 Vietnamese mint leaves
100 g (3¹/₂ oz) pickled vegetables
    (page 34), cut into small dice
¹/₂ red onion, finely sliced

3 cm (1¹/₄ in) piece of lemon grass,
    white part only, finely diced
¹/₂ teaspoon roasted rice powder
    (page 37)
¹/₄ teaspoon fried garlic (page 39)
2–3 tablespoons dipping fish sauce
    (page 33), plus extra to taste
lime wedges, to serve

Finely slice the salmon and transfer straight onto a serving platter. Wash and tear the herbs and scatter evenly over the salmon with the rest of the ingredients, except the dipping fish sauce. Dress with the dipping fish sauce and serve with wedges of lime.

SERVES 6

LUKE NGUYEN: *I am a big fan of lemon-cured dishes. It all started with* Bo Tai Chanh *(lemon-cured sirloin) — a dish I grew up with. Lemon-curing is such a simple and clean way of cooking and the results are amazing. The citrus, when combined with mint, makes the dish refreshing, clean and crisp. At Red Lantern we only serve this kingfish recipe as a 'special' — and the guests love it.*

When I was invited to cook for the Australian Ambassador at a charity dinner for The Asian Society in Manila, I went a little further and added a lemon-cured scallop dish to the menu — it was a winner.

GỎI CÁ KINGFISH
salad of lemon-cured kingfish

100 ml (3¹/₂ fl oz) lemon juice
2 teaspoons fish sauce
1 tablespoon sugar
¹/₂ teaspoon fine white pepper
¹/₂ teaspoon salt
300 g (10¹/₂ oz) kingfish fillet
200 g (7 oz) bean sprouts
1 tablespoon sliced sawtooth coriander
1 tablespoon sliced purple basil
1 tablespoon sliced rice paddy herb
¹/₂ teaspoon garlic oil (page 39)

¹/₂ teaspoon fried garlic (page 39)
¹/₄ teaspoon roasted rice powder
   (page 37)
2 tablespoons fried red Asian shallots
   (page 38)
2 tablespoons dipping fish sauce
   (page 33), plus extra to taste
1 sliced bird's eye chilli, to garnish
1 tablespoon crushed roasted peanuts
   (page 38), to garnish

In a bowl combine the lemon juice, fish sauce, sugar, pepper and salt. Mix well and set aside. Finely slice the kingfish and add to the lemon juice mixture and marinate for 5 minutes. In a separate bowl combine the remaining ingredients except the dipping fish sauce, chilli and peanuts. Squeeze any excess marinade from the fish and add to the salad bowl and mix well. Turn out onto a serving plate, dress with the dipping fish sauce and garnish with the chilli and peanuts.

SERVES 2 AS A MAIN, OR 6 AS PART OF A SHARED FEAST

GỎI CÁ NƯỚNG
salad of chargrilled salmon, pickled vegetables and bean sprouts

200 g (7 oz) salmon fillet, skin on
300 g (10½ oz) pickled vegetables
    (page 34)
100 g (3½ oz) bean sprouts
5 cm (2 in) piece of lemon grass,
    finely chopped
1 handful mixed herbs (perilla, mint,
    Vietnamese mint), torn
2 teaspoons fried garlic (page 39)
½ small onion, sliced
2–3 tablespoons dipping fish sauce
    (page 33)

1 tablespoon chopped roasted peanuts
    (page 38)
1 tablespoon fried red Asian shallots
    (page 38)
1 bird's eye chilli, sliced

SALMON MARINADE
1 teaspoon pickled chilli
1 garlic clove, crushed
2 teaspoons caster (superfine) sugar
1½ tablespoons fish sauce
pinch of salt

At Red Lantern, we like to remove, dry and fry the salmon skin separately as it adds interest and crunch to the salad, but this is purely optional. If using, remove the skin from the salmon and cover both sides liberally with salt and allow to dry for 2 hours in a sunny, well-ventilated position. Alternatively this can be done in a gas oven set to the lowest temperature. Once dry, dust off the salt and fry the skin until it crisps in oil heated to 180°C (350°F), or until a cube of bread dropped in the oil browns in 15 seconds.

Mix all of the marinade ingredients in a bowl, stirring until the sugar dissolves. Add the salmon and marinate it for 30 minutes.

To make the salad, chargrill the salmon over medium–high heat for 2–3 minutes, or until medium–rare, making sure it is well coloured on the outside. Allow the salmon to rest for 5 minutes, then flake the flesh into a bowl. Add the remaining salad ingredients except for the peanuts, shallots and chilli. Mix together well and turn out onto a serving platter. Garnish with the peanuts, shallots and chilli and serve.

SERVES 2 AS A MAIN, OR 6 AS PART OF A SHARED FEAST

TÔM NƯỚNG
soy and honey barbecued prawns

18 large raw king prawns (shrimp)
2 tablespoons soy sauce
2 tablespoons oyster sauce
3 tablespoons honey
2 tablespoons oil

1 tablespoon fish sauce
1 bird's eye chilli, minced in a mortar
1 teaspoon cracked black pepper
1/2 teaspoon salt

Soak 18 bamboo skewers in water for 10 minutes. Peel and devein the prawns, leaving the tail shells intact. Combine the remaining ingredients, mix well, add the prawns and marinate for 30 minutes. Remove the prawns from the marinade, skewer with the bamboo and chargrill over high heat for about 2 minutes, turning once, or until cooked.

SERVES 6

MỰC NƯỚNG XẢ

salad of chargrilled octopus, basil and lemon grass

4 tablespoons fish sauce
2 tablespoons lemon juice
1 tablespoon sugar
1 teaspoon salt
2 garlic cloves, crushed
1 tablespoon oil
500 g (1 lb 2 oz) small octopus,
    cleaned
2 Lebanese (short) cucumbers
5 cm (2 in) piece of lemon grass,
    white part only, finely sliced
1 small red onion, cut into wedges

1 handful Thai basil leaves, torn
10 cherry tomatoes, halved
1/2 teaspoon fried garlic (page 39)
1/2 teaspoon roasted rice powder
    (page 37)
3 tablespoons dipping fish sauce
    (page 33)
2 tablespoons fried red Asian shallots
    (page 38)
1 tablespoon chopped roasted peanuts
    (page 38)
1 bird's eye chilli, sliced

Add the fish sauce, lemon juice, sugar, salt, garlic and oil to a bowl and mix well. Add the octopus and marinate for 30 minutes. To make the salad, halve the cucumbers lengthways, remove the seeds and slice into fine batons. Combine the cucumber, lemon grass, onion, Thai basil, cherry tomatoes, fried garlic and rice powder in a bowl and set aside.

Cook the octopus on a chargrill pan over high heat for 3–4 minutes each side, or until done. The octopus will change colour and be a little charred. Once cooked, add to the salad, dress with the dipping fish sauce and mix well. Serve onto a platter and garnish with the shallots, peanuts and chilli.

SERVES 2 AS A MAIN, OR 6 AS PART OF A SHARED FEAST

PAULINE NGUYEN: *Crab is one of my favourite foods — I love the ritual of donning a bib (debris and finger bowls at the ready), cracking the shell, picking and sucking the meat. It can be a messy and time-consuming process, but the reward is succulent and satisfying. My brothers are not so patient. They would rather have the job done for them or, better yet, eat the whole crab, shell and all. Luke especially loves soft shell crab — most of the crab is edible and you can taste the subtle sweetness of the sea. There are a few species of soft shell crab that are available, but it is the blue crab that is most commonly available. If you can get it, soft shell mud crab is heaven.*

GỎI CUA LỘT
soft shell crab with pomelo and banana blossom salad

1 pomelo
1 banana blossom
40 g (1½ oz/¼ cup) pickled vegetables
    (page 34)
1 small handful Vietnamese mint
    leaves, roughly chopped
1 spring onion (scallion), finely sliced
2–3 tablespoons dipping fish sauce
    (page 33)

2 litres (70 fl oz/8 cups) vegetable oil,
    for deep-frying
4 soft shell crabs
100 g (3½ oz/½ cup) potato starch
1 tablespoon chopped roasted peanuts
    (page 38)
2 tablespoons fried red Asian shallots
    (page 38)
1 bird's eye chilli, sliced

Segment the flesh of the pomelo, making sure to remove the pith. Remove the red outer leaves of the banana blossom to reveal the tender white leaves inside. Tear away the white leaves and finely slice. In a bowl combine the pomelo and the banana blossom with the pickled vegetables, Vietnamese mint and sliced spring onion. Dress with the dipping fish sauce and set aside.

In a deep-fryer or wok, heat the vegetable oil to 180°C (350°F), or until a cube of bread dropped in the oil browns in 15 seconds. Cut the crabs in half, then dust with the potato starch and deep-fry until crisp.

Arrange the salad on a platter, place the crabs on top and garnish with the peanuts, shallots and chilli.

SERVES 2 AS A MAIN, OR 6 AS PART OF A SHARED FEAST

91

PAULINE NGUYEN: *I was first introduced to balmain bugs (the crustacean) when I was supporting myself through university as a waiter at The Balmain Bug (the restaurant). In my naïvety I believed that the chef, a local, went out every morning to catch these strange creatures fresh from Balmain's waters. My admiration for the man grew incrementally when I noticed his signature catch appearing on the menu of many restaurants throughout Sydney. It was not until several years later that I discovered chef Gill's balmain bugs were never caught from Balmain wharf at all — they are found all over Queensland and Western Australia and are sold at the Sydney Fish Markets. Unlike regular rock lobsters, they have wide shovel-like antennae instead of pincers so they can dig deep into the ocean floor to search for food. The flesh of bugs is sweeter and more tender than the regular rock lobster.*

My father has harped on to Mark on numerous occasions that 'stir-fry is stir-fry and soup is soup. You don't stir-fry soup!' However, Mark has included stock in this recipe as he enjoys spooning this delicious sauce over his rice. Leave the stock out if you agree with my father. This recipe is also great with prawns (shrimp) or crab.

TÔM HÙM XÀO TỎI

bugs with garlic and pepper

8 raw balmain bugs, slipper or
   shovel-nosed lobsters
2 teaspoons oil
2 garlic cloves, crushed
4 spring onions (scallions)
100 g (3½ oz) butter
2 teaspoons cracked black pepper
2 teaspoons sugar

½ teaspoon salt
1 tablespoon fish sauce
2 tablespoons rice vinegar
4 tablespoons chicken stock
   (page 36) (optional)
1 lime, cut into wedges
1 large handful coriander (cilantro)
   leaves

Wash the bugs, then cut them in half lengthways. In a wok over medium heat add the oil, garlic, spring onions cut into 4 cm (1½ in) lengths and half the butter. Cook until fragrant but not brown. Add half the bugs, increase the heat and stir-fry for 4 minutes, or until the bugs change colour. Remove the cooked bugs and stir-fry the remaining raw bugs. Return the reserved bugs back to the wok with the remaining ingredients, including the butter. Stir-fry to heat through, or if using the chicken stock, heat until the stock starts to boil. Garnish the dish with lime wedges and a generous handful of coriander.

SERVES 4 AS A MAIN, OR 6 AS PART OF A SHARED FEAST

LUKE NGUYEN: *In Vietnam, fishing is almost impossible from November to April due to high seas. Just as vegetables are pickled for the winter months, fish is dried for the months when seafood is unavailable. Of course, fish can be frozen these days, but dried, pickled and preserved fish are still important ingredients in traditional Vietnamese cooking. Once again, what began as a necessity has now become much prized.*

Following a recent trip home to Saigon, my parents introduced me to this dish. I was blown away by its simplicity. The strong flavours are great with beer — it's the perfect dish to prepare on a fishing or camping trip to impress the boys (or girls).

Most oily fish respond well to sun-drying, although the best fish to use is mackerel, bonito or swordfish. Prawns (shrimp) and squid are also great sun-dried. This method of cooking serves to bring on a concentration of the flavours; however, it does not 'preserve' the fish. The mackerel is only semi-dried, so it should be eaten within 2 days. An alternative to drying in the sun is to dry the fish in an oven on very low heat for several hours.

CÁ MỘT NẮNG
semi-dried mackerel

2 mackerel cutlets (about 300 g/
   10$^1/_2$ oz total)
1 teaspoon sea salt

Wash the cutlets to remove any trace of residual blood and dry well. Massage each side of the fish with sea salt, using a reasonable amount of pressure and making sure not to destroy the flesh. Cover with muslin (cheesecloth) and place the mackerel on a rack to allow moisture to drain away. Dry in filtered sunlight for 4–6 hours. Rinse the mackerel in cold water, then dry well.

To serve, shallow-fry and dress with dipping fish sauce (page 33).

SERVES 2

MARK JENSEN: *This is my favourite dish on the menu. I like to use silver perch for its richness and muddy characteristics. The Vietnamese appreciation for eating meat with the skin and bones transfers also to eating fish. At Red Lantern, we inform our guests beforehand that this dish is served traditionally — the flavours are rich, strong and pungent, and the fish is cooked with skin and bone. Most are undeterred and have come back time and time again for this dish. The fish glistens and melts in the mouth. On simple jasmine rice, it is silky and seductive.*

The clay pot is a primitive but efficient piece of equipment. When used for cooking, a clay pot distributes heat evenly. When presented at the table it maintains heat much longer than a regular serving bowl. The clay pot is often used for caramelizing and braising as it gives the ingredients an earthy dimension, imparting smoky aromas. Like a wok, the clay pot should be looked after.

CÁ KHO TỘ
caramelized silver perch

1 whole silver perch (300–350 g/
   10^1/2–12 oz)
2 tablespoons vegetable oil
1 garlic clove, minced
3 red Asian shallots, diced

75 g (2^3/4 oz/^{1}/3 cup) sugar
2 tablespoons fish sauce
1 spring onion (scallion), sliced
1 bird's eye chilli, sliced
cracked black pepper

Place the silver perch flat on a board. Using a cleaver or large knife, remove the tail, fins and head from the fish. Cut the fish from the tail into 2 cm (3/4 in) sections.

Put the oil in a small saucepan over medium heat, add the garlic and shallots to the oil and fry until the garlic turns golden brown. Strain the oil through a fine metal sieve into a small clay pot, discarding the garlic and shallots.

Add the sugar and 1 tablespoon of water to the clay pot over medium heat. Cook for about 5 minutes to make a rich, dark caramel, then add the fish. Seal the fish on all sides in the caramel, then add the fish sauce and 3 tablespoons of water and bring to the boil. Reduce the heat slightly and continue to cook the fish for about 5 minutes, or until cooked through. Garnish this dish with spring onion, chilli and black pepper.

SERVES 2

LUKE NGUYEN: *This dish pretty much sums up Vietnamese cuisine: clean, crisp, delicate, fresh, textured, fragrant and well balanced. Canh chua is a great introduction to Vietnamese food.*

I introduced my partner, Suzanna, to this dish 7 years ago and she fell in love … with the dish, that is. Today, she cooks canh chua *every Christmas for her family. It has become a permanent addition to their Christmas dinner menu. Suzanna likes to add mussels, prawns (shrimp), pippies, calamari and tofu.*

CANH CHUA CÁ
tamarind and pineapple broth with silver perch

300 g (10½ oz) tamarind pulp
1 litre (35 fl oz/4 cups) fish stock
  (page 99)
4 tablespoons fish sauce
2 x 1 cm (½ in) thick slices of fresh
  pineapple, diced
75 g (2¾ oz/⅓ cup) sugar
1 whole silver perch (350–400 g/
  12–14 oz), cut into 1.5 cm (⅝ in)
  thick cutlets

1 tomato, diced
1 elephant ear stem, sliced on the
  diagonal
10 okra, sliced in half on the diagonal
150 g (5½ oz) bean sprouts
1 bunch rice paddy herb, chopped
1 tablespoon fried red Asian shallots
  (page 38)
2 teaspoons fried garlic (page 39)
1 bird's eye chilli, chopped

Dissolve the tamarind pulp in 250 ml (9 fl oz/1 cup) warm water. Work the pulp until dissolved and then strain the liquid through a fine sieve, discarding the pulp. Combine the fish stock, tamarind liquid, fish sauce, pineapple and sugar in a large claypot and bring to the boil. Add the silver perch pieces to the pot and return to the boil. Then add the tomato, elephant ear stem, okra and bean sprouts to the pot and return to the boil again. Garnish with the rice paddy herb, fried red Asian shallots, fried garlic and chilli. Serve with jasmine rice or vermicelli.

SERVES 2 AS A MAIN, OR 6 AS PART OF A SHARED FEAST

CANH NGÓT

snapper and celery soup

1 whole snapper (1 kg/2 lb 4 oz)
6 Vietnamese celery stalks
6 spring onions (scallions),
    white part only
2 bird's eye chillies
2 litres (70 fl oz/8 cups) chicken stock
    (page 36)

125 ml (4 fl oz/^{1}/$_2$ cup) fish sauce
1 teaspoon sugar
2 large ripe tomatoes
1 large handful bean sprouts
2 limes, cut into wedges

Place the snapper flat on a board. Using a cleaver or large knife, remove the tail, fins and head from the fish. Cut the fish from the tail into 2 cm (^{3}/$_4$ in) sections. Wash the cutlets under cold water, then place the fish pieces in a colander to drain.

Pick the leaves from the celery stalks, reserving them for later use. Using a mortar, pound the celery stalks, spring onions and chillies into a paste. (This can be done with a food processor.) Place the fish cutlets and chicken stock in a large saucepan and bring to the boil, skimming the surface of impurities. Then add the celery paste, fish sauce and sugar. Reduce the heat and simmer for 5 minutes, then add the tomatoes and celery leaves. To serve, divide the soup evenly into the bowls and garnish with the bean sprouts and a wedge of lime.

SERVES 6

NƯỚC LÈO CÁ
fish stock

2 kg (4 lb 8 oz) white fish bones
   (such as snapper or cod)
1 large leek
4 cm (1¹/₂ in) piece of ginger, sliced

4 garlic cloves
2 makrut (kaffir lime) leaves
1 bunch coriander (cilantro), stems
   and roots only

Place the fish bones in a large saucepan with 4 litres (140 fl oz/16 cups) water and bring to the boil. Skim off any impurities, then add the remaining ingredients. Return to the boil, then reduce the heat and simmer for 30 minutes. Strain through a fine sieve and allow to cool. Store in the fridge for up to 3 days, or freeze until required.

MAKES 4 LITRES (140 FL OZ/16 CUPS)

the three big mistakes

The wind grew anxious that afternoon.
It picked up speed to whisper in my father's ear

It's time to wake up now. It was the first sleep he's had in three days — if you could call it that; it was more like a stressful state of unconsciousness. When he woke, he regretted ever going to sleep. Bac Truong had taken over the wheel so that my father could rest. In that time, he had unknowingly steered the boat back in the direction of Vietnam. My father did not sleep again. The blunder added another day to the huge amount of time already wasted in taking the most inefficient route.

We wanted to find Malaysia. Sure, my father could have taken a more direct route but the danger of staying too close to Vietnamese shores was a risk he did not want to take. We went as far south from the coast of Vietnam as possible. Truth be known, my father did not know exactly where he was going, he just knew the rough direction in which to head. By this time, we had no idea how far Bac Truong had steered us back toward Vietnam. 'It could have been worse,' my father consoled, smiling bravely. 'We could have landed in Cambodia.' My father turned the boat back around, hoping desperately that he could deliver his family and his friends safely to the shores of Pilau Bidong, the Malaysian refugee camp rumoured to be the best at the time, with the kindest facilities.

On the fourth day at sea, the wind blew a small gust of hope in our direction. Bac Truong had caught sight of it first — an empty oil barrel bobbing up and down in the distance. 'Over there Lap!' he shouted, excited like a child. 'Over there! Maybe the label can tell us where the hell we are!' The boat could not reach the barrel quick enough before Bac Truong

Previous page: Permission is granted to leave the refugee camp for a day's excursion — my parents stand far left with Lewis and I in front, Bangkok, 1978. Left: My mother, father, Lewis and me, Bangkok, 1978.

jumped into the water. Fear had not yet presented itself to Bac Truong since we left Vietnam. That is, until the cold of the sea shocked his senses, whacking him like a swift sidekick to the stomach, winding him instantly. Only then did he fully realize the severity of our situation.

He suddenly remembered the sharks patrolling the boat's perimeter that morning and his fear solidified. With frantic strokes, he swam for the barrel wanting only to get the task over and done with. He did not dare put his head below the water; it was already pounding from the base of his neck to his temples — the cold throbbed in both ears and made his eyes hurt. The ache in his chest spread to the muscles in his legs and became numbness at the tip of his toes. Soon his shoulders stiffened and he could no longer feel his fingers. He struggled to keep his breathing steady. When he lost control of his jaw, he instantly thought of the wind-up toy he played with as a kid — the plastic set of teeth with pink protruding gums clickety-clacketing all over his mother's dressing table.

When Bac Truong finally reached the barrel he turned to look back at the boat. The sudden vastness of the ocean terrified him — the endless black below dominated his senses. He was never a strong swimmer and positively hopeless at treading water. It was all he could do to hang on tight and stay afloat. It seemed that every motion of a wave swept him farther away from his family. He could see them, his wife jumping up and down like a mad woman, his three children crying like steamed buns over the side of the boat. There was no way he could swim the same distance back. He tried to shout something but his throat produced no sound. The wind moved us farther away from him. He wanted to tell his family that everything was going to be all right. He wanted to tell them that he loved them very much. He wanted to tell them to quit screaming for heaven's sake. Bac Truong knew that my father could not bear to watch him struggle. He had guessed that my father had disappeared below deck. He waited for what seemed like an eternity.

When my father finally reappeared, he carried with him a thick coil of rope draped over his shoulder. With the kind of strength that comes with calm anxiety, he took a run up from one side of the boat to the other, throwing the heavy rope toward his friend. About bloody time, thought Bac Truong, as he wrapped the rope under his armpits and around his chest. Even the children helped to pull him to safety. When he clambered on board, shaking like a flapping mackerel, my father grinned and shook his head. He gently shifted Bac Truong's hair from his eyes and carefully wrapped a blanket around his head and shoulders. He rubbed hard on his friend's back imagining that the short, fast movements would help bring on the warmth. Both men paused for a moment, looked into each other's eyes and broke into a fit of laughter. 'Well, what does it say then man?' Through frozen lips and chattering teeth Bac Truong quickly replied, 'Made in Singapore.'

My father guessed that the oil barrel must have fallen from one of the tankers running gasoline, diesel and jet fuel from Singapore to Hong Kong. My mother contributed that she had heard 'Refugees get put up into hotels in Singapore. But it is almost impossible to gain acceptance. Apparently, they are not as welcoming to Vietnamese refugees.' The reality was, they knew very little about the outside world. Most knowledge of international affairs they received from hearsay, rumours and gossip from their friends. The Vietnamese government had enforced so much censorship that it was hard to know what was fact or fiction. Their world became incredibly insular, filled with communist propaganda and doubt. But it was America they knew most about — The Land Of The Free — the land in which my father had always dreamed of one day settling. Even to this day, my father's greatest regret is missing the opportunity to go to the United States. He still claims that his life would have been easier had he resettled there. This misfortune, he believes, is the result of his own doing. They are what he refers to as, his 'Three Big Mistakes'.

BIG MISTAKE 1

WHEN PLANNING YOUR ESCAPE, DO NOT BE TOO ORGANIZED

We saw the tanker and the tanker saw us. Its majesty loomed before us and created an excitement that inflated like a helium balloon; all giddy, soaring and about to explode. My father had heard about the military ships from the West, plucking refugees from the seas and giving them humanitarian aid and asylum. For this reason, he made sure to study the national flags that could possibly fly from these enormous freighters. The men agreed that it looked like the German flag in the distance. My father chased the ship and, for a long while, it seemed that the ship simply waited for us to catch up. He was happy for so many reasons; they had built a good boat — its engine still in fine condition. They had planned well — his companions still determined and strong. His crew had all maintained high spirits, with his own hope never ceasing. Everyone joined in, jumping up and down, waving their arms, screaming with joy. The banner they had prepared beseeched the words in English, 'Have mercy on us.' It flapped reassuringly in the wind. My father picked up speed because for a moment there, he thought that the ship had started to move away from us. The strangeness of it all, he thought, must be on account of the commotion and excitement of his crew — the more he picked up speed, the more the ship drew farther away. It soon dawned on him that his mind was not playing tricks on him at all. He realized this before the others but continued to chase the ship anyway, risking becoming further lost at sea. It was either that or just give up. Our energy eventually evaporated as disbelief fell upon us. In silence we watched the ship fade to a tiny black dot in the distance.

Four times this happened. Ship after ship ignoring our SOS — a violation of the most basic code of the sea. We thought we saw an American flag among them. My father realized too late what he should have done. He should have killed the engine. He should have told everyone not to display so much energy. He should have made us all appear sick, distraught and helpless. He should have been more cunning.

Why save these refugees when they are clearly not dying? Why rescue a boat that is still in good condition? Only a sinking boat warrants saving. A good boat with a strong engine can continue on its way. Let some other country deal with them.

Our hope had dwindled but had not yet disappeared. We saw land on the sixth day. What started as a blur in the distance soon became a vast expanse of dense jungle. When the trees revealed themselves in greater detail, my father knew we were only about five kilometres (3 miles) away. The black water on which we had floated for so long became a welcoming bright blue. By the time we saw sand, the water turned turquoise. By the time we saw the beach umbrellas, the holiday huts and the manicured pool, the water shone crystal. The sight of Western faces filled us with so much joy we wept in unison. Out of courtesy, my father parked the boat a short distance from the shore instead of beaching it on the sand. He told the rest of us to wait on board while he swam toward the sunbathers. When my father reached the beach, wearing nothing but his faded yellow shorts, a group of Malaysian soldiers came running at him with pistols. When some nearby Western tourists also gathered around, the leader of the soldiers grudgingly asked if there were any sick or injured on the boat. He also asked if the boat suffered engine trouble. My father told the truth and answered 'No' to both his questions. Immediately, the soldier raised his semi-automatic to my father's head, 'Refugee not wanted here!' he shouted. My father obeyed the man's orders and swam back to our boat, his own throat trembling with intolerable despair and frustration.

The villagers also obeyed and waded into the water to push our vessel away from the shore. They threw in a barrel of fuel to get us on our way. With silent embarrassment, the Westerners took pity and swam alongside, throwing in whatever possessions they could spare. My mother remembers two women running from the gift shop waving sunhats, pretty scarves and floral shirts. They told us that we had missed Pilau Bidong by a long shot — in fact, it was on the other side of the Peninsular. 'I was so stupid then,' my father tells me, 'I should have destroyed the boat and sunk it. What were they going to do? Stand there and watch us drown?' My father mustered what was left of his dignity that day and fought hard to hold back his tears. Rather than put his companions through yet another wave of disappointment, he turned the boat around and headed north to the coast of Thailand.

Sheer exhaustion overtook any sense of relief when my father delivered us safely to the shores of Thailand three days later. After nine days at sea, his mind finally allowed his body to collapse as soon as his feet touched the sand. He remained in deep sleep for three days. We had arrived at Pattaya, a beach on the north coast of Thailand — an overcrowded, unsanitary camp with makeshift lean-tos built from sticks and plastic sheeting. By the time my father woke, not one of us felt an inkling of regret when they kicked us out of Pattaya and sent us south to Songkhla on the Malaysian border — 'a less crowded camp', they promised. Duped once again, we discovered Songkhla: a fetid, ant-infested squalor with people sick and dying from lack of food, fresh water and basic hygiene. People would only use the latrines when the tide was high — this way it could be imagined that the falling tide washed away some of the stench. Luckily, we did not stay long.

Under the United States program for refugees, my father fell into a 'Category 3'. This meant that he qualified for entry into America because he held a high-ranking position in the South Vietnamese regime. As well, he collaborated closely with the US military before the war, working as an assistant accountant for the US Air Force. This meant we didn't need to wait for sponsorship from a relative who was already a US citizen. After three weeks at Songkhla,

immigration officials moved us to a transit centre in Bangkok called Dinh Dieng, where they told us we would wait only one month for resettlement into the US. We waited a year.

BIG MISTAKE 2
NEVER GIVE 100 PERCENT UNTIL YOU ARE WORKING FOR YOURSELF

Although slightly better than the refugee camps, living in Dinh Dieng was like living in a low-security prison — the major punishments were worry and boredom. The residents fell into two groups — those who had money and those who did not. Those belonging to the latter group, like my father, worked for free to pass the time. When there is nothing else to do but sit and wait, the mind starts to wander to places that are unwelcome — like that of the past, or perhaps the pessimistic possibilities of the future. For those with money but without the strength of will, alcohol became their only distraction. It helped them to escape the memories of the war and the horrors they had encountered at sea. Trauma was everywhere and alcohol, in many cases, was the only answer. Many attempted suicide — an obvious call that help was needed.

My father made sure to keep himself busy. He spoke English well and liked working with numbers. The United Nations representatives gave him the occasional job of translating menial documents. The decent jobs remained within the embassies — they went to those who were doctors or lawyers back in Vietnam. Typically, it did not take long for the people to elect my father as camp manager. His main duties included the overseeing of camp activities as well as acting as a go-between for the Vietnamese refugees and the Americans who ran the facility. For living expenses, we survived on handouts from the UN. As camp manager, my father worked hard in the hope of impressing the American officials so that we could leave as quickly as possible.

Dinh Dieng had an occupancy of around 800 South-East Asians at the time. Most were Vietnamese, the rest were from Laos, Cambodia and China — every one of us wanting a haven in America. A sleepy, dry and dusty compound, it consisted of a six-storey sleeping facility, a small religious room, a makeshift hospital, an empty gaol cell, less-than-adequate washing facilities, faded demountables for the officials, a restaurant for those who could afford it and a basic canteen for everyone else. Other 'small businesses' of less repute also operated within the compound. The sleeping facilities resembled a multi-level car park where those with money took residence indoors, farthest away from the perimeters. My father, my mother, Lewis and I slept outdoors, on the balcony of the ground floor. A single mosquito net protected us and a small awning hung over our head. When it rained, we were miserable.

A concrete wall surrounded the entire camp. A giant steel gate garnished with a spray of barbed wire locked us in. It was the concrete, steel and barbed wire that caused the greatest problems for the refugees. The Thais and Americans did not understand the tenacity of the Vietnamese. How could they lock the gates on people who value their freedom above all else? How could they keep these people imprisoned — people who have risked everything to escape the oppression of their own country? Inevitably, many escaped over the walls to do as they pleased. Unsurprisingly, they always returned to seek the comfort of their family and friends. Reports of their adventures in the city were an animated delight for those who dared not scale the wall.

In the early hours of another sleepy morning, a Thai soldier caught sight of a Vietnamese boy trying to climb back into the camp. Linh was a beautiful boy — tanned, smooth skinned and agile, with black eyes that lit up with cheek and curiosity at everything he saw. He had studied art before he became a refugee. Linh did not keep secret the infatuation he had with the young 'Thai Princess' who worked at a noodle stand somewhere in the centre of the city. Everybody liked Linh and wished him luck with his conquest. But his luck ran out that day. He found himself on the receiving end of a vicious bashing from the soldier who enjoyed his job a little too much. Naturally, Linh fought back, planting a clean elbow across the soft bone of the soldier's nose. The commotion woke everyone in the compound, including the United Nations representatives.

Clockwise from top: Lewis and I, Bangkok, 1978; my father and mother (left) with Lewis and me enjoying an 'excursion day' with friends outside the compound into Bangkok City, 1978; a photo taken inside the refugee camp, my father stands centre wth everyone prompted to wave American flags.

When my father arrived, Linh was already on his knees with his arms twisted behind his back. He had received such a beating that blood poured freely from his nose and his once slanted eyes swelled like two bloated goose livers. When the soldiers declared that Linh be thrown into the gaol cell, the Vietnamese surged forward in uproar, only to be stopped dead in their tracks by ten heated rifles. My father had not yet wiped the sleep from his eyes when the people started calling his name, 'Do something Lap! They'll listen to you Lap. Help him Lap!' He was wearing nothing but his faded yellow shorts when the mob began pushing him to the fore. When they lifted him onto the table, he wished that he had at least put on a shirt.

'Let him go,' my father demanded. 'No way!' shouted the soldier, nursing his busted nose. 'This one's getting locked up.' The mob pushed forward again, angered that Linh had now passed out. The rifles rose to eye line and my father intervened. 'If he goes to gaol, you will have a fight on your hands. You have only ten guns. There are eight hundred of us. You cannot shoot us all.'

The soldiers lowered their arms when Paul Jones, the program director of the camp, summonsed my father for a private meeting. He was a heavy-set man with big square shoulders to match his square jaw. His dark and neatly-combed hair matched his clean and simple attire. Only his slow words and gentle voice did not quite match his stature.

'The people are angry,' my father told the official, trying to ignore the fact that he was still half-naked in his sleepwear. 'There was no need to beat Linh so badly.'

'He broke the rules. He escaped the compound.'

My father forced a smile. 'He returned didn't he? They always return.'

'The soldiers want him locked up.'

'If you lock him up there will be trouble,' my father warned him.

'I have no choice Lap, he attacked a soldier.'

'The soldier hit him first,' my father seethed at the injustice.

Paul took a deep breath and tried to explain it as calmly as he could. 'You are in Thailand now and you must abide by Thai laws. I promise to have him out in one day. You must understand that I have to lock him up for at least one day.'

My father surrendered to the indignation. 'Can you assure me that he will not be beaten again?'

'Yes, I promise.'

True to his word, Paul Jones released Linh after one day. Linh's wounds, however, took much longer to heal. In protest, the refugees boycotted spending their money with the Thais. Of the businesses within the camp, the restaurant suffered the most. The determination of the Vietnamese to put up with the foul canteen food surprised even the Americans.

Later, the refugees made secret arrangements with street vendors from the outside. Hawker food passed through a secret hole in the compound wall. This delighted my mother enormously. She had craved Vietnamese food for so long. 'They made the best *Bun Bo Xao*!' she tells me. 'I'll never forget those first whiffs of smoky beef and lemon grass. It was pure heaven and so cheap too. We ate it almost every day.' It amazed my mother that, if only for a moment, even homesickness could be remedied with food.

The boycott continued for two weeks, leaving Paul Jones with another problem on his hands. The Thais blamed him for their loss of business. 'I have four children of my own to feed!' complained the restaurant owner. Paul wanted peace within the camp and called my father for another private meeting.

'The Thais are angry.' Paul told him. 'They're not making any money.'

'I know.' My father smiled as he said it.

Paul Jones got straight to the point. 'What do I need to do?'

My father had already prepared the wish list. 'First of all, we want better food in the canteen, not everyone can afford the restaurant food. Half the time, the canteen food is not fit for pigs.' Paul nodded. 'Second, we want our food served to us with respect, not slopped on the plate like a prisoner.'

'Yes, yes.' Paul rubbed his chin and felt relieved that the demands were simple.

My father continued. 'We want to sit on tables and chairs so that we can eat like humans'.

'Okay, okay.' Paul saw his point.

'Third, we want the front gates open.'

'Come again,' said Paul, not believing his ears.

'We – want – the – front – gates – open.'

'That's impossible!' Paul laughed, shaking his head in comic disbelief.

My father explained it simply, 'The Vietnamese climb out, the Vietnamese climb back in. You might as well leave the gates open.'

'I can't do that Lap. You know I can't.'

My father concluded the meeting. 'I know you can.'

And so, permission was granted for one level (of the six levels in the compound) per day to venture out into Bangkok. It was Linh who told my parents about the popular Vietnamese restaurant run by an expatriate couple. This was the highlight of our week, catching that bus to the quiet alleyway on the outskirts of the city — just so we could experience a small taste of freedom and a little taste of home.

Given the poor conditions we lived under, my mother, three months into her pregnancy, seemed to handle it well. My father, however, did not cope well at all with the wait. The time had come to confront Mr Barnes, the US Immigration Officer. Mr Barnes valued his own authority. He was a stern man whose position of power granted him an enormous superiority complex — and a distinct lack of consistency in his compassion. But to get to Mr Barnes you first

Above: A day trip into Bangkok City, my father and mother (left), Lewis and I (front row with hats) and Bac Truong (third from right). Below: Lewis and I at a fun park in Bangkok City, 1978.

encountered his assistant, Miss Callahan. My mother described her simply as 'a big fat woman who ignored us most of the time — in her eyes, we had no rights'.

My father asked Mr Barnes and Miss Callahan why it was that we were still waiting. He reminded them that it should not have been more than a one-month wait. He also reminded them that a 'Category 3' did not require sponsorship from a relative in the US. Miss Callahan did not appreciate my father demanding these questions be answered. She was an American who spoke the Queen's English and liked to elongate her words by curling her 'r's and rounding her 'o's as though her mouth and lips were permanently wrapped around a tight cumquat. 'We know the rrrules Mr Nguyen, we do not need for you to rrremind us of the rrrules.'

'Then why is our name still at the bottom of the list?' my father demanded.

Mr Barnes interrupted. 'That is our business Mr Nguyen. These things take time. You simply must wait your turn.'

Another two months passed and our turn had still not come. My father repeatedly confronted Mr Barnes and Miss Callahan, and they repeatedly ignored him — our file remained at the bottom of the pile. The injustice ate away at my father. He had worked hard for them. He had always given them more than they asked. He had shown them his worth.

This is so unfair. Why isn't our name at the top of that list? Why have all our friends left before us?

The clarity woke him like the painful shock of teeth biting tongue and drawing blood.

What a fool I have been? My hard work and effectiveness is the very thing that is keeping me here. Why would they want to lose someone like me? What a sucker I have been! I can't think of anyone who is more stupid than me. For six months, I have given them my best, and all the while my two young children and my pregnant wife are still hungry and still sleeping outside on the balcony floor.

BIG MISTAKE 3
WHEN STUCK IN A REFUGEE CAMP, DO NOT SPEAK THE TRUTH

Upon hearing of my father's resignation, Paul Jones was the first to express his sincerest regrets. Two days later, he couldn't wait to tell us that we were going to America. My father suspected that Paul had played a big part in speeding up the process. Even Mr Barnes thanked my father for his contribution to the camp and assured us that, 'It would not be long now.'

Around this time, on the other side of the world, a distant aunt on my mother's side had heard about our plight and immediately began organizing sponsorship papers for us to join her in America. 'Eight months in refugee camp, too long, no good!' Knowing that the process was faster for immediate family members, she falsely wrote on the application that my father was her younger brother. Long-distance communication was impossible and our well-meaning aunt had no way of knowing that we were already as good as getting on that plane. When the sponsorship papers arrived, Miss Callahan was quick to bring the discrepancy to her boss' attention.

'Don't think of me as a fool Mr Nguyen!' Mr Barnes slammed the papers down in front of my father's face. 'In one form you state that you are the eldest child in your family …'

'I am the eldest child.' My father couldn't understand it, but the look on Mr Barnes' face told him that the news was grim. Dread settled in his stomach.

'Please don't interrupt me Mr Nguyen. Now, in this other form, it states that you have an older sister in the United States. Now which one is the truth I wonder? You cannot fool us by taking both avenues. You cannot take whichever comes first, that is not how things work around here. These are serious offences Mr Nguyen. Don't think of me as a fool.'

Miss Callahan did not miss a beat. 'Mr Baaarnes does not like dealing with liars.'

'I do not like dealing with liars,' Mr Barnes confirmed.

'I did not lie! I don't know anything about the sponsorship papers. I have no sister in America.'

Hoping that he could find some inkling of compassion between the two of them, my father resorted to begging. He had never begged anyone for anything before that day.

'This is what we do to liars, Mr Nguyen.' Mr Barnes flicked his palm open and right on cue, Miss Callahan dropped the rubber stamp in his hand. With a thump on each document, Mr Barnes permanently assigned the word 'reject'.

It would have been easy for my father to fall into a state of depression, which, he admits, was almost the case. Despite the disappointment — the many disappointments — he knew that he had to remain optimistic; unfailingly optimistic. He owed it to hope — the one thing that had kept his family alive until now. The next plan was to hope for resettlement elsewhere.

Around this time, a correspondent for *Time* magazine had stationed himself inside Dinh Dieng. He conducted interviews and reported on the conditions of the refugees. Mr Barnes had boasted to the reporter that the maximum stay for all refugees was only 20 to 30 days. The reporter approached our family, curiously observing why a heavily pregnant woman, with two young children was living on a verandah. He asked my father how long we had lived under these conditions. Reluctant at first to tell the truth, my father conceded and told the reporter, 'Almost nine months.' Another big blunder! Any hope my father had left soon vanished. Any chance of getting out of there was gone.

Publicly humiliated by the revelation, Mr Barnes spent the next days writing letters to his colleagues around the world. He made sure that no country would accept our family again.

My mother gave birth to Luke and my father's desperation became absolute. It did not go unnoticed that, even after the birth, not one person offered our family a position indoors. My parents have always thought themselves to be resilient and resourceful people, proud and dignified. But they found it hard to be proud about living on handouts. They found it hard to maintain dignity with such a severe lack of privacy.

My parents questioned their strength and wondered how much more they could possibly endure. My father spent his days caring for Luke and my mother. Lewis and I spent our days running around the camp begging for food and harassing anyone we could for their old towels. We cut the worn towels into smaller pieces and made bibs and nappies for our new brother.

Everyone knew about our predicament. Paul Jones continued to express his sympathy. He confirmed that Mr Barnes had successfully prevented any country looking into our application. Still, Paul promised to do all he could to help us. His encouragement was the best he could give to relieve our injured spirits. He gave my father one hundred dollars to help with the baby.

My father usually found it difficult to sleep, often waking up in the middle of the night. If it was not the mosquitoes, it was the worry in his head, or sometimes, his old war wound, giving him chronic sciatica that shot deep into his buttocks and down both sides of his legs. Most of the time, the pain was bearable, but sometimes it was so acute that it nauseated him. On this particular night, something else woke him suddenly. He sat bolt upright. Three questions churned in his head.

Who am I? Where am I? What am I? I am a refugee. I live in a camp. I have no rights. I am the lowest human denominator. I have nothing. I am nobody.

In the night, while the rest of us slept, my father knew what he had to do. He took pen to paper and swallowed hard on his pride. He began to write:

> *Dear Mr Barnes,*
> *I would like to express to you my deepest and sincerest apologies for the humiliation that I have caused you and your people. I accept full responsibility for any trouble caused by my shameful outspokenness. I am so ashamed. I beg that you show mercy for my family, especially for my newborn son. You have the total respect of everyone in this camp and we all think of you as a great and compassionate leader. I hope that you can forgive me.*
> *Yours Sincerely,*
> *Lap Nguyen*

In the morning, my father handed the letter to Mr Barnes — that same afternoon, Mr Barnes informed us that we would be going to Australia.

ERNEST K. MA, B.Pharm., M.P.S., Dip.F.D.A., J.P.
Suite 1, 3/117 John St.Cabramatta 2166 Australia
Tel / Fax: (02) 9724 4293

AUSTRALIAN EMBA

BANGKOK

LETTER OF AUTHORITY FOR TRAVEL TO AUSTRALIA

(Subject to grant on arrival of an entry permit under the Migration Act 1958
as amended)

1. **FULL NAME:** . . . HA Quc Phuong . . . .

2. **DATE AND PLACE OF BIRTH:** . 2.7.1952 . Saigon, Vietnam . . . .

3. **AUTHORITY NO.** . . . . . B 6 71 969 . . . .

4. **TYPE OF AUTHORITY:** . . . . ASSISTED MIGRANT: . . . . .

5. **DATE AND PLACE OF ISSUE:** . . . 28 JUN 1978 . . . . BANGKOK

6. **DATE OF EXPIRY:** . . . . 20 JUL 1978 . . . .

7. **GOOD FOR SINGLE ENTRY FOR** . . FOUR . . . . PERSONS

8. Period of stay in Australia which may be authorised by issue of entry
   permit on arrival: indefinite

9. **CATEGORY:** . . . . . K51 . . . . J.1.   W353 . . . .

NGUYEN, Lap Phuong	9.10.1972	Saigon, Vietnam	K51	J.1	W354
NGUYEN, Lu	11.10.1973	Saigon, Vietnam	K51	J.1	W354
NGUYEN, Lan	4.6.1978	Bangkok, Thailand	K51	J.1	W354

Left: 'Letter of Authority for Travel to Australia'
— my mother (left), me, Lewis and Luke, 1978.
Above: My father outside the American Embassy,
Bangkok, 1978.

BÚN VỚI RAU THƠM
vermicelli salad

250 g (9 oz) rice vermicelli
2 handfuls bean sprouts
1 Lebanese (short) cucumber
1 handful perilla leaves, torn
1 handful mint leaves, torn
80 g (2³/4 oz/1 cup frimly packed)
   sliced iceberg lettuce
125 ml (4 fl oz/¹/2 cup) dipping fish
   sauce (page 33)

4 tablespoons spring onion oil
   (page 37)
4 tablespoons fried red Asian shallots
   (page 38)
4 tablespoons chopped roasted peanuts
   (page 40)

Cook the vermicelli in a large saucepan of boiling water for 5 minutes, or as per packet instructions. Turn off the heat and allow to stand in the water for another 5 minutes. Strain into a colander and rinse under cold water, then set aside to dry at room temperature, covered with a damp towel or plastic wrap.

To assemble the salad, divide the bean sprouts evenly among 4 bowls, then top with the vermicelli. Finely slice the cucumber, then cut it into matchsticks. In a bowl gently mix the cucumber, perilla, mint and lettuce and place on top of the vermicelli. Dress with the dipping fish sauce and garnish with the spring onion oil, fried shallots and peanuts.

SERVES 4

LUKE NGUYEN: *Barbecue dishes are available on most street corners in Saigon, with each vendor specializing in only one dish. For many long moments I have stood there contemplating which dish to choose. Enticed by the thick smoky aroma, the fresh herbs, the chargrilled meat, I would shuffle myself onto a very low communal table and indulge in all. As I ate my way through Vietnam, trying different interpretations of these dishes, I came across various herbs that were not familiar to me. This was one of the many highlights of my first visit.*

Herbs are essential to Vietnamese cuisine — not only are they used for flavour and aroma, but also for their medicinal qualities. When purchasing herbs, choose the freshest bunch you can and wash only when you are ready to use them.

BÚN THỊT NƯỚNG
chargrilled pork with vermicelli salad

1 kg (2 lb 4 oz) pork neck
vermicelli salad, to serve (page 118)

MARINADE
3 spring onions (scallions)
100 ml (3¹/2 fl oz) fish sauce
2 tablespoons sugar
115 g (4 oz/¹/3 cup) honey

1 teaspoon cracked black pepper
4 tablespoons vegetable oil
3 tablespoons dipping fish sauce
  (page 33)

Finely slice the pork neck across the grain into 3 mm (¹/8 in) pieces. To make the marinade, bash the spring onions into a paste in a mortar. Combine the spring onion paste and remaining marinade ingredients, except the dipping fish sauce, in a bowl. Add the pork to the marinade and mix well. Marinate for at least 3 hours, or preferably overnight.

To serve, chargrill the pork and serve on top of vermicelli salad and dress with the dipping fish sauce. Alternatively, wrap the pork and vermicelli in lettuce with fresh herbs, with dipping fish sauce on the side.

SERVES 8

LUKE NGUYEN: *This is such a quick and simple dish to prepare and it is a favourite of mine. At Red Lantern, we serve this as a light lunch. It is also a very popular dish in Cabramatta restaurants. I love that I can taste the flavour of the wok flame on the beef. The heat of the beef and the scent of lemon grass on cool vermicelli noodles and crunchy bean sprouts is a great example of the balance of hot and cold.*

BÚN BÒ XÀO
wok-tossed beef and lemon grass

500 g (1 lb 2 oz) beef sirloin or
  rump steak
3 lemon grass stems, white part only,
  finely chopped
2 tablespoons fish sauce
2 garlic cloves, crushed
2 tablespoons oil
1 small onion, sliced
2 teaspoons sugar

pinch of salt
pinch of fine white pepper
vermicelli salad, to serve (page 118)
1 tablespoon fried red Asian shallots
  (page 38)
1 tablespoon chopped roasted peanuts
  (page 38)
2 tablespoons dipping fish sauce
  (page 33)

Slice the beef into 2 mm (1/16 in) strips and combine in a bowl with 2 tablespoons of the chopped lemon grass, all the fish sauce and half the garlic. Allow the meat to marinate for 10 minutes.

Add half the oil to a wok over medium heat and fry half of the onion and half of the remaining lemon grass and half of the remaining garlic for 1–2 minutes, or until fragrant. Increase the heat to very high and add half the beef and its marinade to the wok. Stir-fry for 2 minutes, then remove the beef from the wok. Repeat the previous process with the remaining beef, onion, lemon grass and garlic. Return the first batch of beef to the wok, season with the sugar, salt and pepper and continue to stir-fry to heat through. Serve on top of vermicelli salad. To finish, top with the essential fried shallots, peanuts and dipping fish sauce.

SERVES 6

MARK JENSEN: *I prepared these delicious pork skewers for my daughter Mia's first birthday party. We had a wonderful picnic by the beach. My mother-in-law took her first bite of one and immediately enquired, 'Who made this?' A sudden nervous silence filled the air as everyone eyed each other, not knowing what to say. After a long lull I spoke up, 'Why do you ask?' 'Oh, because it tastes so good!' she replied.*

You can eat these on their own with dipping fish sauce (page 33), or with a bowl of vermicelli salad (page 118) dressed with dipping fish sauce.

NEM NƯỚNG
chargrilled pork sausage

16 spring onions (scallions), white part
   only, chopped
2 lemon grass stems, white part only,
   chopped
2 teaspoons minced garlic

1 teaspoon salt
2 teaspoons white pepper
700 g (1 lb 9 oz) minced (ground) pork
2 tablespoons fish sauce
2 tablespoons oil

Soak 12 bamboo skewers in water for 30 minutes. Put the spring onions, lemon grass, garlic, salt and pepper in a mortar and pound to a fine paste. Add to a large bowl with the minced pork and fish sauce and mix well. Divide the pork mixture into 12 portions and roll into sausage shapes about 8–10 cm (3¼–4 in) long. Thread the mixture on the prepared bamboo skewers or lemon grass stems, brush with the oil and chargrill for 8 minutes, turning every 2 minutes, until cooked.

MAKES 12

MARK JENSEN: *This recipe works well in a professional kitchen, but at home you may need to cook it in smaller batches. Have all your ingredients ready to go, as with all stir-fries, the action is fast and furious. Fresh bamboo shoots (if available) are relatively easy to prepare and well worth the effort. If pressed for time you will find pre-prepared bamboo shoots in Asian supermarkets.*

BÒ XÀO MĂNG
wok-tossed beef with bamboo shoots and basil

500 g (1 lb 2 oz) beef sirloin or
   rump steak
1 tablespoon oil
1/2 onion, sliced
1 garlic clove, chopped
100 g (31/2 oz) sliced bamboo shoots

2 tablespoons oyster sauce
1 tablespoon fish sauce
1 tablespoon sugar
1/2 teaspoon salt
1 teaspoon cracked black pepper
1 handful basil leaves, torn

Slice the beef into 4 cm x 5 mm (11/2 x 1/4 in) pieces. Heat a wok over very high heat. Add the oil, beef, onion and garlic, tossing to seal the beef. Add the bamboo shoots, oyster sauce, fish sauce, sugar, salt, pepper and finally the basil. Stir-fry the beef for 2–5 minutes, depending on how well cooked you like it, then turn out onto a serving platter. Serve with jasmine rice.

SERVES 2 AS A MAIN, OR 4 AS A SHARED FEAST

LUKE NGUYEN: *Certain varieties of coconuts are harvested for their sweet juice, which is often used in making coconut drinks or as a cooking liquid — such as in this recipe. When purchasing coconut juice from Asian supermarkets, ask for the variety that can be used for cooking. The drinking variety is often not appropriate as it is usually sweetened and contains coconut flesh. Be sure not to confuse coconut juice with coconut milk.*

GÀ RÔ TI

soya chicken drumsticks

2 kg (4 lb 8 oz) chicken drumsticks
3 tablespoons fish sauce
3 tablespoons soy sauce
125 ml (4 fl oz/1/2 cup) shaoxing
   (Chinese cooking wine)
250 ml (9 fl oz/1 cup) coconut juice
1 tablespoon sesame oil
95 g (3 1/4 oz/1/2 cup) soft brown sugar
1 tablespoon cracked black pepper

1 onion, diced
8 garlic cloves, chopped
1 tablespoon finely sliced ginger
250 ml (9 fl oz/1 cup) oil, for frying the
   drumsticks, plus 2 tablespoons extra
500 ml (17 fl oz/2 cups) chicken stock
   (page 36)
2 spring onions (scallions), sliced
1 handful coriander (cilantro) leaves

Clean the drumsticks of excess fat, wash and pat dry with paper towel and put in a large bowl with the fish sauce, soy sauce, shaoxing, coconut juice, sesame oil, brown sugar, black pepper, 1 tablespoon of the diced onion, 1 tablespoon of the chopped garlic and the ginger. Mix to combine the ingredients well and marinate for 4 hours in the refrigerator.

Remove the drumsticks from the marinade and pat dry with paper towel, reserving the marinade for later use. Add the oil to a wok or large saucepan over high heat and fry the chicken in small batches until golden brown. Remove and set aside.

Once all the chicken is cooked, discard the oil and clean the wok. Add the extra oil to the wok and fry the remaining onion and garlic until golden, add all of the chicken back to the wok along with the reserved marinade and chicken stock. Cover with a lid and simmer for 15 minutes.

Remove the lid and increase the heat slightly. Reduce the sauce by half, turning the drumsticks regularly as the sauce reduces, about 30 minutes.

Once cooked, the chicken should fall off the bone. Remove the chicken to a serving platter and boil the sauce for a further 5 minutes before pouring it over. Garnish with the sliced spring onions and coriander. Serve with jasmine rice, sticky rice or a fresh baguette.

SERVES 4 AS A MAIN, OR 6 AS PART OF A SHARED FEAST

LUKE NGUYEN: *Growing up, we went to a lot of family barbecues — but not the sausage and T-bone kind. Our barbecues offered beef wrapped in betel leaf, chicken wings marinated in soy and honey, satay chicken skewers and spiced quail. And for some Vietnamese authenticity, a suckling pig or a baby goat would be turning on a spit.*

Try preparing a Vietnamese dish for the next barbecue you go to. You'll add such excitement to the party — maybe not so much with a baby goat in tow — but Nem Nuong or Bo La Lot are so much fun.

BÒ LÁ LỐT
beef and lemon grass wrapped in betel leaf

750 g (1 lb 10 oz) minced (ground) beef
100 g (3½ oz) pork fat
3 lemon grass stems, white part only, finely chopped
8 spring onions (scallions), white part only, finely chopped

1 garlic clove, crushed, finely chopped
3 teaspoons salt
3 teaspoons fine white pepper
2 bunches betel leaves

Combine all the ingredients except the betel leaves in a bowl and mix well. Allow the flavours to infuse for 15 minutes. Meanwhile, pick the individual betel leaves and wash in cold water. Lay the leaves flat on a cloth to dry.

To form the rolls, lay a large betel leaf (or 2 smaller leaves), shiny side down, on a board with the stem of the leaf pointing towards you. Spoon approximately 1 tablespoon of the beef mixture onto the bottom edge of the leaf. Work it into a sausage shape, then roll the leaf from bottom to top and place the seam flat on your bench to stop the leaf unrolling. Repeat this process until you have used all of the beef. The mixture should make about 40 rolls.

Cook the parcels, seam first, on a chargrill or barbecue hotplate over medium heat, turning to colour all over, for about 5 minutes, or until done.

MAKES 40

LUKE NGUYEN: *This is one of my mother's favourite desserts. I have introduced this dessert to many Red Lantern guests and it has become a favourite for many.*

Sugar bananas are the best to use because they are starchier, sweeter and won't collapse when cooked. Be sure to stir the pan consistently during cooking so that the tapioca pearls don't stick to the base of the saucepan.

CHÈ CHUỐI CHƯNG
tapioca pudding with banana and cassava

40 g (1¹/₂ oz) tapioca
100 g (3¹/₂ oz) cassava, cut into
   1 cm (¹/₂ in) dice
140 g (5 oz/²/₃ cup) sugar
250 ml (9 fl oz/1 cup) coconut cream
3 sugar bananas

1¹/₂ teaspoons salt
250 ml (9 fl oz/1 cup) sweetened
   coconut cream (page 129)
3 tablespoons chopped roasted peanuts
  (page 38)
1 tablespoon toasted sesame seeds

Bring 1 litre (35 fl oz/4 cups) water to the boil in a saucepan. Add the tapioca, stir to separate them and cook on a rapid boil for 4 minutes. Strain into a fine sieve or colander, rinse under cold water and set aside.

Meanwhile, put 600 ml (21 fl oz) water, the cassava, sugar and half the coconut cream in a large saucepan over high heat and bring to the boil. Reduce the heat and simmer for 15 minutes.

Peel and slice the bananas crossways into 5 mm (¹/₄ in) slices. Add the tapioca and bananas to the pan and stir constantly for 10 minutes. (This is important, otherwise the tapioca pearls will sink and burn on the bottom of the pan.) Add the remaining coconut cream and salt and continue to simmer for 2 minutes. To serve, divide evenly into 6 bowls and garnish with sweetened coconut cream, roasted peanuts and sesame seeds.

SERVES 6

CHÈ KHOAI MÔN
black sticky rice with taro

100 g (3¹/2 oz) taro, cut into
   1 cm (¹/2 in) dice
250 g (9 oz/1¹/4 cups) black
   glutinous rice
250 ml (9 fl oz/1 cup) coconut cream
1 teaspoon salt

145 g (5¹/4 oz/²/3 cup) caster
   (superfine) sugar
250 ml (9 fl oz/1 cup) sweetened
   coconut cream (see below)
1 tablespoon toasted sesame seeds

Cook the taro in salted water for about 5 minutes, or until *al dente*. Rinse under cold water and set aside.

Put the rice in a large saucepan and cover with cold water, agitate the rice with your hand to release excess husks and impurities, then carefully strain off the water. Repeat this process three times. Then, add cold water to cover the top of the rice by 2.5 cm (1 in) and add half the coconut cream to the saucepan. Bring to the boil, then reduce the heat and simmer for 30 minutes, stirring occasionally. The rice should be tender but still maintain its shape.

Add the taro and cook for a further 5 minutes. Stir through the remaining coconut cream, salt and sugar. To serve, divide into 6 bowls and garnish with sweetened coconut cream and toasted sesame seeds.

SERVES 6

NƯỚC CỐT DỪA
sweetened coconut cream

250 ml (9 fl oz/1 cup) coconut cream
1 tablespoon sugar

1 teaspoon potato starch

Add the coconut cream, sugar and potato starch to a saucepan and mix well. Heat the mixture slowly, stirring constantly. Do not allow it to boil. Once hot, remove from the heat and serve.

MAKES 250 ML (9 FL OZ/1 CUP)

the chinks
in his armour

Compassion fatigue had not yet set in when our family arrived in Australia.

It is widely acknowledged that the most comprehensive, and arguably the most successful, effort to integrate the Vietnamese people was made by the Australian government. Prime Minister Malcolm Fraser led the country at the time — his campaign represented a radical break from the once notorious 'White Australia' policy, where the colour of a person's skin determined an immigrant's chance of selection. Upon arrival, the government housed us at Westbridge Migrant Hostel — a place in south-west Sydney especially constructed for new migrants and refugees. It provided a supportive environment to help set us up for the difficult transition into an alien society. These days, the hostel lays baron next to Villawood Detention Centre — a colourless, uncompassionate place where hundreds of asylum seekers from across the world remain locked up behind the razor wire of prejudice and bureaucracy.

Westbridge Migrant Hostel consisted of dozens of small, brown brick houses containing two-bedroom apartments — our family had an apartment to ourselves. As a family, we were entitled to stay at the hostel for one year, though my father was determined to get out sooner. During this time, he took up orientation classes to help him find work and learn more about Australian systems and way of life. Kitchens did not exist in the apartments — instead, we queued up and ate all our meals in the canteen. If I close my eyes hard enough, I can still conjure the smells of tepid beef stews, soggy mashed potatoes and rubbery, overcooked carrots. In fact, my earliest memory of living in Australia is sneaking outside to

Previous page: Luke and I, 1981.
Left: Luke (age 5) on Uncle Thuan's car at Bonnyrigg, 1983.

sit under the concrete stairs of our apartment — a secret place where I could sit alone and suck on tiny dried shrimp that I had kept hidden in a small film canister. Sometimes Lewis would join me in savouring a chilli sauce sandwich — anything for a taste of Asia.

My father quickly found a job working on the production line at the Sunbeam factory in Campsie, assembling electric food mixers, toasters and kettles. He had to work harder than most — not only were we a one-income family with not a cent in the bank, we were also a family with two fussy children who refused to eat any of the canteen food provided for us. We found the cheese sandwiches served at lunch particularly hard to comprehend. We were not alone in our dislike of the food. The residents objected to not being allowed to cook the food of their homeland. Thankfully, the downtime provided opportunities for clandestine cooking of more culturally acceptable food.

For my father, the culture shock of his new environment was incalculable. He had served in a war, survived an ordeal at sea and endured the degrading conditions of a third-world refugee camp. Now, he was confronted with the demoralizing aspect of working in an environment that not only demanded skills well below his capabilities but that was also rife with bigotry and racism. Sunbeam gave my father the graveyard shift from 2pm to 2am. 'The train ride home was the worst,' says my father. 'Every night was dangerous. The locals wanted to beat me. They shouted, "Go home to your own country!" I cried every night coming home on that train. Those bigots … they have never known suffering or what it means to risk everything … they didn't understand why we were here. A lot of us cried in those days. Just like a newborn, we started our lives the day we got here, we came with empty hands; no house, no job, no money. We didn't know the laws or the systems — many of us didn't even know the language. We had absolutely nothing. There was so much pressure … so much pressure and stress.'

There were few people in the Vietnamese community actually working at jobs compatible with their level of educational attainment in Vietnam. With limited resources, there was not much in the way of training, retraining, or even recognition of overseas skills and qualifications. 'So much skill and potential wasted,' says my father, 'but we had no choice, we took the least popular jobs — the ones the Australians didn't want.' My father's friends at the hostel found jobs as fruit pickers, labourers and cleaners. Although the strain was immense, my father remained determined to adapt and succeed.

For my mother, the first few months were possibly the most painful of her life. She received a telegram with news that her father had passed away while we were still in Bangkok — a month before we arrived in Australia. My grandfather died of worry. He couldn't stand not knowing the fate of his daughter and his grandchildren. No-one knew whether we would live or die. My grandfather turned to chain smoking; with tobacco eventually poisoning his lungs. My mother's siblings in Vietnam had kept the news from her to avoid adding further stress to an already difficult pregnancy. Mourning the loss of her father so long after his death had added to the emptiness she had brought with her to this foreign country. Her grief could not be shared with her mother, brothers or sisters — all of whom she missed so much.

During the day, while my mother cared for our baby brother, Luke, Lewis and I explored the hostel surrounds. One day we peeped into a neighbouring apartment and laid eyes on our very first television set. We were mesmerized — we had to have one no matter what. After almost continuous badgering, my father gave in and borrowed $50 from a friend to buy our first TV — a huge amount of money for anyone at the time. My father sighs as he confesses, 'This was the first in a long chain of debts … I was forever signing debt papers.' He bought a secondhand Philips with Hi-Fi Spatial Stereo and 4-Speaker Super Selection. It stopped functioning many years ago, but my father refuses to get rid of it. It still sits in his livingroom today to remind him, he says, 'of how we got here and where we came from.'

Around the same time as the television arrived, I laid eyes on my very first head of bright red, curly hair — belonging to a woman working at the hostel. I loved it, and was determined to have the same locks. Although my parents couldn't afford to change the colour, they finally gave into the harassment for the curls. At the age of five, I received my first perm and looked fabulous.

We finally won our independence and left the hostel after four months. My father found a white-brick two-bedroom unit in Berala in south-west Sydney. He left Sunbeam and, somewhat ironically, landed a job at the nearby Westbridge Hostel as the kitchen hand. The graveyard shift was the only position offered. In the afternoon, he peeled potatoes and made chips. After dinner service, he washed dishes and scrubbed the pots and pans. At night until 3am, he chopped a mountain of vegetables. On his first day in the kitchen, the head cook had given him specific instructions to shred lettuce and julienne vegetables for salad. My father couldn't understand why this crazy woman made him perform such a time consuming and arduous task. She must be crazy, he thought, either that or she is torturing me. Why would anyone want to waste so much time cutting vegetables into tiny sticks? Thinking that he knew better, my father quickly tore the lettuce into smaller pieces and chopped the vegetables into rough chunks. So much faster, he thought, and left to take the 3.30am train home. When he arrived for his second shift, an impatient greeting awaited him. 'This is for pigs!' the head cook shouted, throwing his handy work back at him. My father learned his first culinary lesson that day — 'Australians like their food pretty.'

Back at Berala, the only food concern my mother had was that her food be eaten — every single mouthful. As children, my mother would feed Lewis and myself a banquet of no less than four or five dishes at a time. Our meals consisted of the usual meat, fish, vegetable and soup dishes with rice — too much food for any young child to sit with. Usually, around the three-hour mark, we began to nod off. Our heads would jerk back and forth from momentary sleep, our mouths still full of food, and always some sort of drool escaping from the corners — if not because we were already full to the brim, then because we were bored beyond consciousness.

After a short kip, I would open one eye, making sure Lewis was still humped over the table and, with the speed of a ferret, I would scrape the remainder of my food into Lewis' bowl declaring to my mother that I had finished. Poor Lewis, my mother never listened to his complaints about the injustice he had been served.

'Even when you and Lewis were babies, we fed you nothing but the best,' my father tells me, referring to 'Guigoz', the infant formula known as 'liquid gold' — a Swiss brand so rich, it is also sold as 'milk for coffee lovers'. It cost ten times more than the average infant formula and was very much a status symbol in Vietnam. The strong aluminium tin even became a collector's item. My parents stored all sorts of things in the tins, from tea leaves and coffee beans, to herbs and spices. Later, my father used the container to hide his life's savings, turning the 'liquid gold' into solid gold —

a back-up plan in case we failed in our escape. If the communists imprisoned my father, my mother was to use this gold to buy his freedom. Before leaving Vietnam, my father transferred what remained of his assets into thin gold bars and diamonds. The Guigoz container was strong, waterproof and airtight — the perfect size and shape for fitting into the drainpipe of the bathroom sink. My grandmother later spent the secret Guigoz fortune on the safe passage of two uncles, three aunties and one cousin to Australia. My father sponsored the relatives under the 'family reunion' program. He would quickly need a bigger house to welcome them.

~

We eventually moved into a large four-bedroom house in the nearby suburb of Regents Park. The rent was cheap because we lived directly across the road from the railway tracks. The house had a huge backyard with a derelict car thrown in as part of the package. The pleasant things about that house I remember with a smile. The dark green trimming around the top gutter stood out charmingly against the white paint of the timber façade. It matched the green iron leaf trim that wrapped around the front verandah, giving the house a quaint, colonial feel. In the backyard, a wild choko plant thrived, its vines had strangled the life from the abandoned car and kept the suffocated vehicle in its place. In the front grew a stocky pomegranate tree bearing fruit so sour we winced at the sensation every

Clockwise from left: My mother and father making new friends, 1979; my mother, Luke, Lewis and I (with my fabulous perm) in front of our new TV, Westbridge Migrant Hostel, 1978; Lewis and I at the hostel after the recent death of our maternal grandfather, 1978.

time. In the mornings, I watched my father perform his daily exercise — he liked to roll every major joint in his body clockwise then anti-clockwise. I joked that he secretly practised for the under 40's Hula Hoop finals. Once a month my father gave haircuts in the backyard. He always used the same technique and equipment — a round plastic bowl to place over our heads and a pair of industrial-strength scissors to cut around it.

On the weekends, my father and his friends went diving for shellfish at Kurnell in southern Sydney. I would watch the men dive with uneasy admiration as I impatiently waited for them to come up for air. On the edge of panic every time, I compared my own breath-holding ability to their experienced lungs. When they finally resurfaced, I would burst into tears of relief and they would laugh at my distress — crooked teeth beaming at me through wet smiles, handing me hairy mussels, pippis and periwinkles so spiky I thought my little hands would bleed. At home, we soaked the shellfish in buckets of cold water, adding chopped chillies so the pippies would spit their sand. We lay down two heavy electric heaters my mother bought at a garage sale. With the heat bars facing up to the ceiling, we placed the periwinkles on top of the grill and savoured the unmistakable aroma of barbecued shellfish. My mother gave each of us a sewing needle to pick out the sweet, yielding flesh. With a quick dip into some fish sauce with ginger, the clean flavour of the sea and the subtle richness of these succulent creatures invaded my mouth so completely that for the duration of that meal, I could pretend that I had not a worry in the world.

Eleven people lived in our house at Regents Park. Uncle and Aunty Five lived in one room with their two-year-old daughter, Thu. Uncle and Aunty Seven lived in another. Lewis, Luke and I shared a third room with my Aunty Ten. My parents slept in the front room, closest to the consuming noise and vibrations of the passing trains. To support us all, my father took on extra jobs. He came home one day in a dark green second-hand Ford Escort. I thought it strange that the car only had two doors. Attached to the top of the car stood a professionally painted sign, 'Lap's Driving School', while the number plates read 'LAP 888'. My father became the first Vietnamese driving instructor in Sydney. 'There were so many Vietnamese but no one to teach them how to drive.' In the mornings he taught and in the afternoons he worked in the hostel kitchen. As well, he acted as an interpreter on the side. I rarely saw my father, but the few times that I did, I could see that uneasiness agitated his brow and tension weighed so heavily on his shoulders, his whole being sank closer to the ground. He grunted at the people he lived with and seemed annoyed at the world in general. We did our best to stay out of his way.

My father soon acquired a reputation within the Vietnamese community for being a 'special' kind of driving instructor — one who liked to yell abuse and add derogatory innuendo into the mix. The fact that he was the only Vietnamese driving instructor must have contributed largely to the student's perseverance. The lessons often ran over schedule as it usually involved the student having to pull over for a cry, or my father demanding complete attention when he told them how grateful they should be, to be exposed to such a fine teacher with tactics as hard as his. Sure enough, most of the students passed their driving examinations at the first attempt — a fact he still brags about on occasion. For the few who didn't pass the initial test, he motivated them to persist until they did. In his book, *The Dragon's Journey*, sports masseur to the stars, Duy Long Nguyen ('Longy'), respected for his magic healing hands, recounts of how my father consoled him with words of encouragement. 'A lot of people don't pass first go. It's just the way it is. You know you can drive — all you have to do now is learn to drive safely.'

At home, my father was always angry. He had an anger in him that neither he nor anyone else could explain. He became like a faulty pressure cooker, always on the boil — a rolling heat building up inside waiting to explode in the most destructive way. Perhaps the accumulated weight of responsibility grew too much for him, perhaps the hurdles of adaptation had become too difficult to cope with; perhaps having to support so many people all living under the same roof strained his patience and drained his resources. Maybe the sciatic nerve pained him again, pinching from hours of sitting in a hot car. It was not the first time I witnessed my father offload his anger upon my mother, but it was the first time that he had inflicted permanent physical damage. I was six-years-old at the time.

'I had nightmares.' My father tells me, 'The same dream over and over. I am back in Vietnam making plans for the escape. The dream is so real. I am back in the water with nowhere to go, and then I wake up.' My father had constant flashbacks to the war. Part of his job as a lieutenant in artillery was to count the dead bodies after the kill. He would assess the damage so he could better calculate his aim for next time. 'I don't know how many I killed, one shell killed so many.' The scars from his own bullet wounds resemble a question mark covering the length of his spine.

Many of my father's friends came to him with the same sorts of flashbacks, with some memories far more horrific. Visitors came to ask for his advice about the laws and the language. Often they came to ease feelings of loneliness and isolation. Some struggled to cope with the scars of past experiences, finding it hard to simply function, let alone provide for their families. 'Many had symptoms of depression,' says San Duy Nguyen, a Vietnamese-born psychiatrist who dealt with many Vietnamese refugees at the time, 'but if you consider the hardships they have endured you would expect a higher incidence of mental health problems.' I have spoken recently to my father about this phenomenon and asked if he would agree; that he and his friends might have benefited all those years ago from

Clockwise from left: Lewis and I at the Sydney Opera House, 1981; Lewis, me, my cousin Thu and Luke at another 'freebie' event my father read about in the paper (hosted by Barbecues Galore — cow on a spit); a family picnic at the Botanical Gardens, my mother (left), me standing alongside Aunty Ten (as always) in the distance, Luke in his pram, Uncle and Aunty Five, their daughter Thu and Lewis.

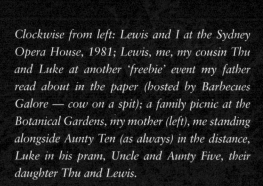

seeking professional guidance, if not to allow some sort of healing then at least to acknowledge the darkness that festered within. In typical fashion, my father responded, 'What for? What was the point? We just got on with it.'

The level of perception young children can possess is a constant source of amazement for me. I look at my own daughter and the ease at which she can sense the mood of her surroundings — whether it is from the observation of a small gesture, a tone of voice, or something as simple as a sombre silence. Is it any wonder that some of us are able to remember minute details of our own childhood, storing the memories, both good and bad, in the back of our mind's archive for later contemplation?

Of the adults in the household, it is only my Aunty Ten who treated us with the kind of respect and tolerance that any child deserves. She is called Aunty Ten because she is the ninth child in her family. The strong respect for position in Vietnamese culture requires that each child be referred to by the number in which he or she is born into the family. To confuse matters slightly, there is never a 'Number One' child — as it is the parents who come first and foremost. The eldest child therefore starts at 'Number Two', the second child 'Number Three' and so on. My father is 'Number Two' in his family, as am I.

Aunty Ten was the sister I never had and, at times, the mother I never had. She always made an effort. She took us out on excursions and chaperoned a day's escape from the prison my father had created for us. She wanted us to have fun, to enjoy moments of laughter and to experience a little freedom, however temporary that moment might be. She took us to see our first movie, *Annie* — the orphan girl with bright red curly hair who wished she could have a better life. She made sure to take us with her when she visited her friends and she bought us chocolates just to see a smile on our faces. Aunty Ten's departure from my life would later be the source of a piercing sadness that took me many years to overcome. I cannot blame her for leaving us. She has her own family now and resides in the United States.

Around this time, Aunty Ten studied to become a hairdresser. The doll heads she brought home to practise on terrified me. The heads differed in skin colour and hairstyle, but all had the same big, bulging eyes with scary teeth smiles so wide the cheeks were enormous in proportion. Aunty Ten liked to clamp the heads to the dining table so she could study them while she ate. The dining room led to the backyard and to the only toilet we had. The outhouse scenario was scary enough in the middle of the night without having to confront a possessed mannequin head on the way. I would wake Lewis to share my fear and every night, half-asleep, he would accompany me obediently. I do not know if Aunty Ten was ever a good hairdresser, but if the length of time she took to cut one head of hair equated to her level of ability, then she was indeed the finest hairdresser that I had ever met. We looked forward to my Aunt's haircuts with as much trepidation as glee. Trepidation because the sitting would last for at least three hours (without a break) and glee because the matching flat top mullets and rat tails with tinted blonde tips were such a welcome change from my father's five-minute bowl.

One thing remained certain; Aunty Ten never had a flair for cooking, especially when it came to our school lunches. She did not understand that a frozen beef patty from Franklins required defrosting before cooking — which is actually beside the point, as there was never any attempt to either defrost or cook the frozen disc of meat she stuck between two pieces of thin, white bread. On our way to school, Lewis and I would throw our raw, wet sandwiches in the same spot over the side of the railway bridge. Occasionally we tiptoed over the rails to check on the progress of our mouldy pile, which had over the months grown into an impressive mound. At the other end of the spectrum, my mother made lunches for us that were too elaborate to be considered socially acceptable at school. While the other six-year-olds brought the standard ham and cheese sandwiches, my mother forced Lewis and I to carry a four-tiered contraption made of shiny aluminium — a 'lunch box' much too large to conceal in our school backpacks. Each tier contained a different dish — she gave us meat for protein, rice for basic carbohydrates, vegetables for vitamins, and always, a tier of soup for easy digestion. When stacked up, the tiers clamped together for efficient maintenance of heat and portability. With chopsticks in one hand, a soup spoon in the other, and our lunch spread out before us, Lewis and I would cop the usual taunts.

> You've got funny eyes,
> and we've got our meat pies.
> We are the bestest bunch,
> cos you've got a smelly lunch.

We found it surprisingly easy to shut out the teasing and the laughter. It was because we had each other and because we knew that those kids had no idea what they were missing. Recently, I spotted a fancier version of our tiffin carrier on a 'must have' page of a popular style magazine. Made of shiny chrome, it came encased in dark brown leather complete with detailed stitching. It is amusing to me now that something so 'un-Australian' in those years is considered a lunchtime style accessory today.

Sometimes my mother would accompany us on school excursions. Instead of packing pre-made sandwiches from home just like everybody else, she liked to bring along every piece of equipment, utensil and ingredient necessary to make our lunches fresh. 'So much better this way,' she would say, 'No soggy bread, no bruised vegetables ... everything so fresh.' Her bag of tricks included a chopping board, a serrated bread knife, a sharp cutting knife, a bottle of soy sauce, salt and pepper shakers, crisp Vietnamese bread rolls, home-made pâté, pork terrine, mayonnaise, cucumbers, stalks of spring onions (scallions), fresh chilli, pickled vegetables and fresh coriander (cilantro). Come lunchtime, we needed space for this spread and could be seen squatting on the ground, Vietnamese style, making our *banh mi thit* (Vietnamese pork rolls). I have no doubt that some of the kids envied us but mostly they just stared and made fun.

These days, everyone eats *banh mi thit*. I can declare with confidence that a *banh mi thit* is undoubtedly the healthiest, tastiest, most satisfying and best value sandwich I can get at anytime. There are at least ten Vietnamese bakeries in Cabramatta alone that sell *banh mi thit* — each having their own version of crisp bread, mayonnaise, pork and pickled vegetables. The constant demand has called for some bakeries to remain open 24 hours a day. The bread is baked on the premises and the rolls are made to order. In twenty years, inflation has hardly affected this cheap and wholesome food.

We went our separate ways once my uncles and aunties could support themselves. The New South Wales Housing Commission enabled my parents to afford a house in Bonnyrigg, a suburb in western Sydney. It is within these walls that most of our childhood occurred. To help make ends meet, my mother found work in a sewing factory as soon as Luke was old enough to go to school. Lewis and I thought it hilarious that Luke cried so much on his first day. My father scolded us for laughing as we helped peel Luke's arms away from our father's neck. During the day, my mother sewed in the factory. At night and into the early hours of the morning, she sewed at home for a different textile company using an industrial sewing machine and overlocker my father had bought from a friend. My father quit his kitchen job at the hostel as he had far bigger plans to pursue.

The high success rate of examinees meant that Lap's Driving School had more students than it could handle. In the early eighties, my father invested in a second vehicle — same make, same model, same secondhand dealer, the only difference was the colour — a deep purple with number plates that read GUN 771. My father had a new recruit, his younger brother Thuan. Uncle Thuan is not called by his position number in the family because we decided one day that it would be easier to use his real name. Uncle Thuan came to Australia with his best friend Dung. They escaped from Vietnam together on a wooden raft they had built by hand. Standing at six foot, Dung was the tallest and skinniest Vietnamese man that we had ever met. We thought him amazingly strong for his lack of body mass. He towered over us and could carry all three kids at the same time, swinging us around until we laughed with dizziness. Uncle Thuan, on the other hand, was a man far more serious — an ex-junkie, ex-inmate and ex-philanderer, he had the capacity to become so severe there was no doubting he was indeed my father's brother. I admired Uncle Thuan, not so much for his ability to inflict pain at the drop of a hat, but for his absolute faith and loyalty to my father.

My father always had a way of commanding a strange and consuming loyalty from all his friends — a knack that I have acknowledged since I was very young. It was not only the way he spoke — when he had something to say, the delivery of his speech could quieten a room — it was the thought he gave to the things he said. When he had nothing to say, he kept quiet. With the encouragement of his friends, my father realized the need to create a safe place for the men within the community to frequent, to be with each other and to keep away from trouble. He opened an amusement centre in Yagoona, not far from Regents Park. The main attraction for the business was three French Billiard tables. Nowhere else in Sydney at the time offered French billiards — a game much loved by the Vietnamese. Unlike snooker, there are no pockets on the table and only three balls; two white and one red. The objective is to hit both the opponent's white balls as well as the red ball in a single stroke, hitting at least two rails before the first ball is struck — clearly a game of skill and geometric challenge. People came from everywhere and booked the tables several days in advance. To avoid any arguments among the patrons, my father mounted a blackboard clearly scheduling the line-up for the tables. The customers were happy to wait. The pub across the road offered a space for them to drink while they waited their turn to play.

Those who had no interest in billiards came to play the other games my father offered. We had Pacman, Space Invaders, Ladder, Solitaire and chess. Many came just to avoid being alone. From the loft, my mother sold *banh mi thit* as well as strong, instant coffee with condensed milk — Vietnamese style. The business thrived and we hardly saw our parents at all — a circumstance that did not bother us in the slightest. After school, I cooked dinner for my brothers and hassled both of them to do their homework. Lewis would always comply but Luke never listened. On the weekends, we helped at the amusement centre. Lewis polished the billiard tables and computer games, Luke emptied the bins and ashtrays and I washed all the dishes.

The customers felt a great sense of regret when my parents closed the business. It followed the night they came home with bloodstains on their clothes. The bikie gang who frequented the pub across the road didn't like Asians drinking in 'their territory'. On this particular night, just as my parents were closing up, one of my father's friends came running from the pub and collapsed in their arms. Covered in blood, he came to warn them that there was trouble ahead and that they should go home as quickly as possible. He waited

Clockwise from left: Uncle Thuan, looking deadly serious with Lewis, Luke and I, as well as Lucky our Great Dane and Lucy our Pekingese, 1983; Luke and my father, 1980; Luke's fourth birthday, 1982.

for my parents to drive off before he ran back into the pub to continue the fight alongside his friends. Fuelled by racism, the brawl had brewed for a long time. When my parents arrived the next morning, they found police tape surrounding the shop and several police cars parked in front of the pub. Someone had thrown a garbage bin through our shopfront window, the equipment had been smashed and the billiard tables destroyed. The owner of the pub came to apologize to my parents for the damage the bikie gang had caused. He also came to tell them that their friend had died in the brawl. The bikies had stomped him to death.

While my parents thought about their next business venture, my father taught people how to drive and my mother sewed full-time from home. By this time, my father's reputation for practising the very firm but fair approach had spread to people of non-Vietnamese backgrounds. His student base included Italian, Chinese, Cambodian, Laotian, Yugoslavian and Australian. Uncle Thuan's help enabled my father more time to pay attention to the kids. Thursdays became 'eat out' day. Whether it involved getting up at 6am to go to yum cha before school, dining in a fancy seafood restaurant at night, or just going to Kentucky Fried Chicken to guess the Colonel's secret herbs and spices, my father made sure that we ate out at least once a week. It was important for him that we discovered new flavours and appreciate the techniques used in creating the food. 'Before you know how to cook, you must learn how to eat,' my father would tell us. It was important for him that we learned how to behave in different restaurant environments. He became obsessed with exposing us to as many new tastes and textures as we could possibly handle. Sometimes I think that he enjoyed it just a little too much. My father got a big kick out of watching us discover, with tears in our eyes, the burning sensation of a fiery chilli. He took pleasure in watching us overcome the psychological challenge of stomaching a hairy duck embryo, still intact. He laughed at us when we held our noses and swallowed hard on a stinking, one-hundred-year-old egg.

One day, we came home from school to the house filled with a warm, enticing, yet curious aroma. Clearly, the pot on the stove had simmered for a long time. My father made Lewis, Luke and me wash our hands before sitting down in our places at the dining table. Still in our school uniforms, he placed a small ceramic bowl with its lid on in front of each of us. He did not allow us to lift the lid until he said so. He waited until our eyes rested solely on him before he began.

'Now, I want you all to try something new today. It has taken me a long time to cook this.'

Impatiently we chanted, 'What is it Dad? What is it?'

He teased us, 'I can't tell you until you try it. Maybe you can guess what it is.' He paused for effect then gave us the go ahead. 'Okay, you can lift the lids now.'

My father can cook a broth for many hours, sometimes days, without the liquid becoming cloudy. The clarity of this broth was no exception. When I lifted the lid the fragrant steam gently touched my face and made my mouth water. A slight hint of something familiar tickled my nose. I closed my eyes, inhaled the aroma and held my breath briefly before softly exhaling. Inside the clear mahogany broth floated five pieces of meat sliced into uniform discs. Three paper-thin onion rings lay on top with a restrained sprinkle of spring onion (scallion) and a small scattering of cracked black pepper to finish.

'Can you smell it?' He asked.

'Yes Dad,' we replied in unison.

'Well, what can you smell?' He directed the question at Luke.

'Beef and five-spice.' Luke answered quickly.

'Yes, that's right. That's right. What else can you smell?' This time he looked at Lewis for a response.

'... Ahhmmm ... some ... herbal medicine?'

'Yes that's right, that's right.' My father couldn't contain his excitement and gave us permission to taste.

The flavours were truly divine. So delicate was the broth that my tongue shivered and left me speechless for a while. My father was right — I had never tasted meat like this before; firm yet marvellously soft and ever so slightly gelatinous. The vibrancy of the spring onion lifted the broth perfectly. 'Yum,' was all that we could muster.

Impatience showed on his cheeky grin. 'Well, what do you reckon? What is it?'

Knowing that it was my turn to answer, I gave it a guess. 'Is it beef tendon?'

'Nope.' He tried to suppress a giggle and shook his head mockingly.

'Ahhmm ... beef cheeks?'

'Nope, you've got one more guess. Come on, what is it, what is it?' He began laughing out loud — I began to worry.

The three of us eyed each other with nervous anticipation. We stopped chewing at the same time and wondered if it was such a good idea to swallow.

With genuine concern, I finally blurted, 'I give up, I have no idea. What have you just fed us?'

At those words my father spat out a laugh so loud, it filled our small house like a firecracker. His eyes wet with hysterics, he told us that we had just eaten our very first aphrodisiac — the ancient dish *ngao binh*, 'broth of bull's penis'.

My parents love to make eating an occasion. For them it is a shared ritual that brings together family and friends. Many dishes are served at the same time, conveying the sense of a communal table. The dishes we enjoy most are those that require preparation at the table. Some involve rolling in rice paper or wrapping with lettuce — this is very much an individual feature

Clockwise from left: Luke's fifth birthday, all of us with matching bowl haircuts, 1983; Lewis and I in front of our Regents Park home, 1979; Lewis, Luke, Thu and I with Aunty Ten and my mother, Regents Park, Christmas 1979.

of Vietnamese cuisine. We like to cook the ingredients in a hotpot placed in the centre of the table or watch the food sizzle on a hotplate as we eat. Our obsession with freshness is satisfied by the mountain of fresh herbs consumed and continually replenished. Not only is this hands-on style of eating interactive and fun, it also enables us to taste the different combinations of flavours, allowing us to play around with a variety of ingredients. My father greatly enjoyed having his friends come to graze with him over a long lunch, sharing their stories with one another. Having yet to finish one meal, they were already planning the next. Lunches often led into dinner.

One of my father's friends, who we called Uncle Nghia, came around every Saturday morning in his beaten-up yellow station wagon. Uncle Nghia always drove to our house first, straight from his fishing boat in Botany Bay. With feverish excitement, we would rush out to greet the delights he had brought to us. It was a treat to see the fish glisten with such freshness. I particularly liked to mimic my mother when she picked up the squid and dangled it up and down like a puppet, testing the bounciness of its peculiar tentacles. I'm still not sure if she performed this ritual for my amusement or hers. I didn't mind the prick of the prawn heads as I helped her to select the largest ones. I watched the crabs writhing with life and wondered if they stopped to think about the doomed future that awaited them. Uncle Nghia later died at sea.

The television news reported that his body and that of his three fishing companions could not be found. He left behind four beautiful children. His wife soon lost her mind. I saw her sometimes, roaming the streets of Cabramatta, rambling to herself and asking the locals if anyone had found her husband yet.

My father's obsession with 'goodness' and 'quality' spilled over into areas other than food. A health freak, he instilled in us at a very young age a great awareness of nutrition and maintenance of wellbeing. He forced the three of us to run close to 5 kilometres (3 miles) each morning, covering six long blocks. Sometimes we caught him spying on us (with good reason) to see if we were playing in the park instead. Before dinner, he made us take turns on the stretch machine so that we could further enrich our lives with the ability to do the splits. Before bed, we practised compulsory meditation. He coached us in the art of yoga breathing and breath retention, '… breathe in as slowly as you can through the nose, slowly, slowly, slowly, fill your lungs and expand your navel. Visualize the breath of life travelling through your body. Now, hold your breath, pull in your stomach and hold, hold, hold …'

The breathing part almost bored us to tears. We did, however, enjoy his martial arts demonstrations on how to manoeuvre defensively in one swift movement 'like a panther'. Each move was counter balanced by a deft swipe of an arm ending in a pose more comic than

Kung Fu. Luke would always finish this manoeuvre Bruce Lee style, with a quick thumb swipe of his nose and a short flick of his chin, urging on his fantasy opponent with the inviting flicker of his fingers and a high pitch, cat-like whine.

'The defensive moves,' my father told us, 'are far more effective than the offensive moves.'

We would nod in obedience, pretending that we had not heard this speech a hundred times before.

'It takes far less energy to move out of the way … than it takes to block your enemy.'

We continued to nod.

'When you see that boulder rolling down the waterfall to kill you, it is better to move to the left,' in slow motion he moved to the left, 'or to the right,' in slower motion he moved to the right. 'But whatever you do, do not try to block that boulder … because it will kill you.'

In unison, we would continue nodding, making sure to acknowledge the profound revelation my father had enlightened us with.

My father also insisted that we studied martial arts. Three times a week for six years we went to Cabramatta Police Boys Club to practise Viet Quyen Dao — a Vietnamese art form created by Master Ngoc, a university professor from Saigon. We trained under Master Man, a gentle, committed and passionate teacher who taught us that martial arts was not about fighting and winning, but about something far more

gratifying — that of self competition. 'To compete with oneself in order to maintain spiritual harmony with the mind, body and spirit.' At first, we found the commitment a little strange, but after a time, we took the form seriously and it became an important part of our lives. By our mid teens, Lewis and I earned our first black belts — Luke received his at the age of eleven. A year later, we each acquired a second black belt in the not-so-spiritual style of Tae Kwon Do.

Of all the strict disciplinary regimes that my father enforced upon us, breakfast filled me with the most dread. A tall glass of pure aloe vera juice, which literally tasted like bile, preceded several large bowls of warm milk with raw egg. My father insisted that two litres of milk per day would be 'good for my bones' and that my 'bones would become strong' so as to 'effectively block my enemies'. The bile stuff I could handle — it was the full-cream milk that caused me the most grief. The reason why very little dairy product is used in Asian cooking is because most Asians are lactose intolerant. This is why there is a prolific use of soy products and coconut milk instead. Lewis, Luke and I suffered terribly from the effects of having to ingest so much milk — a fact my father did not want to know about. In a fit of frustrated rebellion, I began making a habit of disposing the six litres that we had delivered to our doorstep each day. I poured the contents of each bottle into our great dane's enormous drink bowl. Lucky loved the milk so much he stopped drinking water altogether. We successfully escaped the trauma of lactose for many weeks before Luke informed my father of my wasteful actions. Luke's spite was the result of a silly quarrel between siblings — of which I was the eventual loser.

For punishment, my father maintained three instruments of torture. The first was a thick metal billiard stick that he had kept as a souvenir from the amusement centre days. The second, a flexible cane whip that smarted so sharply it sliced my buttocks like a knife cutting the red flesh of a watermelon. The third, and most effective weapon he had, was fear. For this particular instance, he chose the cane whip to fit my crime. As usual, the ritual was drawn out. As usual,

I swallowed the pain without dropping a tear — the only sound that filled the room that day was the fast whoop of the cane followed by a sharp clap on contact with my skin. Had I learned my lesson? Yes. Did I deserve it? No. For years we had been forced to ingest and endure my father's extremities — testing our tolerance and pushing our bodies to its farthest limits. This incident only served to cement a thought that I had kept to myself for a long time. It was the notion that, as receptive and malleable as my body had become, there were limits to how much it could endure. If my body were forced to continue receiving that which it is not built for, then, the day will come when its rejection of these bad things will be a violent and dramatic one.

151

July 30, 1979

Dear Lap:

I have received your letter dated 16 July 1979, and I am very
happy to hear from you. I am glad things are going well for
you in Australia and I know that you all will do very well.

Regarding your younger brother, I will be very happy to try to
locate him. I will go to both the UN and US Embassy name list
and I will be able to check Malaysia and the Philippines for you.
If he is in any of these locations I will find out and I will let
you know immediately. If he is in Thailand, I know that we can
be of assistance to him here.

Thanks again for your letter and I will let you know as soon
as I can find out anything about your brother.

Sincerely,

Paul W. Jones
Program Director.

PWJ:ch

Left: A personal letter from Paul Jones to my father regarding the whearabouts of my Uncle Thuan, 1979. Above: Luke, me and Lewis with our dogs, Lucky and Lucy, at Bonnyrigg, 1985.

ỐC LUỘC
steamed cockles or periwinkles

1 kg (2 lb 4 oz) cockles or periwinkles
garlic mayonnaise (page 161), to serve

Pour 250 ml (9 fl oz/1 cup) water into a wok, add the cockles or periwinkles and cover with a lid. Bring to the boil over high heat and steam for about 10 minutes. Don't allow the wok to boil dry — add extra water if required. Strain off excess water and place the cockles in a serving bowl. To eat, remove the flesh from the shell and dip it into garlic mayonnaise or a mixture of dipping fish sauce (page 33) and finely sliced ginger.

NGHÊU HẤP VỚI ỚT TỎI VÀ RAU HUẾ

steamed pipis with chilli, garlic and basil

500 g (1 lb 2 oz) pipis (vongole)
250 ml (9 fl oz/1 cup) chicken stock
   (page 36)
2 tablespoons oil
2 spring onions (scallions), white
   part only, chopped
1 garlic clove, crushed
1 tablespoon oyster sauce

1 tablespoon fish sauce
2 teaspoons sugar
1/2 teaspoon salt
1 handful basil leaves, shredded,
   plus extra to garnish
1 teaspoon potato starch
1 bird's eye chilli, sliced

In a wok or large saucepan, add the pippis and chicken stock, cover and steam for about 5 minutes, or until the pippis open. (Discard any that do not open.) Strain the cooking liquid from the pippis and reserve for later use.

Return the wok to the heat, add the oil and gently fry the spring onions and garlic. Once softened, increase the heat and add the pippis, oyster sauce, fish sauce, sugar and salt. Stir or toss the wok to combine the ingredients. Add the basil and 125 ml (4 fl oz/1/2 cup) of the reserved cooking liquid and bring to the boil. Once boiled, add the potato starch mixed with 1 tablespoon of cold water to the wok. This will thicken the sauce slightly. Turn out onto a serving plate and garnish with extra basil leaves and chilli.

SERVES 4 AS PART OF A STARTER

MARK JENSEN: *This dish is cooked at the table in a claypot over a portable gas cooker. Butane gas cookers are relatively inexpensive and are available in Chinese supermarkets. They are fun to have on hand and are a compact piece of cooking equipment for seaside picnics.*

BÒ NHÚNG DẤM
beef cooked at the table in a coconut, lemongrass and vinegar hotpot

1 kg (2 lb 4 oz) beef eye fillet
1 butter lettuce, leaves peeled
1 Lebanese (short) cucumber, cut
   into matchsticks
1 small red onion, finely sliced
1 handful perilla leaf
1 handful mint leaves
1 handful coriander (cilantro) leaves
100 g (3¹/2 oz) bean sprouts
200 g (7 oz) cooked vermicelli

250 ml (9 fl oz/1 cup) white wine
   vinegar
250 ml (9 fl oz/1 cup) coconut juice
1 lemon grass stem, finely sliced
20 sheets of 16 cm (6¹/4 in) rice paper
dipping fish sauce (page 33) or
   anchovy and pineapple sauce
   (page 199), to serve

Slice the beef very finely across the grain, about 2 mm (¹/16 in) thick, and lay flat on a large plate. Arrange the lettuce, cucumber, onion, perilla, mint, coriander and bean sprouts on a separate platter with the cooked vermicelli.

Add the wine vinegar, coconut juice, 250 ml (9 fl oz/1 cup) water and lemon grass to the clay pot and bring to a slow simmer over low heat.

To serve, each person prepares their own rice paper by dipping it in a bowl of warm water, shaking off the excess water and laying it flat on a plate. Place a piece of butter lettuce, a few leaves of perilla, mint and coriander, along with some onion, cucumber, vermicelli and bean sprouts on top of the rice paper.

Each person then picks up pieces of beef with chopsticks and dips it into the clay pot. (Cook for as long or as little as you like.) Place on top of the rice paper, roll up tightly and dip into your chosen dipping sauce.

MAKES 20

MARK JENSEN: *Pauline first introduced me to this wonderful creation 5 years ago. It has the richness of pork meat, liver pâté and mayonnaise, but is balanced so wonderfully with lightly pickled carrots, fresh cucumber, spring onion (scallion), coriander (cilantro) and chilli. Banh Mi Thit are very addictive and so inexpensive. No trip I take to Cabramatta is complete unless I have one ... or two.*

BÁNH MÌ THỊT
vietnamese pork rolls

4 fresh Vietnamese bread rolls
4 tablespoons chicken and pork
    liver pâté (page 160)
4 teaspoons garlic mayonnaise
    (page 161)
100 g (3½ oz) pork terrine (page 159),
    finely sliced
100 g (3½ oz) pork belly (page 162),
    finely sliced

200 g (7 oz) pickled carrots
    (page 163)
2 Lebanese (short) cucumber, cut into
    batons the length of the rolls
2 spring onion (scallion), cut to the
    length of the rolls
coriander (cilantro) sprigs, to taste
2 bird's eye chilli, chopped, or to taste
soy sauce, to season

Slice the bread rolls lengthways and open out flat. Spread with the pâté and mayonnaise, and layer with terrine and pork belly slices. Place the pickled carrots, cucumber and spring onion on top. Garnish with coriander and freshly chopped chilli. Dress with a dash of soy sauce and season with salt and pepper.

MAKES 4

CHẢ LỤA
pork terrine

1 kg (2 lb 4 oz) pork leg, minced
   (ground)
1 tablespoon sea salt

2$\frac{1}{2}$ tablespoons fish sauce
1 large banana leaf

Ask your butcher to put the pork leg through the mincer on its finest setting. Fry the salt in a dry wok for a few minutes until aromatic. Place the pork, fish sauce and salt in a food processor and pulse until it forms a very fine paste.

Soak the banana leaf in water for 5 minutes, dry and lay it flat on a bench. Cut the leaf in half and cross one piece over the other. Place the pork paste in the centre and draw up all sides to form a tight parcel. Secure with string and cook in simmering salted water for 1 hour. Allow to cool, remove the banana leaf and slice the pork when needed. Refrigerate for up to 1 week.

MAKES 1 TERRINE. THIS IS A COMPONENT OF BANH MI THIT
(PAGE 158) AND IS ALSO ENJOYED AS AN APPETIZER.

MARK JENSEN: *This is a French-influenced recipe that I can immediately relate to. The Vietnamese prefer a pâté with more substance and texture, hence the inclusion of the minced pork. If you prefer a smoother consistency, eliminate the mince and increase the quantity of the liver by 100 grams (3¹/₂ oz). Finally, pass the pâté through a fine sieve, then refrigerate.*

BA TÊ GAN GÀ HEO
chicken and pork liver pâté

200 g (7 oz) pork livers
200 g (7 oz) chicken livers
100 g (3¹/₂ oz) butter, softened
100 g (3¹/₂ oz) minced (ground) pork
2 red Asian shallots, finely diced
2 garlic cloves, finely diced

2 tablespoons brandy or Cognac
4 tablespoons pouring (whipping)
    cream
1 teaspoon sugar
1 teaspoon salt
¹/₂ teaspoon fine white pepper

Clean the livers of fat and sinew and cut the pork livers to match the size of the chicken livers. Wash under cold water, dry well with paper towel and set aside.

Add 2 teaspoons of the butter to a frying pan over medium heat and once it starts to bubble, add half of the livers to the pan and fry for 1–2 minutes, until browned, then turn them over and brown the other side for 1–2 minutes, keeping them quite soft in the middle. Remove to a plate, then repeat the process with the remaining livers.

Add 1 tablespoon of butter to the pan and gently fry the pork for about 2 minutes, or until cooked through but not browned.

Wipe the pan clean with paper towel, add 2 teaspoons of the butter and gently fry the shallots and garlic for 5 minutes, or until very soft and slightly caramelized. Increase the heat and add all of the livers back to the pan, pour over the brandy or Cognac and ignite the alcohol. Once the flame subsides, pour the liver mixture into a food processor and process until smooth. With the motor running, add the remaining butter and the cream.

Finally, season with the sugar, salt and white pepper, taste and adjust the seasoning if necessary. Pour into a container and refrigerate for about 2 hours, or until set. Before serving, remove from the fridge and let stand at room temperature for 30 minutes.

MAKES 1 PÂTÉ. THIS IS A COMPONENT OF BANH MI THIT (PAGE 158)
AND IS ALSO ENJOYED AS AN HORS D'OEUVRE.

SỐT MA-DÔ-NE TỎI
garlic mayonnaise

3 garlic cloves
2 egg yolks
1 tablespoon lemon juice
1/4 teaspoon salt

1/4 teaspoon fine white pepper
200 ml (7 fl oz) vegetable oil, mixed
    with 50 ml (1 3/4 fl oz) light olive oil

This quantity of mayonnaise is best made in a bowl using a whisk. Make sure the bowl is secure on the bench. (A good tip is to roll a damp cloth into a circle on the bench and then place the bowl in the middle.)

Bash the garlic into a paste in a mortar. Combine the egg yolks, lemon juice, crushed garlic, salt and white pepper in a bowl and whisk well. Continue to whisk slowly, adding only a few drops of oil to the egg yolks at a time. Once you have added about 50 ml (1 3/4 fl oz) of the oil, you can continue to add the oil in one slow, steady stream.

Place into a container, cover with a lid or plastic wrap and refrigerate for up to 1 week.

MAKES 250 ML (9 FL OZ/1 CUP). THIS IS A COMPONENT OF BANH MI THIT (PAGE 158).

THỊT BA RỌI
pork belly

1/2 teaspoon Chinese red food
    colouring
1 kg (2 lb 4 oz) pork belly
2 tablespoons soy sauce

1 tablespoon five-spice
4 garlic cloves, finely chopped
1 tablespoon salt
1 litre (35 fl oz/4 cups) coconut juice

Mix the Chinese red food colouring with 1 tablespoon of cold water and mix to dissolve. Brush onto the pork belly until well coloured. Combine the soy sauce, five-spice, garlic and salt. Massage this mixture into the pork, then leave to marinate for 1 hour.

Bring the coconut juice to the boil in a large saucepan over high heat. Meanwhile, lay the pork flat, skin side down, and roll up tightly from the bottom in an upward direction. Tie the pork with string and place into the boiling coconut juice, cover, reduce the heat and simmer for 1 hour, turning the pork regularly.

Once cooked, allow the pork to cool in the juice before slicing the amount you require. As well as using pork belly in Vietnamese pork rolls, it can also be chopped and layered over rice or rice noodles and served with dipping fish sauce (page 33). This dish will keep for up to 4 days in the refrigerator.

MAKES 12 ROLLS. THIS IS A COMPONENT OF BANH MI THIT (PAGE 158) AND IS ALSO ENJOYED AS AN APPETIZER.

CÀ RỐT CHUA
pickled carrots

375 ml (13 fl oz/1½ cups) rice vinegar
220 g (7¾ oz/1 cup) sugar

2 teaspoons salt
3 large carrots

Add the rice vinegar, sugar and salt to a saucepan over high heat, stir to dissolve the sugar and bring to the boil. Remove from the heat and set aside to cool.

Coarsely grate the carrots and add to a pickling jar, pour over the pickling liquid and leave to mature overnight.

MAKES ENOUGH FOR 12 ROLLS. THIS IS A COMPONENT OF BANH MI THIT (PAGE 158).

MARK JENSEN: *In Vietnam, this dish is cooked at the table in a small frying pan over a charcoal grill. If you have a tabletop gas cooker, you can prepare this dish in a similar fashion. Cook the fish in smaller quantities and assemble the vermicelli salad at the table.*

CHẢ CÁ
ling fillets marinated with dill and turmeric

1 kg (2 lb 4 oz) ling fillets
8 spring onions (scallions)
4 garlic cloves
1 tablespoon ground turmeric
2 teaspoons hot curry powder
   (such as 'Ayam' brand)
2 tablespoons plain yoghurt
125 ml (4 fl oz/^{1}/$_2$ cup) fish sauce

3 tablespoons sugar
3 tablespoons vegetable oil
1 bunch dill
125 g (4^1/$_2$ oz) rice vermicelli
250 ml (9 fl oz/1 cup) fish stock
   (page 99)
1 lemon
300 g (10^1/$_2$ oz) bean sprouts

Cut the ling fillet into 4 cm (1^1/$_2$ in) pieces, place in a bowl and set aside. Put the white heads of the spring onions (reserving the stalks) and garlic in a mortar and pound to a paste. Add the turmeric, curry powder, yoghurt, fish sauce, sugar, 2 tablespoons of the oil and a third of the dill, roughly chopped, to the fish and mix well. Cover and marinate in the refrigerator for 1 hour.

Meanwhile, cook the vermicelli in boiling water for 5 minutes, turn off the heat and let sit for a further 5 minutes. Strain into a colander, refresh under cold water and set aside to dry.

Thinly slice 4 of the green spring onion stalks. Heat a large frying pan over medium heat, add the remaining oil, then fry the fish fillets on one side for 30 seconds. Turn the fillets over, add the fish stock and simmer for 3–5 minutes, until the fish is cooked through. Remove the fish and squeeze over the juice from the lemon. Mix the bean sprouts, sliced spring onion, remaining dill and vermicelli together. Place into bowls and spoon over the fish fillets and sauce.

SERVES 6

BÁNH CUỐN CHẢ LỤA NEM CHUA

steamed rice noodles with pork terrine and cured pork

pork terrine (page 159), as required
cured pork (page 169), as required
400 g (14 oz) rolled sheet of
  rice noodles
1 Lebanese (short) cucumber
1 handful perilla leaves
1 handful mint leaves
1 handful Vietnamese mint leaves

100 g (3½ oz) bean sprouts
3 tablespoons dipping fish sauce
  (page 33)
2 tablespoons spring onion oil
  (page 37)
2 tablespoons fried red Asian shallots
  (page 38)
2 bird's eye chillies, sliced

Slice as much of the terrine and cured pork as you require and set aside. Cut the rice noodles into 2 cm (³/4 in) wide sections and separate into ribbons. Slice the cucumber into batons and roughly chop the herbs.

Place the noodles on a steaming tray and steam for 2–3 minutes, until hot. Alternatively, place the noodles in a microwave and warm through for 1 minute. Turn the noodles out onto a serving platter, blanch the bean sprouts and arrange them with the cucumber over the noodles. Scatter with the herbs and arrange the meats on top. Dress with the dipping fish sauce and spring onion oil, and garnish with fried shallots and chilli.

SERVES 2

NEM CHUA
cured pork

500 g (1 lb 2 oz) pork leg, finely
    minced (ground)
250 g (9 oz) pork skin (pre-cooked
    and cut variety)
1/2 bag nem powder (from Asian
    supermarkets)
2 tablespoons sugar

1/2 teaspoon salt
1/2 teaspoon cracked black pepper
4 garlic cloves, finely sliced
4 bird's eye chillies, finely sliced
    lengthways
10 Vietnamese mint leaves

Ask your butcher to mince the pork leg as finely as possible (it's best to put it through the mincer at least 3 times). In a large bowl, combine the pork leg, pork skin, nem powder, sugar, salt and pepper. Mix well and knead the ingredients together, occasionally lifting the mix and throwing it down hard into the bowl. This slightly aerates the mix and gives the desired texture.

Line a tray just large enough to hold the mixture with plastic wrap, scatter the pieces of sliced garlic across the plastic, then press the pork mixture into the tray. Arrange the chilli and Vietnamese mint across the top, cover with plastic wrap and place a same sized tray on top. Weigh it down with a light weight (such as a tin of coconut cream) and refrigerate for 2 days.

To serve, remove from the fridge and allow to sit for 30 minutes at room temperature before slicing into 4 x 3 cm (1½ x 1¼ in) rectangles.

SERVES 10. THIS IS A COMPONENT OF BANH CUON CHA LUA NEM CHUA (PAGE 168) AND IS ALSO ENJOYED AS AN APPETIZER. (IT IS GREAT WITH COLD BEER!)

CHẢ GIÒ
red lantern crisp parcels

80 g (2³/4 oz) dried glass or cellophane
   noodles
50 g (1³/4 oz) dried mushroom strips,
   such as wood ear mushrooms or
   Chinese black fungus
250 g (9 oz) minced (ground) pork
250 g (9 oz) minced (ground) chicken
500 g (1 lb 2 oz) carrots, grated
¹/2 onion, finely diced

1 tablespoon sugar
3 teaspoons salt
2 teaspoons fine white pepper
1 tablespoon fish sauce
1 packet spring (egg) roll papers,
   22 cm (8¹/2 in) square
dipping fish sauce (page 33), to serve
   (optional)

Soak the noodles and mushroom strips separately in cold water for 20 minutes, then drain and dry. Cut the noodles into 4 cm (1¹/2 in) long pieces, then combine with all of the filling ingredients in a large bowl and mix well.

Cut the spring roll papers diagonally to form 2 triangles, then separate the paper into single sheets. Place a piece of paper on a plate with the base of the triangle facing you. Spoon about 1 tablespoon of the mixture onto the middle of the bottom edge of the paper and fold the two adjacent sides, one on top of the other into the centre. Roll towards the apex to form a nice firm roll, and secure with a dab of flour mixed with some water. Repeat until you have filled all of the papers.

When freshly rolled, the *cha gio* can be deep-fried in oil at a temperature of 180°C (350°F), or until a cube of bread dropped in the oil browns in 15 seconds. Alternatively, you can store them in the freezer and cook when required.

These can be cooked and eaten on their own, dipped in dipping fish sauce, or placed on top of a dressed vermicelli salad (page 118). At Red Lantern, we like to wrap the parcels in lettuce with herbs and serve with dipping fish sauce.

Note: Ensure you use the spring roll papers as soon as they thaw.

MAKES 40

MARK JENSEN: *The technique required to make this dish made sense to me the first time Sifu — a Vietnamese master chef — demonstrated it. With a background in French cuisine, I understood the technique of making and steaming 'farce' meat. However, I found the use of sugar cane unusual. Here it is used to skewer the prawn (shrimp) farce. Once the chao tom is steamed and chargrilled it is cut off the sugar cane skewer into strips, then rolled up in rice paper with lettuce and herbs. You chew the sugar cane afterwards, as the sweet juice provides a refreshing palate cleanser.*

CHẠO TÔM

prawn paste wrapped around sugar cane

PRAWN PASTE
1 garlic clove
10 spring onions (scallions), white
    part only, chopped
3 teaspoons salt
2 teaspoons fine white pepper
1 teaspoon sugar
900 g (2 lb) raw prawn (shrimp) meat
2 tablespoons fish sauce

1 egg white
1/2 teaspoon bicarbonate of soda
    (baking soda)
1 tablespoon cornflour (cornstarch)

10 thick sugar cane skewers
oil, for brushing
dipping fish sauce (page 33), to serve

Pound the garlic and spring onion in a mortar with the salt, pepper and sugar. Transfer to a bowl and combine with all the other prawn paste ingredients.

Add small quantities of the mixture to a food processor and process until smooth. Repeat this process with the remaining mixture.

Weigh the prawn paste into 125 g (4 1/2 oz) amounts (you should have 10 in total). Using your hand, pick up each portion of the paste and throw it down hard onto your work bench several times. This aerates the paste and gives it a smooth, glossy appearance. Repeat this process with all the paste.

Roll each portion of paste into sausage shapes and skewer with the sugar cane. Brush with some oil and place on a steaming tray over high heat for 10 minutes. To serve, brush with some oil and chargrill until golden brown.

This dish is assembled at the table. Cut the *chao tom* into four strips and eat with vermicelli, lettuce and fresh herbs wrapped in rice paper, with dipping fish sauce.

Chao tom can be made well in advance — it will keep for 3 days in the refrigerator and up to 3 months in the freezer.

MAKES 10

MỰC NHỒI TÔM THỊT

twice-cooked calamari stuffed with pork, prawn and water chestnuts

50 g (1³/4 oz) dried mushroom strips,
    such as wood ear mushrooms or
    Chinese black fungus
50 g (1³/4 oz) glass noodles
6–8 calamari (1.5 kg/
    3 lb 5 oz in total)
4 large raw king prawns (shrimp),
    peeled
250 g (9 oz) minced (ground) pork

3 spring onion (scallions), chopped
2 tablespoons chopped lemon grass,
    white part only
2 tablespoons chopped water chestnuts
1 tablespoon sugar
2 teaspoons salt
1 teaspoon white pepper
dipping fish sauce (page 33), to serve

Soak the mushrooms and glass noodles separately in cold water for 20 minutes, then drain and drip dry in a colander. Clean and wash the calamari, set the tubes aside and cut the tentacles into 2 cm (³/4 in) long sections. Dice the prawns and combine the remaining ingredients in a bowl with the mushrooms and noodles.

Lay the calamari tubes flat on a board and pierce the tip of each tube with a knife. (This allows trapped air to escape when the tube contracts during cooking, helping to prevent it from exploding.)

Now stuff a quantity of mixture into the calamari, allowing room for contraction and secure with a toothpick. Repeat until all the tubes are filled.

Place on a steaming tray and steam over high heat for 20 minutes. Once steamed the calamari well keep for 3 days in the refrigerator. When ready to serve, deep-fry until golden in oil heated to 180°C (350°F), or until a cube of bread dropped in the oil browns in 15 seconds.

This dish is assembled at the table. Cut the calamari into 5 mm (¹/4 in) slices and wrap with lettuce and fresh herbs, and serve with dipping fish sauce.

SERVES 6

CHEM CHÉP XẢ ỚT
mussels with lemon grass, chilli and garlic

500 g (1 lb 2 oz) black mussels
250 ml (9 fl oz/1 cup) chicken stock
    (page 36)
2 tablespoons oil
2 lemon grass stems, white part only,
    finely sliced
1/2 onion, chopped
2 garlic cloves, chopped
1 bird's eye chilli, sliced

1 tablespoon oyster sauce
1 tablespoon fish sauce
1 teaspoon potato starch
2 teaspoons sugar
1/2 teaspoon salt
1/2 teaspoon black pepper
1 handful coriander (cilantro) leaves
1/2 lemon

Scrub and de-beard the mussels, then set aside. In a wok over high heat, add the chicken stock and mussels, cover with a lid and cook for 5 minutes, or until the mussels open. (Discard any that do not open.) Strain the mussels, reserving the cooking liquid for later use.

Put the wok back over medium heat, add the oil and gently fry the lemon grass, onion, garlic and chilli. Once golden, add the mussels and increase the heat. Toss through the oyster sauce and fish sauce, then add 125 ml (4 fl oz/1/2 cup) of the reserved cooking liquid. Mix the potato starch with 1 tablespoon water and toss it through the mussels to thicken the sauce. Season the mussels with the sugar, salt and pepper, turn out onto a serving platter, garnish with the coriander and squeeze the lemon over them.

SERVES 2

pho cay du

'I look forward to the day when the Asians of Cabramatta spread their influences beyond their own suburbs. After all, who is better placed to establish the trade links with Asia, which both political parties insist are so important to our future. They have the contacts, they have the language skills, they have the cultural understanding and they have the financial base in Australia from which to grow. All we need is time and tolerance.'

John Newman, Member for Cabramatta, 1993

We lived in the unremarkable suburb of Bonnyrigg — a 15 minute drive from the very remarkable suburb of Cabramatta. But 68 John Street, Cabramatta, is where we really grew up. Some 32 kilometres (20 miles) south-west of central Sydney, Cabramatta falls within the Fairfield City local council. The land is flat and is known, among other things, as 'the burbs' or 'way out west'. No less than 130 different nationalities live in this bustling multicultural suburb, with Italians and immigrants from the former Yugoslavia comprising the largest ethnic grouping in the wider Cabramatta–Fairfield area — a fact at odds with the overwhelming Asian appearance of the suburb's commercial centre.

Cabramatta has never been an 'Australian' suburb, it is simply an area that housed one wave of immigrants after another. The European contingent comprises Dutch, German, Polish, Serbian, Croatian and Macedonian. The Asian overlay comprises Vietnamese, Laotian, Cambodian, ethnic Chinese from mainland China and South-East Asia, as well as Russian-speaking Chinese. Timorese, Turkish, Lebanese, Latin American and Australians also share the suburb. The churches and temples, all within close proximity, cater for a wide range of denominations and faiths including Russian Orthodox, Catholic, Baptist, Anglican and Buddhist.

My father chose Cabramatta for its strong sense of community. He liked the idea that a number of his friends had already set up a life for themselves in such a short period of time. He understood that the

Previous page: Hon. Barry Unsworth, my father and John Newman MP at a charity function in Cabramatta, 1992. Opposite, clockwise from left: Freedom Plaza, Cabramatta; my parents outside Pho Cay Du, 1992; my father proudly delivering his famous crispy garlic chicken wings to the bank next door, New Year, 1990.

secret to their success was hard work and unconditional dedication — often fuelled by an underlying desperation. It did not surprise him that many of his friends had become astute business people; showing great aptitude as small shopkeepers.

In the mid-eighties, as Lap's Driving School continued to operate on the side with its steady stream of students, my father fed his sudden urge to open a video library. 'Asians love action movies,' he would say. The blockbuster releases at the time were *Full Metal Jacket*, *Platoon*, *Born On The Fourth Of July* and *Good Morning Vietnam*. He found a prime location right in the centre of bustling John Street — the spinal chord to Cabramatta's pumping commercial centre. The front of the huge two-storey building loomed over the busy pedestrian crossing on the main street. The side of the premises, with floor to ceiling windows, stretched back along John Street Boulevard — another major capillary joining Cabramatta Road to John Street.

'But why a video library?' I asked my father.

'Same as the driving school,' he said, 'no-one else in Cabramatta was doing it.' My father liked to be 'the first' at most things that he did.

In an excited moment of discovery, my father called upon Uncle Thuan to look after the video library for a day. He had read in the paper about a food and wine fair being held at Darling Harbour in the city. Guessing that there would be food samples galore, he made sure that the family were scrubbed, combed and polished before taking us into town for some freebies.

There were many things we hadn't seen before as a family, and this occasion topped our list of new favourite things. We stood in amazement at the entrance to the exhibition hall and gawked like circus clowns at the wonderment around us. We had never before experienced a magical world like the one we saw that day. I felt like a princess in a wonderland full of free food, smiling faces and shiny equipment. Happy people were everywhere. 'Wow Dad!' were the words of the day. I ran my fingers along each sticky stall counter to savour every moment of this fairytale occasion. Everything went into our mouths: salad dressings, dessert toppings, pasta sauces, seafood sticks, cheese sticks, sugar sticks. My parents showed more restraint than I had expected, standing back to laugh at us instead. I noticed that they spent more time at stalls with names I found unfamiliar — Norgen Vaas, Häagen-Dazs, Royal Copenhagen, Carpigiani. At each stall, I could hear my father say, as his eyes rolled blissfully to the back of his head, 'This is the best ice cream I have ever tasted.' Intoxicated by the occasion, he decided that making ice cream would be his next calling.

For three weekends in a row, we helped our father research his newfound passion. Cramped inside the tiny Ford Escort, he drove us to the remotest suburbs of Sydney in search of the 'perfect ice cream'. It surprised me that ice cream came in so many exotic flavours —

more than simply chocolate and vanilla. By the end of each day's research, we became sick from the mass consumption of dairy.

My father's ice cream dream became a reality when Mr Carpigiani, of Carpigiani Ice Cream fame, made a timely guest appearance, all the way from Italy, to hold courses on Italian-style homemade ice cream. My father fell in love with Mr Carpigiani and borrowed more money from the banks to purchase a Carpigiani Pasto XP pasteuriser and Labo XP batch freezer, as well as two shiny cabinets to display at the front of the video library. With no say in the matter, I became chief ice cream maker, Lewis, the official ice cream scooper and Luke, head ice cream rotator.

Foremost Natural Ice Cream was the first in Cabramatta to sell exquisite real fruit natural ice cream. We created our own exotic flavours to satisfy both Western and Asian palates. My personal favourite would have to be durian for its glorious creamy pungency. Luke especially did not share my love for this exotic fruit — not only would he have to leave the room immediately after we cracked open a fresh durian, he would cross the road and not return until we assured him that the smell had dissipated. Luke's favourites were hazelnut and banana. It perplexed some of the customers that our banana ice cream was a dense white colour with tiny seeds through it. 'Banana should be bright yellow,' they would say. We politely asked them to close their eyes and 'think about it'.

Lewis loved coconut and passionfruit but simply hated the lonesome chore of scooping boxes upon boxes of these fruits from their husks. My father's favourite was avocado — 'pure and simple'. My mother greatly enjoyed working around the abundant fresh fruit. Making ice cream allowed her to utilize the fresh produce skills she had inherited from the family business in Vietnam. She would insist on using only the ripest and most flavoursome fruit. I am not afraid to admit that we really did make the best ice cream that I have ever tasted.

Inspired by Mr Carpigiani and infected by the learning bug, my parents joined The Australian Gas Cooking School. In case they didn't already have enough to do, they travelled by train in the evenings to the school in North Sydney and left us kids in charge of the business until they returned late at night. At first, I didn't understand why my father often insisted that I attend the cooking classes in his place — at the age of thirteen, I was the youngest class member. However, his intentions soon became clear when he opened Pho Cay Du underneath the video store, and made me the assistant cook.

I learned a lot in that time — we all did. Although we Nguyen children can all lay claim to growing up in the restaurant business, it is our youngest brother, Leroy, who was born into and truly grew up in our family restaurants. My mother fell pregnant just before we opened Pho Cay Du and worked non-stop up until the day of his birth — and returned to work three days later. Leroy inconveniently arrived on a day of another martial arts tournament. My father insisted that we honour that commitment and so my mother gave birth alone. 'He was an accident,' she would say. Leroy remains the ugliest baby we have ever laid eyes on. Friends and neighbours would recoil in horror when they came to visit him. My mother blamed Lewis, Luke and I for this. She was convinced that we had put a curse on him.

It was during my mother's pregnancy that Uncle Thuan dated a woman who looked like a witch with the nose of a swine. As we secretly made fun of her, my mother would verbalize her superstitions. 'You had better stop saying such nasty things, otherwise Pamela will be born just as ugly as she.' Yes indeed, *Pamela* — it was also Uncle Thuan who convinced my mother that she was having a baby girl. 'I can tell by the angle of your belly button,' he told her. And so, 'Pamela' became Leroy — the ugly baby boy who had nothing but pink dresses to wear for most of his early days.

The 'curse' lifted, of course, and Leroy grew to be the cutest, most adorable (and most dramatic), baby brother. 'Growing up in Pho Cay Du,' says Leroy, 'I became deeply fond of ice cream, which probably explains the terrible addiction that burdens me today.' Leroy's favourite ice cream flavours were pandan and coffee. It was the unique muskiness of pandan combined with the rich intensity of coffee that he liked best. He begged us to hide his clandestine consumption from my mother — it upset her immensely that her five-year-old baby boy could be addicted to caffeine.

In the mornings before school, we helped our parents set up the restaurant. Luke swept the inside and outside areas before setting up the tables and chairs. Far too big for him to manage alone, he would call for help when the time came to put up the outdoor shade umbrellas. Lewis cleaned and presented the ice cream cabinets and made sure to inform me of the flavours I needed to make on the weekend. In the kitchen, I helped my mother set up the *mis en plus* while my father greeted his regular breakfast customers.

Each morning, at the last quiet hour before the streets began to swell with people, the same group of customers would wait impatiently for us to open the doors. They needed their first hit of caffeine. My parents made sure to have completed a barista course before purchasing their first espresso machine in the mid eighties. Pho Cay Du was the first Vietnamese restaurant in Cabramatta to sell espresso coffee instead of the instant stuff most people had grown accustomed to. We sold mostly Vietnamese coffee, espresso served hot with condensed milk or cold on ice. Coffee sales averaged around 300 glasses a day. Naturally, my father created his own secret blend and became famous in Cabramatta for his coffee. His good friend Nino from Brasilero Coffee has roasted my father's secret blend for the last 25 years.

For many reasons, my father was considered a pioneer within the business community. Prior to opening the restaurant, he had dared to approach the local government about such matters as outdoor seating and shop renovation — a considerable feat for a new Vietnamese migrant at the time. Along the outside of the restaurant on John Street Boulevard, my father had successfully sought council permission to set up outdoor tables — each with a brightly coloured umbrella to complete the kitsch aesthetic. He became the first in Cabramatta to offer alfresco dining and it proved to be a huge success. He named the restaurant Pho Cay Du: *Pho* being the traditional 'beef noodle soup' that is his specialty and *Cay Du*, or 'umbrella', to mark his bureaucratic achievement. Around this time, my father also became a Justice of the Peace and continued to give advice on social, legal and personal matters. Pho Cay Du offered a place for lonely migrants to meet and chat in their new and native tongues over a shared meal or a cup of coffee and ice cream as they sat and watched the world go by. It made my father happy that his contribution and participation had helped so many of his peers to rebuild their lives with confidence and hope.

My father displayed enormous pride and became fiercely protective of the small enterprise he had created. He usually employed one or two staff members, but it was the family who provided the major support. My mother worked permanently in the kitchen with me as her helper. Luke, who was not yet eight years old at the time, worked the floor with my father, serving customers and selling ice cream. Lewis had the easiest job, stationed upstairs in the video library watching his favourite films.

In the early hours of another long and busy day, we noticed an unusually tall and formal-looking man, wearing beige ironed chinos, a stiff white shirt and a slim sky-blue leather tie. His hair had been clipped into an immaculate military-style flat top — similarly symmetrical to his perfect moustache. We watched as he scanned the perimeters, observing the restaurant from various angles. We could tell by the look on his face that he was not contemplating our extensive menu. Without warning he made his approach and began folding down my father's outdoor umbrellas, stacking up his tables and chairs. I saw the look on my father's face and instinctively braced myself for what was going to happen next. 'Hand me that cleaver', my father shouted. With dread, I knew that he meant his favourite — the biggest and sharpest one.

As I watched my father march outside, cleaver swinging at his side, I felt sorry for the other poor fellow who was either very brave or incredibly stupid. Without an introduction, my father wrenched the man's tie and firmly twisted it around his fist. He yanked it with such force that the man stooped down to his eye level. What my father lacked in inches, he made up for in fearlessness. I couldn't tell if the man had raised his hands in an attempt to release the pressure from his throat, or to protect himself from the wielded cleaver — but from afar it looked as though he was praying.

'I'm from the council!' the man yelped, 'You need permission to put these tables out here. You people think you can just come here and do whatever the hell you like ...'

My father tightened his grip, this time pulling the man to his knees. He pulled the cleaver above his head. 'I have permission you bastard. Touch another piece of my property without my permission and I'll chop both your bloody hands off.'

The man saw the rage in my father's eyes and knew that he meant every word. He turned a pasty green colour and spoke not another word. As soon as my father released his grip, the man stumbled to his feet, straightened his tie and sprinted full speed into the distance. The council never bothered us again.

I confess that I have not always agreed with the maniacal strategies of my father but it is clear from the outcomes, that there is indeed a method in his madness.

It was Saturday, an hour into lunch service when the team of late adolescent soccer players took full occupancy of the outdoor tables and chairs. Still pumped full of adrenaline and bursting with pubescent testosterone, it was evident that their morning football match could not have been anything less than the complete annihilation of the other team. I recognized some of the faces from the Croatian Social Club further along the boulevard. They had never wanted to eat in our restaurant before. Lunch service had already started to heat up. Customers filled inside, taking advantage of the air-conditioned relief from the scolding humidity outside. Luke and Lewis had together attempted to take the soccer players' order but the self-assured boys with their cocky attitude and bravado smiles had told them both to 'piss off'. They made it clear that they wanted nothing to eat or drink — they just wanted to sit there and 'chill out'.

When I overheard this information relayed to my father, my throat dried up a little and my stomach shrunk. I watched as my father whispered words of assurance to himself, nodding his head in firm agreement with the next plan of action. I cleared the way as he shuffled past me into the kitchen. I watched as he patiently began boiling three large pots of water while calmly continuing to look after his customers inside. When the water reached boiling point, my father shuffled outside, wiping his hands on the cloth that always hung freely from the string of his apron. He asked the soccer players once more if they wanted anything to eat or drink. 'Piss off old man,' they laughed at him. 'Go back inside your shop and leave us alone. We just want to sit here and chill out okay!' I could hear them mocking him from inside the kitchen. I could only close my eyes and wait. The little old man did as he was told and went back inside his shop. He picked up the first pot of boiling water with both hands and carried it carefully outside. The warning was

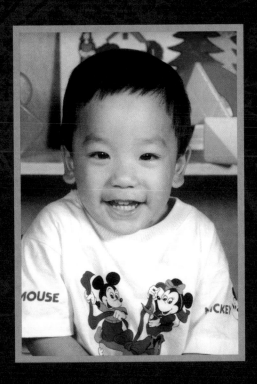

Clockwise from left: Leroy (age 1), 1985; my mother, Leroy, Lewis and I on our front verandah at Bonnyrigg, 1984; Lewis, me, Luke, my cousin Dung and my mother at Lap Bros Video Library, 1984.

non-existent. In a giant sweeping motion, he flung the steaming liquid in one glorious arc all over the 'chilled out' boys. As planned, he shuffled back inside and did the same with the second pot. By the time he came out with the third, the last of the young men had already fled as fast as his soccer legs could take him.

It was not that my father enjoyed a violent remedy every time; it was just that he had a severe aversion to a lack of courtesy and respect. Roger, the real estate agent from a few doors down, found this out the hard way. As well as sporting an impressive shiny black quiff, Roger had all the attributes of a rodent — shifty, greasy, self-absorbed and desperate. He liked to ask for credit on his coffees. For a long time, Roger had been trying to sell an empty shop situated at the back of John Street Boulevard. He didn't have any luck because the shop's location did not sit in clear view of the pedestrians on the main road. Roger decided that he would better his chances if he planted the 'For Sale' sign on the top level awning of my father's building — a helpful arrow would point down into the laneway.

Roger came one morning, loitering with a ladder under one arm and a 'For Sale' sign under the other. Of course we all saw him, how could we not? He was just too self-interested to realise it. He waited until my father stepped out of sight before he scurried up the ladder. My father waited until he climbed all the way up and, without hesitation, fetched his trusty meat cleaver and removed the ladder. Roger realised too late.

'Hey! Whacha doin' wif me ladder? Put it back, how'm I gonna get down?'

'Shut up,' my father shouted. 'You can't put that sign there. Everyone will think my restaurant's for sale.'

'Come on Mr Lap, the law's the law. I can put this sign wherever I want. You can't stop me.'

If it angered my father at first that the real estate agent had shown disrespect for himself and his property, it now incensed him that his intelligence had been insulted. Too often he had seen others equate the colour of his skin with ignorance. Barking from the stomach, he delivered his message loud and clear. 'If you come down from there you bastard, I'll chop both your bloody feet off!'

We shouldn't have found it funny when Roger's quiff melted in the sun or laughed when his pants had wet from distress. His cries for help fell onto the deaf ears of passers by. A good three hours passed before his colleagues came to rescue him.

My father's unorthodox methods of negotiation naturally gained him a vicious reputation within the community. Many respected him, some did not — but all knew not to mess with him. I admired his fearlessness, but it was hard for a teenage girl to watch her father commit such acts of cruelty and humiliation. This is not how they do it in Australia. I had to hand it to the old man, he was fair — everyone got the same treatment, even his children. If outsiders knew how severe my father was, they wouldn't have come between him and his business. My father prided himself on being a hard working, family man.

Everybody works hard in Cabramatta. Seven days a week the commercial centre pumps at full steam. There is no day off. Rest time comes once a year in February to celebrate the Lunar New Year. For most of their lives, my parents have worked seven days a week from 6.30am until 10.30pm. In all the years, my father had closed the restaurant only once — when my grandmother passed away. Like many of their friends, my parents are workaholics who don't know what to do with spare time. It is only now, in retirement, that they have learned what it means to relax a little.

In the early years, when the Vietnamese community had begun to firmly plant its roots, we suffered much criticism from outsiders. They wondered with envy and scepticism how the refugees who came with nothing could afford to buy new cars, new houses and run successful businesses. They didn't understand that people who have lost everything, have no choice but to work hard. 'We aim high because we must. People are always afraid of what they don't understand. Take my friend Minh for example,' says my father, 'he's been washing dishes for almost thirty years. When he came here, he had no friends, no money, no social life. Working hard was the only thing he could do. He now owns four houses. He works eighty hours a week, he goes home to his family, he never eats out, he never goes on holidays. He doesn't drive an expensive car. He saves every cent of his pay to secure a future for his children. All he does is work, work, work. That is his life.'

A significant feature of Cabramatta's dynamic commercial centre is that the Asian business people have not confined themselves to the traditional trade outlets. The newsagent, the tobacconist, the electrical goods store, the internet cafe or the lingerie shop is likely to have an Asian entrepreneur. In the late eighties, Asians were buying up large parts of Cabramatta's decaying shopping centres owned by the previous wave of migrants, and turning it into a profitable, vibrant and exotic shopping destination. The most important factor of these transformations was that it provided an employment lifeline for those who would otherwise find it impossible to get a job. It is through diligence and hard work that the proudly self-sufficient refugees of Cabramatta have turned adversity into success in such a short time. As my father's friend Tuan Anh says, 'We are working. We are not living on handouts. All our charm, humour and dignity have returned. We are no longer just survivors.'

The reason why the Asian impact is so complete in Cabramatta was due to the housing of refugees in the nearby Villawood and Cabramatta migrant hostels at the time. Much like the Italian and Greek migrant groups before us, the Indo-Chinese refugees arrived poor, unskilled and with little English.

Cabramatta offered employment, cheap housing and more importantly, the comfort of fellow refugees who offered some semblance of the old ways, helping to make their lives more bearable in a foreign country.

People have criticized the Vietnamese for sticking together, but there are pockets of nationalities in every country. I have visited Chinatowns in New York, Paris, Barcelona, Rome, London, Sydney and Melbourne. I have seen Little Italys everywhere in my travels. I have even stayed in patriotic Australian villages in Vietnam, Paris and London. All over the world, various races and cultures group together. Having been through what the refugees have been through, it is only human nature to seek solace, companionship and mutual support among our own people. Indeed, there are Vietnamese in Cabramatta and, yes, we have made an impact on the community. We have had our fair share of problems but this has been the case with every new wave of immigrants in every country of the world.

One of the biggest myths about Cabramatta is the belief that the suburb is a ghetto full of Vietnamese who are unable or unwilling to adapt to Australian society. This coincides with the even more popular myth that Cabramatta is a drug-saturated hot spot, full of junkies, corruption and Asian criminals. The rise of gangs and drugs during the mid-nineties had deeply wounded the community, but it was the media who inflicted the most harm. Even today, if there is a crime in Cabramatta, it receives a huge amount of publicity — a crime in another suburb hardly warrants the same exaggeration.

The media frenzy reached its peak following the violent murder of the local Member of Parliament (MP) John Newman in 1994. A gunman had shot him dead in his driveway. The headlines described it as Australia's first political assassination. Deeply saddened by the news, I realized too well the repercussions of his death and the field day the journalists would have.

John Newman had been a crusader for the Vietnamese people and a strident campaigner against Asian crime and Asian gangs. A dominant force for tourism in Cabramatta, he had a vision for the suburb as being a thriving multicultural metropolis. My father considered him a friend. As expected, the bad publicity escalated after his murder, bruising the community on both a social and economic level. Business revenue dropped terribly and the area lost over $10 million in tourism. Worst of all, the bad reputation incited fear and misunderstanding, tarnishing our prospects at school, in the workforce and in society.

When the media linked the assassination with events that happen in Cabramatta every day of the week, they neglected to mention the decent people — the honest, law abiding, hard working people who had chosen to work, raise their families and make a life for themselves in this multicultural suburb. Negative press continued and, for a time, even the residents became too scared to walk the neighbourhood streets after dark. Media beat-ups and xenophobia are nothing new to the Vietnamese people. The real story was that we were down but not out. How could they dampen the spirit of people who have been through so much to get to where they are? How could they expect to keep down a community of survivors dominated by a race who have a history of surviving?

Over time, the wounds healed and the bruises faded as the entire community banded together, determined to fix the issues affecting it. Residents walked the streets with members of the local government, pointing out areas that needed attention. The state government's participation saw the installation of closed circuit security cameras, improved street lighting, widening of footpaths, removal of vegetation and the increase in pedestrian police. The most significant factor that helped to stem the tide of crime (a factor that barely existed before) was the higher level of courtesy and respect paid to the locals by the police — an attitude naturally reciprocated.

In the rare downtimes, the suburb is calm, quiet and peaceful. Otherwise, it swarms with activity as people weave in and out of the maze of alleyways in search of great bargains, competitive prices and Asian delights. These days, there are other pressing local government issues, such as increased parking to deal with the congestion caused by daytrippers who flock to the suburb on the weekends. As with our family, most

Vietnamese who work in Cabramatta actually live elsewhere. Many have come from the South Vietnamese middle class and, as they have acquired more wealth, they have risen above their low socio-economic place in Australian society and swiftly moved to more affluent areas. While immigrants from Laos and Cambodia tend to concentrate in Fairfield, the Vietnamese are widely dispersed and have a high degree of geographic mobility. The presence of each ethnic group in Cabramatta is exaggerated somewhat by the ethnic visibility of the business area. Far from being a ghetto, Cabramatta is a place where thousands of people visit, or like me, return, in search of great company, amazing produce and excellent cuisine.

I regret that I do not return to Cabramatta as often as I would like. I miss that I cannot eat there every day, just as I did when I was a young girl. For me, going back is always a special time where I am comforted by the familiar faces of my childhood and resuscitated by the reassuring food of home.

It took a number of years for the Vietnamese people of Cabramatta to repaint the maligned canvas that had portrayed them. These days, Cabramatta is back on track to being recognized as the ultimate destination for lovers of Asian cuisine. It is just as well for my food-obsessed parents that market day in Cabramatta is every day of the week. Fruit, herbs and vegetables arrive crisp, firm and fresh every day, direct from the market gardens nearby. Most stalls carry the full range of Australian and Asian produce. Seafood and meat is fresh and reasonably priced. The butchers offer familiar cuts, as well as the Asian preference of meat closer to the bone. The offerings at the fish markets are extensive, with almost every type of fish imaginable on display.

There are more than eighty eateries in Cabramatta — offering authentic Vietnamese, Thai, Laotian, Cambodian, Chinese and vegetarian cuisine. There is even an Eastern European delicatessen, an Italian coffee house and my favourite Lebanese kebab shop. This is the spirit of Cabramatta, where racial harmony exists against a backdrop of a thriving economy, rich with cultural life.

For my parents, it was always business as usual. The negative press did not affect our restaurant as much as it had that of their friends' businesses. Pho Cay Du relied mainly on the loyalty of the locals who knew the real story — those not swayed by the media hype. My parents continued to work hard on the business, determined to expand their knowledge of all things culinary. They became obsessed with mastering their trade. My father even purchased a professional waffle cone maker to perfect the ice cream experience. This also meant staying back several hours each night after closing time, to mix the perfect batter to create the perfect cones — the imperfect ones we ate appreciatively. It had become clear by this stage that my parents had created too much work for themselves to enjoy life in any way. While my mother tackled the waffle cone maker, my father nursed his most important asset — *pho*.

There is a great fondness and respect dedicated by food writers and *pho* obsessives alike to the national soup of Vietnam. The art of making *pho* has been described by authors and avowed *pho*-natics Cuong Phu and Mai Long as 'symbolizing a Vietnam whose people and history are as varied and complex as the preparation of a bowl of *pho* itself — a dish that has travelled across the oceans and continents, transforming itself to survive'. *Pho* has integrated so completely into Australian society that there is no longer the need to refer to it as 'beef noodle soup' — everyone knows what *pho* is.

For me, *pho* represents a dish of tolerance and freedom of expression. Why have so many *pho* restaurants in Cabramatta survived for over 20 years? It is because there are enough varied palates and personal preferences to keep the vendors alive. Some prefer the Southern version, embellished with herbs, chilli, lemon and sauces. Others will eat only *pho bac*, the Northern version, unadorned with extra condiments. Some like a complex broth sweetened with herbs and spices, while others prefer the subtler flavours of white radish and charred onion. Some enjoy the fresh noodle; soft, slippery and delicate. Others prefer the re-hydrated kind, which is chewier in consistency. Whether it is *pho ga,* with chicken, or *pho dac biet,* with the lot, there is a style to reflect the fussiest palates.

No-one in my family is alike. My father likes the classic *pho tai nam,* with just a hint of lemon in his fish sauce to dip. He doesn't like MSG in his broth but my mother insists upon it. I prefer more noodles and less meat in my bowl and, like my mother, I like to leave the herbs and sprouts crisp on the side — my father allows the herbs to soften in his bowl. Lewis likes *pho dac biet* — without any fat, of course. He insists that the addition of any sauce is a crime: 'It takes away the purity of the *pho.*' Luke eats his with *gau*; beef flank marbled with some fat. He prefers just a hint of lemon and a sliver of chilli to infuse the broth. Leroy, on the other hand, loves plenty of lemon, basil, sawtooth coriander and chilli in his bowl, dipping his beefy goodness in a mess of hoisin and chilli sauce.

For a dish steeped in such history and tradition, it is unprejudiced and wholly accepting of individual evolvement and personal interpretation. Known among his peers as 'The Godfather of Pho', my father has dedicated a lifetime to mastering this dish and, indeed, it has taken him a lifetime to master. 'The secret is in the broth,' says my father. 'It takes up to 24 hours to make the soup and every cook adds his own special herbs. The broth demands constant nurturing and patience, skimming it of impurities. It is labour intensive and physically tiring to make but ultimately so rewarding.'

Although it is not my favourite food, it is certainly a special one for me. It had been my father's livelihood for most of his life — a recreation of the resilient flavours of his home. I have, since childhood, tasted many different versions of my father's *pho.* As I have witnessed the changes in my father's broth, I have witnessed the changes within my father. Most noticeably in these recent years, I watch as he strives to modify old habits and adapt to the new — always searching for a way in which to improve. On a recent trip home to Bonnyrigg, I tasted what I can call true perfection — the best my father has ever given me. The experience was nurturing, nourishing, soothing and painfully delicious. For many reasons I prefer my father's *pho* of today than that of past. Those days were dark, cloudy and complicated. Today, although still complex, there is more clarity and understanding. The most precious thing about today is his overpowering desire to make things better than before.   ■

Left: Our family business — Pho Cay Du, Lap Bros Video Library and Foremost Natural Ice Cream — Cabramatta, 1986. Clockwise from top right: Food scenes in Cabramatta; my father prepares to light firecrackers outside Pho Cay Du, New Year's Day, 1986.

LUKE NGUYEN: *This traditional salad is a perfect starter. It is a 'rare' treat — so refreshing, crisp and aromatic. Described by some as 'Vietnamese carpaccio', Bo Tai Chanh is a particular favourite in Suzanna's and my family.*

Rice paddy herb and sawtooth coriander (cilantro) are essential for this dish and should not be substituted. The rice paddy's sharp citrus character and the sawtooth's powerful aroma perfectly match this lemon-cured dish.

BÒ TÁI CHANH
lemon-cured sirloin

400 ml (14 fl oz) lemon juice
1 tablespoon fish sauce
1 teaspoon salt
2 teaspoons sugar
1 teaspoon fine white pepper
500 g (1 lb 2 oz) sirloin, trimmed of
    fat and sliced as thinly as possible
1 garlic clove, finely chopped and fried
1/2 teaspoon garlic oil, reserved from
    frying the garlic

1 large handful sawtooth coriander,
    roughly chopped
1 large handful rice paddy herb,
    roughly chopped
1/2 small red onion, finely sliced
1 large handful bean sprouts
2 tablespoons chopped roasted peanuts
    (page 38)
1 bird's eye chilli, sliced
dipping fish sauce (page 33), to serve

Combine the lemon juice and fish sauce, then mix through the salt, sugar and pepper. Arrange the sirloin in a single layer on a plate and marinate in the lemon mixture for 10 minutes, ensuring all the meat is covered. Remove the sirloin from the lemon mixture and gently drain the excess juice. Combine with the garlic, garlic oil, herbs, onion and bean sprouts.

Transfer to a serving plate and garnish with the peanuts and chilli. Dress with dipping fish sauce at the table.

SERVES 6

CÁNH GÀ CHIÊN TỎI

crisp garlic chicken wings

4 kg (9 lb) chicken wings
3 tablespoons salt
3 tablespoons soy sauce
8 garlic cloves, crushed
2 tablespoons plain (all-purpose) flour

1 egg
500 g (1 lb 2 oz/4 cups) cornflour
  (cornstarch)
oil, for deep-frying

Cut the chicken wings into three pieces by slicing through at the joints. Combine the salt, soy sauce and garlic in a large bowl. Add the chicken wings and mix well. Allow to marinate in the fridge for 1 hour.

Combine the plain flour with the egg and 2 tablespoons of water, add to the bowl of chicken wings and mix well. In a large wok or saucepan, pour in enough oil to deep fry the chicken and heat to 180°C (350°F), or until a cube of bread dropped in the oil browns in 15 seconds. Put the cornflour in another bowl and coat each piece of chicken thoroughly with it. Deep-fry in small batches until golden brown and cooked through. Remove from the oil and drain on paper towel.

Serve with salt, pepper and lemon dipping sauce (page 302) or dipping fish sauce (page 33).

SERVES 6, OR UP TO 12 PEOPLE AS PART OF A SHARED FEAST

LUKE NGUYEN: *My mother used to cook this dish for the family at least once a week. One of my duties as a child was to lay sheets of newspaper on the floor in front of the stove to catch any oil splatter. In my Vietnamese squatting position, I would get sidetracked by the newspaper articles and then told to hurry up with a flick behind the ear from Mum as the oil got hotter.*

Mum's preferred fish is silver bream or sand whiting. Snapper is my personal choice. I enjoy the texture of its crispy golden skin when fried, allowing me to crunch, suck and chew on all the bones. Don't believe your parents when they tell you that eating the fish's eyes helps to improve your eyesight. It's not true. The Nguyen clan have eaten fish eyes our entire lives and we all wear glasses.

CÁ CHIÊN DÒN

crispy-skin snapper with ginger and lime fish sauce

1 whole snapper (300–500 g/
    10½ oz–1 lb 2 oz)
2 tablespoons potato starch
1 egg white
oil, for deep-frying

1 large handful shredded green papaya
    or green mango
4 tablespoons ginger and lime fish
    sauce (page 199)
1 tablespoon spring onion oil (page 37)

Wash and dry the snapper thoroughly and place on a cutting board. Make 3 diagonal cuts along each side of the fish, making sure not to cut right through to the bone. Mix the egg white with the potato starch to form a batter and set aside. In a large wok or deep-fryer, heat the oil to 180°C (350°F), or until a cube of bread dropped in the oil browns in 15 seconds.

Coat the snapper thoroughly with the batter. Wipe off any excess batter and carefully slide the snapper into the oil. Cook the fish for 5–7 minutes, or until done. The skin should be crisp and the fish slightly underdone, as it will continue to cook once removed from the oil.

Place on a serving platter, cover with the shredded green papaya or mango, spoon over the ginger and lime fish sauce and spring onion oil.

SERVES 2

LUKE NGUYEN: *This is a great dish to share at the table. Have plenty of butter lettuce, perilla and mint available, along with some vermicelli noodles and rice paper. Once the fish is cooked, roll pieces of fish with the salad and noodles in rice paper and dip in the anchovy and pineapple sauce (next page). Be warned: the sauce is strong and pungent — it is an acquired taste. Substitute it with dipping fish sauce (page 33) if you prefer something less intense.*

CÁ NƯỚNG
chargrilled barramundi

1 whole barramundi (500–700 g/
   1 lb 2 oz–1 lb 9 oz)
1 tablespoon oil
salt and white pepper

Wash and dry the barramundi thoroughly and lay it flat on a cutting board. Make 3 diagonal slices on each side of the fish, making sure not to cut right through to the bone. Brush with the oil and season with salt and pepper. Grill the barramundi over high heat on a chargrill pan for 5–7 minutes each side, or until the flesh is opaque through to the bone.

SERVES 4

NƯỚC MẮM GỪNG

ginger and lime fish sauce

100 ml (3¹/₂ fl oz) dipping fish sauce
   (page 33)
juice of ¹/₂ lime

2 teaspoons finely chopped ginger
1 teaspoon pickled chilli (from Asian
   supermarkets)

Combine all of the ingredients together and mix well.

MAKES 125 ML (4 FL OZ/¹/₂ CUP)

MẮM NÊM

anchovy and pineapple sauce

1 tablespoon sugar
2 tablespoons boiling water
1 tablespoon fermented anchovy sauce
2 tablespoons unsweetened
   pineapple juice

1 tablespoon crushed fresh pineapple
1 teaspoon finely sliced lemon grass
1 garlic clove, crushed
1 bird's eye chilli, finely sliced

Dissolve the sugar in the water and allow to cool. Combine with the rest of the ingredients and mix well.

MAKES 125 ML (4 FL OZ/¹/₂ CUP)

LUKE NGUYEN: *Steaming fish is so simple and healthy. It is such a quick and clean method of cooking. It encloses all the freshness and sweetness of the fish, giving it a very delicate quality. A good substitute for silver perch is barramundi. Be sure that the water is rapidly boiling before placing the fish in the steamer.*

CÁ HẤP

steamed silver perch with shiitake mushrooms, ginger and spring onion

1 whole silver perch (500 g/1 lb 2 oz)
3 dried shiitake mushrooms,
   soaked in hot water for
   30 minutes then julienned
2 tablespoons julienned ginger
1 garlic clove, crushed
125 ml (4 fl oz/½ cup) fish stock
   (page 99)

1 tablespoon oyster sauce
½ teaspoon dark soy sauce
2 teaspoons sugar
salt and fine white pepper
½ teaspoon potato starch
2 bird's eye chillies, seeded and julienned
1 spring onion (scallion), sliced on
   the diagonal

Wash and dry the silver perch thoroughly and lay it flat on a cutting board. Make 3 diagonal slices on each side of the fish, making sure not to cut right through to the bone. Using a large bamboo steaming tray with a lid, or a purpose built metal steamer, fill with water and bring to the boil.

Meanwhile, add the shiitake mushrooms, ginger and garlic to a saucepan with the fish stock, oyster sauce and soy sauce and bring to the boil. Simmer for 5 minutes, then season with sugar, salt and pepper. Remove from the heat.

Place the fish on an oiled piece of foil, season with salt and pepper and steam for about 10 minutes, or until the flesh is opaque through to the bone. To serve, mix the potato starch with a little water to dissolve it, then add it to the sauce and reheat. Place the fish on a serving platter and scatter with chilli and sliced spring onion, pour the sauce over the fish and serve with steamed jasmine rice.

SERVES 4

LUKE NGUYEN: *Crabs are adored in all Asian countries. In Vietnam, many different varieties of crab are available — species that I had never seen before I visited. They ranged in size from 5 cm (2 in) to an enormous 70 cm (28 in) in diameter — of course, I had to try them all.*

For this recipe a 1 kg (2 lb 4 oz) 'muddy' is substantial. Remember to fry the crab in two batches so that the oil stays hot and the crab keeps its texture.

Make this dish when you really want to impress, as it has definite wow factor. Be sure to eat the roe from inside the shell — it's one of the best parts of the crab.

CUA SỐT ME

crab in tamarind and plum sauce

1 whole mud crab (1–1.5 kg/
   2 lb 4 oz–3 lb 5 oz)
6 spring onions (scallions)
2 long red chillies
200 g (7 oz/1 cup) potato starch
1 teaspoon salt
1 teaspoon fine white pepper

3 litres (105 fl oz/12 cups) oil,
   for deep-frying
250 ml (9 fl oz/1 cup) tamarind
   and plum sauce (page 207)
1 large handful coriander
   (cilantro) leaves

To kill your crab humanely, place it in the freezer for 1 hour. Remove the crab from the freezer and lay it on its back on a cutting board. Take a heavy cleaver and place the top 4 cm (1½ in) of the blade between the eyes along the middle of the body. Using enough force to split the body — but not the outer shell — hit the back of the cleaver with your fist.

Remove the hard body shell, making sure to keep the roe (if any) intact. Remove the gills and discard, scrub the crab under cold water with a brush to remove dirt and mud. Place the crab on a cutting board and, using a cleaver or large knife, cut the crab in half from top to bottom. Cut the claws from the body, then cut them in half at the elbow joint. Using the back of your cleaver, gently tap on the claw shells until they shatter slightly (this aids the cooking process). Cut in between each leg of the crab, so each portion contains 1 leg and a piece of the body.

Cut the spring onions into 4 cm (1½ in) lengths and finely slice the chillies on the diagonal and set aside. Combine the potato starch, salt and pepper in a bowl. Pass each piece of the crab through the potato starch to lightly cover, then shake off any excess starch.

Meanwhile, put the oil in a wok or large saucepan and heat over high heat until the temperature reaches 180°C (350°F), or until a cube of bread dropped in the oil browns in 15 seconds. Add the pieces of the crab to the wok in quick succession (you may have to do this in small quantities to maintain the high heat in the oil). Cook for 3–5 minutes, or until the crab sits high in the oil, then remove to a colander to drain off excess oil. Carefully strain the hot oil from the wok into an appropriate container for discarding and place the wok back on the heat.

Add the spring onions, chilli and crab to the wok, and toss well to combine the ingredients. Add the tamarind and plum sauce. Bring it to the boil and reduce the sauce while occasionally tossing the wok to coat the crab with the sauce. Once the sauce has coated the crab and reduced by half, about 1–2 minutes, turn it out onto a serving platter and garnish with the coriander leaves.

SERVES 2, OR 4 AS PART OF A SHARED FEAST

GỎI BÒ

beef, mushroom and glass noodle salad

1 sirloin steak (200 g/7 oz)
100 g (3¹/₂ oz) glass noodles
10 g (¹/₄ oz/¹/₄ cup) dried mushroom
 strips, such as wood ear mushrooms
 or Chinese black fungus
1 small handful mint leaves
1 small handful basil leaves
1 small handful coriander
 (cilantro) leaves
1 small handful Vietnamese mint leaves
2 makrut (kaffir lime) leaves, finely sliced
2 long red chillies, julienned
1 red onion, sliced
1 Lebanese (short) cucumber, halved
 lengthways and sliced into 2 mm
 (¹/₁₆ in) wide pieces
1 teaspoon roasted rice powder
 (page 37)
1 tablespoon chopped roasted peanuts
 (page 38)
1 tablespoon fried red Asian shallots
 (page 38)

BEEF MARINADE
1 garlic clove, crushed
1 tablespoon soy sauce
1 tablespoon fish sauce
2 teaspoons sugar
1 teaspoon sesame oil

SALAD DRESSING
45 g (1¹/₂ oz/¹/₃ cup) grated palm
 sugar (jaggery)
4 tablespoons lime juice
2 tablespoons fish sauce
2 tablespoons soy sauce
1 garlic clove
1 tablespoon chilli oil
1 tablespoon sliced lemon grass,
 white part only
1 small handful coriander
 (cilantro) leaves
2 tablespoons olive oil

To marinate the beef, mix all the marinade ingredients together in a bowl, add the sirloin steak and coat well. Leave refrigerated for 2 hours.

Soak the glass noodles and mushrooms separately in hot water for 20 minutes, strain and dry with paper towel. Cut the glass noodles into 4 cm (1¹/₂ in) lengths and set aside. Put all of the salad dressing ingredients in a food processor and blend to combine.

Cook the sirloin to your liking on a chargrill or frying pan. Allow to rest for 5 minutes, then finely cut the sirloin across the grain into 5 mm (¹/₄ in) slices. Combine the beef with the rest of the salad ingredients, except the peanuts and shallots in a large bowl. Add the dressing, then toss well to combine. Turn the salad out onto a serving platter and garnish with roasted peanuts and fried shallots.

SERVES 4 AS PART OF A SHARED FEAST

GỎI TÔM VỚI HỦ QUA

stuffed bitter melon and prawn salad

1 bitter melon
250 g (9 oz) cha gio chay filling
   (page 231)
6 cooked king prawns (shrimp), peeled,
   deveined and sliced in half
50 g (1¾ oz) bean sprouts
100 g (3½ oz) pickled vegetables
   (page 34)

1 small handful chopped mixed herbs
   (perilla, Vietnamese mint and
   coriander/cilantro)
3 tablespoons dipping fish sauce
   (page 33)
1 tablespoon chopped roasted peanuts
   (page 38)
1 bird's eye chilli, chopped
1 tablespoon spring onion oil (page 37)

Lay the bitter melon flat on a board and cut it in half across the middle. Take a spoon and hollow out the centre of the melon. Fill with the *cha gio chay* stuffing and wrap in plastic to seal. Place in a steamer and steam over high heat for 20 minutes, remove and allow to cool, then place in the refrigerator for 30 minutes. This makes it easier to slice later.

To assemble the salad, slice the bitter melon into 5 mm (¼ in) wide pieces and lay flat on a plate. In a bowl, combine the prawns, bean sprouts, pickled vegetables, herbs and mix well. Place the salad on top of the bitter melon, dress with dipping fish sauce and garnish with peanuts, chilli and spring onion oil.

The bitter melon can also be served in pork broth (page 56). In this case you would stuff the melon, then gently poach in the broth until tender.

SERVES 6

LUKE NGUYEN: *I always have a container of this sauce ready-made in my fridge at home. It's so versatile — team it with king prawns (shrimp), crab, roast duck, marinated chicken or a simple green vegetable stir-fry.*

NƯỚC SỐT ME
tamarind and plum sauce

125 g (4^1/$_2$ oz) tamarind pulp,
   without seeds
375 ml (13 fl oz/1^1/$_2$ cups)
   boiling water

185 ml (6 fl oz/^{3}/$_4$ cup) plum sauce
185 ml (6 fl oz/^{3}/$_4$ cup) oyster sauce
200 g (7 oz) caster (superfine) sugar

Put the tamarind pulp in a heatproof container and pour over the boiling water. Once it is cool enough to handle, break the pulp up with your hands, then pass the entire mixture through a sieve, to make a smooth sauce.

In a saucepan, combine the tamarind sauce, plum sauce, oyster sauce and sugar, and bring to the boil. Remove from the heat and allow to cool. Store in an airtight container in the fridge for up to 1 month.

MAKES 625 ML (21^1/$_2$ FL OZ/2^1/$_2$ CUPS)

LUKE NGUYEN: *The day I learned to use chopsticks, there was a bowl of pho waiting for me. We all grew up on this national treasure. When my folks had Pho Cay Du in Cabramatta, I would have a bowl of pho everyday. In those years, I thought my father's pho had already reached perfection — how wrong I was. Dad's pho continues to improve each time I am invited home for his heavenly broth. His spice combination and cooking methods become more and more complex and he takes his broth to a higher level every time. I simply cannot keep up with him. He is a true pho-natic.*

Everything I know about pho I have learned from my father — this is the priceless recipe he has passed down to me. I am convinced, however, that it is not the complete recipe — somehow it never tastes as good as his. I'm sure he still keeps many little secrets from me.

PHỞ BÒ TÁI NẠM
beef noodle soup

1 litre (35 fl oz/4 cups) beef stock base
   for pho (page 210)
800 g (1 lb 12 oz) fresh, thin rice
   noodles (bahn pho)
200 g (7 oz) beef flank, reserved
   from beef stock base for pho
   (page 210), finely sliced
200 g (7 oz) beef sirloin, finely sliced
1 small white onion, finely sliced
   into rings

2 spring onions (scallions), finely sliced
1 bunch sawtooth coriander (cilantro),
   sliced
1 bunch coriander (cilantro)
100 g (3 1/2 oz) bean sprouts
1 bunch Vietnamese basil
2 red chillies, finely sliced
1 lemon, quartered

Have a saucepan of boiling water on the stove. Bring the *pho* soup base to the boil in another saucepan. Divide the noodles into 4 portions, then blanch them individually in the boiling water for 30 seconds. Add the noodles to serving bowls, then layer the pieces of beef flank, then sirloin over the noodles. Pour over the boiling *pho* soup base and garnish with the white and spring onions, sawtooth and coriander.

Serve the *pho* with fresh bean sprouts, Vietnamese basil, chilli and lemon on the side. Additional condiments could include chilli sauce, hoisin and fish sauce.

SERVES 4

NƯỚC PHỞ BÒ

beef stock base for pho

4 beef shin bones
4 kg (9 lb) beef flank
1 whole chicken, cut into quarters
2 tablespoons table salt
350 g (12 oz) dried ginger (from Asian
    supermarkets)
50 g (1³/4 oz) cinnamon stick
12 star anise

6 cloves
230 g (8 oz/1 cup) caster
    (superfine) sugar
160 g (5¹/2 oz/¹/2 cup) rock salt
300 ml (10¹/2 fl oz) fish sauce
1 large bulb of ginger (150 g/5¹/2 oz),
    cut in half and chargrilled
4 large onions, chargrilled in their skin

Place the shin bones, flank and chicken in a very large saucepan or stockpot and cover with cold water. Add the table salt and leave for 2 hours. This will clean the meat and bones. After 2 hours, discard this water and scrub the shin bones under cold water. Add the meat, bones and chicken back to the saucepan and cover with 15 litres (525 fl oz/60 cups) cold water. Wrap the dried ginger, cinnamon, star anise and cloves in muslin (cheesecloth), add to the pan and bring the water to the boil over high heat. Constantly skim the impurities from the surface as the water comes to the boil, then reduce the heat to a simmer and cook for 1 hour, continuing to skim.

After 1 hour, add the sugar, rock salt and fish sauce to the broth and simmer for another 2 hours, frequently skimming. Remove the beef flank and place it in a large container, cover with some broth and allow it to cool.

Fill the pan back up with cold water to get it back to 15 litres (525 fl oz/ 60 cups) and return it to the simmer, cover with a lid, reduce the flame to low and cook overnight. The broth should barely be moving.

The next morning, pass the broth through a double layer of muslin into another pan. Wrap the chargrilled ginger and onions (with skin removed) in muslin, add to the pan and cook for a further 2 hours. Remove the muslin bag and allow the stock to cool. Portion into smaller quantities and refrigerate or freeze until required. The reserved beef flank is sliced into 2 mm (¹/16 in) wide pieces and added to the *pho* (page 208).

MAKES 15 LITRES (525 FL OZ/60 CUPS)

LUKE NGUYEN: *This very popular dessert is a classic in Vietnamese households. Influenced by the French* flan au caramel, *the Vietnamese recipe uses coconut milk. At Red Lantern, we steam rather than bake the crème caramel. This gives it a much smoother and silkier finish.*

Be sure to allow the caramel to cool in the moulds before pouring in the coconut mixture and avoid getting hot caramel on your skin. It really hurts!

BÁNH GAN
coconut crème caramel

425 g (15 oz) caster (superfine) sugar
6 eggs
425 ml (15 fl oz) coconut cream

200 ml (7 fl oz) milk
2 tablespoons toasted desiccated
  coconut

Put 250 g (9 oz) of the sugar and 100 ml (3½ fl oz) water in a saucepan, without stirring, then bring to the boil over high heat. Cook for 5–8 minutes, until the sugar syrup turns a golden caramel colour. Pour the caramel carefully into six 250 ml (9 fl oz/1 cup) caramel moulds, using tongs to hold the moulds and swirling them around so the caramel coats the sides as well as the bottoms of the moulds. Half fill a metal steamer large enough to cook the caramels and bring to the boil.

Meanwhile, break the eggs into a bowl, add the remaining 175 g (6 oz) of sugar and whisk well to combine. Add the coconut cream and milk and mix thoroughly. Pour the coconut mixture into the moulds, then place in the steamer, cover and reduce the heat to low and steam for 40–45 minutes, or until the mixture sets. Check regularly as the caramel can easily overcook, giving a bubbled appearance when turned out onto the serving plate. To check if the caramel is set, tap the mould with your finger — the surface of the caramel should be firm and wobble slightly.

Once cooked, remove from the heat and allow to cool. To serve, gently run a knife around the edge of the mould, turn upside down and allow the caramel to fall out onto a serving plate. Sprinkle with the toasted desiccated coconut.

MAKES 6

CHUỐI CHIÊN
banana fritters

200 g (7 oz/1²/₃ cups) self-raising flour
300 ml (10¹/₂ fl oz) cold soda water
2 teaspoons oil
pinch of salt

4 cavendish bananas
oil, for deep-frying
2 tablespoons chopped roasted peanuts
    (page 38)

Mix the flour, soda water, oil and salt together and set aside for 10 minutes. Cut the bananas in half across the middle and add them to the batter, coating them well. Heat the oil in a wok or large saucepan to 180°C (350°F), or until a cube of bread dropped into the oil browns in 15 seconds.

Using a fork, skewer the banana pieces, and add to the oil one at a time. Cook for 3–5 minutes, or until golden brown. Serve with your favourite ice cream and garnish with roasted peanuts.

SERVES 4

LUKE NGUYEN: *I am the only member of my family who is not in love with* sau rieng *(durian). I totally understand why airlines and hotels forbid this 'king of fruits' — its strong aroma really packs a punch. Its fragrance, or should I say, odour, will fill the whole house within seconds. And the persistent stench promises to stick around for days. Mum would describe this delicacy as 'custard-like flesh, rich, creamy and smooth ... like nothing else on earth'. Dad would simply say, 'Tastes like heaven, smells like hell.' For durian lovers, this ice cream recipe is delicious. When choosing a durian, go for one with a big solid stem — a sign of freshness. Use a heavy cleaver to open the fruit, as it's impossible to cut without one.*

KEM SẦU RIÊNG
Durian ice cream

400 g (14 oz) durian pulp
1 lemon, zest only, in large pieces
500 ml (17 fl oz/2 cups) milk
500 ml (17 fl oz/2 cups) pouring
   (whipping) cream

6 egg yolks
250 g (9 oz) caster (superfine) sugar

Remove the seeds from the durian and lightly pulse the flesh in a food processor to loosen the fibres of the fruit. Put the durian, lemon zest, milk and cream in a saucepan and bring to the boil over medium heat. Remove the lemon zest.

Meanwhile, place the egg yolks in a bowl, add the sugar and whisk well until light in colour. As soon as the mixture in the saucepan comes to the boil, pour it over the egg yolks, whisking constantly. Pour the mixture back into a clean saucepan and cook for about 5 minutes over medium heat, stirring constantly, until the mixture thickens slightly and coats the back of a wooden spoon. Remove from the heat and pour it into a bowl and place over ice to cool.

Put half the mixture in an ice cream machine and churn until frozen, or place in the freezer and whisk it every half hour until frozen. Repeat with the second batch. It will take 4–5 hours to freeze.

MAKES 2 LITRES (70 FL OZ/8 CUPS)

KEM CHUỐI DỪA
banana and coconut ice cream

2 *very ripe lady's finger bananas*
250 *ml (9 fl oz/1 cup) coconut cream*
250 *ml (9 fl oz/1 cup) milk*

4 *egg yolks*
100 *g (3½ oz) caster (superfine) sugar*

Blend the banana with the coconut cream and milk until very smooth, then add the mixture to a saucepan. Place the saucepan over medium heat and bring to the boil. Meanwhile, whisk the egg yolks with the sugar until light and fluffy. Pour the boiled coconut cream and milk over the egg mixture while continually whisking. Pour the mixture back into a clean saucepan and cook for about 5 minutes over medium heat, stirring constantly, until the mixture thickens slightly and coats the back of a wooden spoon. Remove from the heat and pour it into a bowl and place over ice to cool.

Put the mixture in an ice cream machine and churn until frozen, or place in the freezer and whisk it every half hour until frozen. It will take 4–5 hours to freeze.

MAKES 750 ML (26 FL OZ/3 CUPS)

KEM TRÁI BƠ
avocado ice cream

125 ml (4 fl oz/¹/₂ cup) milk
375 ml (13 fl oz/1¹/₂ cups) pouring
   (whipping) cream
1¹/₂ very ripe avocados
1 tablespoon lemon juice

2 tablespoons condensed milk
1 teaspoon salt
4 egg yolks
100 g (3¹/₂ oz) caster (superfine) sugar

Put the milk and cream in a saucepan and bring to the boil over medium heat. Meanwhile, remove the flesh from the avocados and blend it in a food processor with the lemon juice, condensed milk and salt. As soon as the cream comes to the boil, blend it through the avocado in the food processor. Whisk the egg yolks and sugar together until light and fluffy, then pour the avocado mixture over the yolks while continually whisking. Pour the mixture back into a clean saucepan and cook for about 5 minutes over medium heat, stirring constantly, until the mixture thickens slightly and coats the back of a wooden spoon. Remove from the heat and pour it into a bowl and place over ice to cool.

Put the mixture in an ice cream machine and churn until frozen, or place in the freezer and whisk it every half hour until frozen. It will take 4–5 hours to freeze.

MAKES 750 ML (26 FL OZ/3 CUPS)

the missing years

Gratitude is something of high importance to the Vietnamese people.

My father says 'If someone does right by you, show your gratitude, give thanks, never forget the gesture and return it tenfold.' The Vietnamese community has much to be grateful for. We are grateful to the Australian government for giving us an opportunity we would never have had — the opportunity to make a better life for our children, our children's children and ourselves. Given that our entire history is one of oppression and turbulence, we are grateful to the country that took us in, and allows us to retain our cultural heritage and identity. As my father says, 'When you have been to where most refugees and Vietnam veterans have been, you feel gratitude.' In turn, the Vietnamese have given a great deal back to Australia, further enriching this multicultural society.

The year 2005 marked 30 years since the first Vietnamese refugees arrived in Australia. While it took previous waves of immigrants at least two generations to achieve wealth and social status, the first generation of Vietnamese have already climbed that ladder. Consistently over-represented at universities, the Vietnamese, who make up less than 1 percent of Australia's population, occupy more than 7 percent of law, medicine and engineering places. Vietnamese are participating in higher education at more than double the rate of students with English speaking backgrounds. There is an enormous emphasis placed on education and a great motivation to succeed. The Vietnamese community is highly visible outside of Cabramatta in high white-collar and blue-collar positions. In a short period, we have secured a presence in the world of film, art,

Previous page: My mother in the final days of Pho Cay Du. Left: My parents 'giving thanks' at a Buddhist temple in Cabramatta, 2005.

literature, law, medicine and even politics. Diligence, conscientiousness and sheer determination has seen the Vietnamese community participate and contribute greatly to Australian society.

Like his peers, my father wanted desperately to raise four high achievers, believing that the sacrifices he and my mother have made are far too great for us not to be. We aimed high because we had no choice. We were made acutely aware (and never forget) that he and my mother fled Vietnam not for their own future but for ours — to ensure that we could lead a prosperous life and have a better education. 'You are like cars with no direction ...' my father would say, '... and I am your steering wheel, leading you in the right direction.' He taught us to always hold high aspirations and maintain strong ambitions for our future. He reminded us never to forget where we came from and drilled into us the value of freedom. To do well was our way of recognizing and honouring our parent's sacrifice.

My father feared that his children would lose the old culture. At home, we spoke Vietnamese to our parents and English to each other. We practised all the formal traditions and lived the pious Vietnamese way. We upheld filial obedience and dutifully worshipped our long lost ancestors. We paid the consequence for forgetting to respect our elders in any way.

My father had hoped that the two very different cultures could blend into one well-adjusted whole. In theory, this sounded better than when it was put into practice. We worked at the restaurant seven days a week before and after school, stopping only to finish our homework and complete household chores. Outside activities included maths school, Vietnamese school, cooking school, debating and martial arts. We did all this and had to get top grades as well.

My father placed tremendous pressure upon us from an early age — any average result was a failure in his eyes. The knowledge of this lingered over our heads like a cheerless cloud that never lifted. He sent us to strict same-sex private Catholic schools, which was a challenge in itself. But report time was the worst. Twice a year from the age of seven until thirteen, we would bring home our school reports with total fear and loathing. Assisted by his favourite billiard stick, the stiffest, shiniest one, my father would cane us once for every 'B' grade that we held. For every 'C', he caned us twice. This ritual required us to lay flat on our stomachs and not budge a millimetre as we waited for our father to deliver his wrath. Our polished floorboards, as hard and shiny as they were, offered no support as my father's stick sliced the skin of our buttocks and hacked at the flesh of our thighs. When my father was done, and as we lay there in a bloody heap, he threw us a dollar for every 'A'.

With teeth clenched and fists squeezed until our knuckles turned white, I sometimes stared out the window and wondered what the neighbours would think if they ever heard us scream. What did it matter? To shed a tear or release a whimper at anytime throughout this ritual meant a further beating to nullify our weakness. I cried only in private, knowing that the pain and bruising usually got worse before it got any better. Mostly I cried for Lewis who, no matter how hard he tried, could never get anything higher than a 'C' for handwriting and physical education.

Fear dominated every day of my childhood. Fear and the dog shit covering the yard, were the smells of my youth. I cannot remember any time when fear did not lurk over my shoulder. Fear seeped through every window, rose up from each shiny floorboard and spilled through the dead cracks in our walls. It hovered over our beds while we were sleeping.

My dearest Aunty Ten tried her best to ease our pain. It was all she could do when report time came, to stay at our house for as long as possible to delay the beatings. It comforted me to know that there was another Vietnamese adult in this world who thought that my father's actions were cruel and unacceptable. 'They are only children for Christ's sake.' Her kindness only made matters worse — elongating our agonizing wait; our nerves singed to the flashpoint. Eventually the time would come for her to leave. She had her own life, her own home — she couldn't stay with us forever. With desperate weeping voices we would beg, 'Please Aunty, please stay … just a little bit longer.'

'I'm so sorry honey I must go … I'm so sorry.'

It made no difference to my father what time my Aunty left. He was a patient man and especially good at playing this game. As soon as Aunty Ten walked out the front door, my father would, with the enthusiastic glare of an executioner, cock his head once in our direction, and we knew what we had to do. The regular beatings ensured that I eventually brought straight 'A's home to my father and secured a permanent position within the top three students of my grade — a habit I kept for every one of my dreary school years. By the time we reached high school, the private canings stopped and a new punishment was introduced — public humiliation. While our friends lived their teenage years going out, discovering life and having fun, my father forbade us to go anywhere. He installed deadlocks on every major door of our house — front door, back door, living room door, dining room door and bedroom doors. It would have been impossible for a thief to penetrate — let alone for any child to escape. Our lives consisted of school, restaurant, sanctioned activities and home. He tolerated nothing else. My father controlled every hour of our day and when any situation fell out of his control, we suffered the full force of his anger.

I can still recall the stench of my fear when I stepped onto the wrong train going home from school one day. It was overcast — the claustrophobic clouds had already descended with an air of nervous anxiety. In a flutter of lateness, I had mistakenly caught the express train at Liverpool station. It shot past Cabramatta and didn't stop until half an hour later at Town Hall. Distressed and severely panicked at the thought of having to explain the lateness to my father, I carelessly jumped onto the first train I saw heading back. Unfortunately for me, it was the 'all stops' peak hour train delivering me back to Cabramatta another two hours later. Walking to the restaurant that evening to face my father, was like losing control behind a car wheel — I am heading at full speed into a brick wall and there is no way of stopping. All I can do is grit my teeth, clench my fists and brace myself for the impact.

My parents didn't want to know about my version of events, accusing me instead of secretly meeting with the phantom boyfriend they had concocted in their heads. My father confirmed my fear with three clean punches to my face followed by his usual torrent of poisonous words, 'You'll grow up and amount to nothing more than a common whore!' He made sure his friends were watching.

The reality of our lives was unkind, unfair and affectionless. Over the years, our skin grew thick and our pain tolerance high. My father had successfully created three tough, working machines. No parent could have wished for better children. We were disciplined, obedient, hardworking, sensitive, caring, polite and always respectful. There was never any room to breathe, let alone misbehave. Mentally and physically we were strong — emotionally and spiritually we were a mess.

One of my father's well used and memorable quotes was, 'I created you and I have the power to destroy you.'

What problems my father must have had within himself, to treat his innocent children with such contempt — his explosive anger, completely out of proportion to any incident at hand. As I searched for a way of understanding the reason for the bleakness of our lives, I came to realize that it wasn't that my parents didn't love us; it was just that they had never known how to love themselves. The idea of enjoyment had completely passed them by. I regret that my parents saw no other alternative but to work constantly. I regret that they blamed their children for the pressures they had created. I wish that my parents had learned how to be kinder to themselves — taking time to step back, breathe a little, relax, and truly enjoy their own achievements.

My father, like many Vietnamese men in the early years, could not escape the old tradition where the man's word is the law. Born into a Confucian culture that values fragile women, my father believed that a woman must first obey her father and then her husband. If her husband dies, then she must obey her son. Confucianism decrees that the father totally rules the family home. My mother, also a product of Confucian culture, grew up believing that it is her duty to remain submissive and obedient. When a Vietnamese woman is badly treated by her husband, she cannot speak out. My mother believes that 'speaking out brings the family shame'.

Oh my dear sweet mother, how it pains my soul that you are sad and lonely. How it aches my heart that your tears are dry. How my body trembles, that you cry only deep inside.

It is only in my adult years that I found the courage to approach the subject with my father. I asked if he thought about seeking the help of community support groups offered by other refugees and war survivors. His answer: 'We were too busy working.'

I know for certain that my mother would have treasured a kind ear and a shoulder to cry on and I have no doubt that my father would have benefited greatly from community groups dealing with the trauma of war and escape.

Although my parents did not seek guidance, many in the community found it necessary. Realizing the need for awareness, compassion and understanding, the Vietnamese community set up a vast network of support and self-help services for refugees subjected to torture during the war and the trauma of losing family and friends, as well as being uprooted from their homes and their livelihood. These holistic services not only helped, and continue to help, to facilitate the healing process for soldiers of war but civilians alike — those subjected to rape by pirates on the high seas, those who have watched others killed or starving next to them and those hopeless and hungry for days just drifting in the water. These psychological and physical fears have a huge impact — they are all trauma.

It has been documented that the children of Vietnam veterans maintain the highest rates of suicide. We Nguyen children have all thought about it at some time. I had long fantasized that post-traumatic stress disorder was ultimately the reason for the unreasonable nature of my father's rage.

The modern term for 'battle fatigue' or 'shell shock', post-traumatic stress disorder can present to combatants of all wars, but is most common with Vietnam veterans. This is due to the stress of guerrilla warfare, unspeakable human atrocities, terrorism and the vague military objectives of the war. Doctors who have studied veterans with 'psychic wounds you cannot see' say that the victims report nightmares, flashbacks, irritability with children, anger, depression, anxiety and panic attacks. They exhibit erratic behaviour from instant rage to sudden remorse. They suffer fits of jealousy at the happiness of others and show intense feelings of fear, sadness and guilt. Destruction has a lasting impact — the pain and human suffering continues long after the battles have ceased. While some numb the pain with alcohol and drugs, others, like my father, hide behind unending work.

When I dare ask my father about the stress he suffered after the war, he shrugs off the notion and replies, 'I don't think about it. Why do I want to think about the past for? I think about the here, the now. I cannot ask myself, "Who was I?" I ask only, "Who am I?" I cannot think about the things I did thirty years ago, twenty years ago or even ten years ago. I did so many bad things. Life is still about survival. In order to survive I must think only about today, not yesterday.' Indeed the sheer passage of time has helped to heal some wounds. It is only now, in my early thirties, that I see my father begin to make peace with the inner demons that haunt him. On a recent occasion I overheard him say, 'My children, they understand me now, I was very strict, I lost my temper very easily … very easily … I was so jealous of other people and angry all the time … sometimes I need to be alone, to ease the pressure and release my stress.'

Paul A. Witteman, in his 1991 *Time* article 'Lost in America', describes a change in approach over time: 'When Roman Legionnaires returned from war, they were encouraged to settle in quiet rural areas to decompress quietly. Greek Spartans recouped with their families to the seclusion of the tranquil mountains. Japanese literature tells of Samurai retiring to seek inner peace and tend to the "perfect garden".' For the path laid out for my father, I question, could there ever have been a natural positive reaction to such a string of abnormal events?

My father fled Vietnam to escape the oppression of the communist regime. It is ironic that we in turn have had to escape the tyranny and oppression of his rule to find freedom for ourselves. With the help of a close friend and with the support of my brothers, I ran away from home just as soon as I was old enough and immediately, I went into hiding. My brothers, who always knew of my whereabouts, warned me by phone if my father or any of his henchmen came close to finding me. He had spread the word that there could be only two reasons for my leaving: one, that I had become a drug addict too ashamed to face the world; and two, that I had fallen pregnant to the phantom boyfriend he had concocted in his head. These egocentric conclusions were so typical of his nature. He had never attempted to get to know or understand his children in any way. What assumptions he did come up with, he did so with anger and venom in his heart. I do not know which fact is sadder.

That morning, after the rain and just before December, I packed a lone suitcase, said goodbye to my brothers and walked out the tired front door. Leroy, only five-years-old at the time and already displaying a knack for all things dramatic, had pleaded with me to stay. 'If you leave me sis, I will get a knife and stab myself in the stomach!' Poor Leroy, how confused he must have felt to be abandoned by his sister.

With the courage of soldiers my brothers ventured out to the restaurant to face the firing line. They presented my father the farewell letter I had written — a soft, compassionate letter outlining all the reasons I had to leave. My brothers told my father that they had 'found' the letter after 'discovering' that I had gone. He hastily read my words and put them in his pocket. He ordered my brothers to join him at the table. He picked up four square, stainless steel napkin dispensers and placed them neatly on top of one another. With steel in his voice, he said, 'These represent each one of you.' He pointed to each dispenser as he spoke, resting his finger on the bottom. 'This one is your sister, she is meant to be the foundation for the four of you.' After a long, deliberate pause and his backhand at the ready, he took a sudden violent swing at the bottom dispenser, sending it flying through the air and smashing it against the tiled wall. As the top three dispensers came crashing to the ground, he shouted, 'Instead, she has chosen to wreck the family home!' My brothers tell me that the restaurant was full of customers and that he digested not one word of my letter — 'She is wrong,' he said, 'to do what she has done.'

Leaving my three brave brothers was the most painful part of running away — leaving them to face the consequences and pick up the pieces once I had gone. Life only got worse for them as the damp vapour of sadness filled every corner of our family home, lingering persistently over their heads, seeping into their clothes and skin. The pain between my mother and father followed them even to the restaurant, like a translucent shadow, leaving an unnatural mist for all

to see. If little dialogue existed between them before, even less existed once I had gone. Communication shut down all together — not out of hatred for one another, but out of despair. 'Every day was like walking on thin ice,' Luke tells me. My brothers' workload grew heavier as they picked up the duties I had left behind. 'Every day we were afraid — afraid of not working hard enough, afraid of coming home late from school, afraid of letting any chores go amiss, afraid of stepping out of line in any way. We made sure that we did nothing wrong. Dad's wick was constantly on fire.'

My mother suffered the most, Lewis tells me. 'She briefly lost her mind when she lost her only daughter.' She became emaciated, letting grief eat away at her. 'She sighed constantly, wore a permanent frown and never smiled at all.' She became a vegan and vowed not to eat meat until she could see me again.

For many Buddhists, vegetarianism is a means of cleansing not only the body, but also the spirit and mind. It is a way of asking the gods for forgiveness, guidance and strength. It is custom to abstain from meat twice in every lunar calendar month. My mother's tears fell at last, as she prayed every day for my return. After two long years of waiting, my parents emptied of all hope, every ounce of inspiration drained out of them. They finally surrendered to their own sorrow and closed down the family business. They stopped working altogether. With their livelihoods packed up, they began living a monastic existence, trying the best they knew how, to make amends with the three boys still living at home.

For me, life was also about survival. In order to survive I could not allow myself, not even for one moment, to think about the tremendous shame that I had dumped upon them. The months passed slowly as I moved around to avoid detection. Truly fearing for my life, I hid in a quiet beach suburb in Newcastle, a city north of Sydney — one of the last places anyone would think of looking. But my spirit grew weary of living in fear and my body tired of being on the run. I made up my mind to return to Sydney and finish my degree.

By this time, I had found a new strength. My fear of the future was nothing compared to my fear of the past. Even so, out of habit, I would look over my shoulder everywhere that I went. I completed my arts degree in 1995. Looking back, I find it amusing that even years after leaving home, I still felt compelled to inform my father of my academic achievements. Each year, I would cut away my home address and send him my results — to let him know that there were some things, I would never forget. 'Aim high; hold strong ambitions for your future. Remember where you came from and above all else, never forget the true value of your freedom.'

Graduation Day, 1995

BÌ CUỐN CHAY
soft vegetarian rice paper rolls

1 *quantity* chay gio chay *filling*
  (next page)
1 *tablespoon roasted rice powder*
  (page 37)
2 *tablespoons fried red Asian shallots*
  (page 38)
1 *small potato, grated and deep-fried*
  into potato straws

50 g (1³/4 oz) bean sprouts
18 sheets of 22 cm (8¹/2 in) rice paper
1 large handful perilla leaves
1 large handful mint leaves
¹/4 iceberg lettuce, shredded
vegetarian dipping sauce (page 243),
  to serve

Mix the *chay gio chay* filling with the roasted rice powder and combine with the fried shallots, potato and bean sprouts. Soak a sheet of rice paper in hot water and lay it flat on a work bench. Place some perilla, mint and lettuce on a sheet of rice paper and lay about 1 handful of the filling on top. Fold over the sides and roll up to form a tight roll. *Bi cuon chay* is assembled in the same way as *goi cuon* on page 27 — for more detailed rolling instructions, refer to the earlier recipe. Serve with the vegetarian dipping sauce.

MAKES 18

CHẢ GIÒ CHAY
crisp vegetarian parcels

50 g (1³/4 oz) split yellow mung beans
50 g (1³/4 oz) glass noodles
25 g (1 oz) dried mushroom strips,
   such as wood ear mushrooms or
   Chinese black fungus
vegetable oil, for frying
1 carrot, grated
1 celery stalk, finely sliced
50 g (1³/4 oz) bamboo shoot strips
100 g (3¹/2 oz) store-bought deep-fried
   tofu, finely sliced

2 tablespoons soy sauce
2 teaspoons dark soy sauce
1 tablespoon sugar
1 teaspoon salt
1 teaspoon white pepper
1 teaspoon sesame oil
12 spring roll papers, without egg
oil, for deep-frying
vegetarian dipping sauce (page 243),
   to serve

Soak the mung beans in hot water for 1 hour, then steam for 15 minutes, or until tender. Soak the noodles and mushrooms separately in cold water for 20 minutes, drain and dry well with a cloth. Cut the noodles into 4 cm (1¹/2 in) lengths.

Add 2 tablespoons oil to a wok set over high heat, add the grated carrot, celery, mushrooms and bamboo strips. Stir and toss well to combine, and cook for 3 minutes. Add the noodles, mung beans and tofu to the wok and continue to stir-fry, combining the ingredients. Cook for a further 3 minutes, then add both soy sauces, sugar, salt, pepper and sesame oil. Taste for seasoning, adjusting if necessary, then remove from the heat and allow to cool. The vegetables should still retain some crispness.

To make the parcels, cut the spring roll papers in half diagonally and separate the sheets. With the longest edge of the paper facing you, place 1¹/2 tablespoons of the mixture on the bottom centre of the paper. Draw the left side of the paper over the filling, then the right side up and over. Now roll the parcel from the bottom to the top and secure by placing a dab of water on the paper before you complete the roll. Repeat until you have used all of the filling. The parcels can be fried immediately or frozen for up to 1 month.

Put enough oil in a wok to deep-fry the parcels and heat to 180°C (350°F), or until a cube of bread dropped in the oil browns in 15 seconds. Fry the parcels in small batches for about 5 minutes each, or until golden brown and crispy.

These parcels can be eaten on their own, with vegetarian dipping sauce on the side, wrapped in butter lettuce with mint, perilla leaf and bean sprouts or served on vermicelli salad (page 118).

MAKES 24 PARCELS

BÁNH XÈO CHAY
crisp vegetarian rice flour crepe

RICE FLOUR CREPE
100 g (3¹/2 oz) rice flour
25 g (1 oz) plain (all-purpose) flour
¹/2 teaspoon salt
1 teaspoon ground turmeric
150 ml (5 fl oz) coconut cream
150 ml (5 fl oz) cold soda water

MUSHROOM AND TOFU FILLING
50 g (1³/4 oz) mung beans, soaked
  overnight, until doubled in size
50 g (1³/4 oz) store-bought deep-fried tofu
100 g (3¹/2 oz) oyster mushrooms

20 g (³/4 oz) dried shiitake mushrooms,
  reconstituted, stems removed
100 g (3¹/2 oz) enoki mushrooms
1 tablespoon vegetable oil
pinch of salt and fine white pepper

1 spring onion (scallion), finely sliced
50 g (1³/4 oz) bean sprouts
8 butter lettuce leaves
1 handful perilla leaves
1 handful mint leaves
100 ml (3¹/2 fl oz) vegetarian dipping
  sauce (page 243)

Sieve the rice flour and plain flour into a bowl, add the salt and turmeric and mix well to combine. Pour the coconut cream and soda water into the bowl and mix well with a whisk to form a smooth batter. Allow to rest for 10 minutes before use. This makes enough batter for three 32 cm (12¹/2 in) crepes. The remaining batter will keep refrigerated for 3 days.

To make the mushroom and tofu filling, steam the mung beans until soft and set aside. Finely slice the tofu and oyster and shiitake mushrooms, and cut the enoki mushrooms into 2 cm (³/4 in) long pieces. In a very hot wok add the oil and stir-fry the mushrooms and tofu for 2 minutes, or until they are browned on the edges but not cooked through. Season with salt and pepper, then remove to a colander and drain off any excess liquid.

To make the vegetarian crepe, place a non-stick frying pan over medium heat and sprinkle half of the spring onion into the pan. Pour about one-third of the batter into the middle of a 32 cm (12¹/2 in) frying pan, pick it up by the handle and ease the batter over the entire surface of the pan and pour the excess back into the original batter. (The crepe should be quite thin.) Scatter the mung beans and cooked tofu and mushroom mixture, bean sprouts and remaining spring onions over one half of the crepe. Reduce the heat to low and cook until the crepe is crisp and browned.

Using a spatula, fold the crepe in half and slide it onto a large plate. Cut the crepe into 6–8 pieces, pick up a piece of lettuce, a couple of perilla and mint leaves, place the crepe on the lettuce, roll it up and dip in vegetarian dipping sauce. Repeat with the remaining batter to make 2 more crepes.

SERVES 2, OR 6 AS PART OF A SHARED FEAST

MARK JENSEN: *This dish is easy to prepare, a great accompaniment to crabmeat, chargrilled prawns (shrimp) or a substantial vegetarian dish on its own. This is also a great dish to throw on the barbecue or even over some hot coals.*

CÀ TÍM NƯỚNG
chargrilled eggplant with shallot and chilli

4 long, purple (Japanese) eggplants
   (aubergines)
2 tablespoons vegetable oil
3 tablespoons dipping fish sauce
   (page 33)
1 tablespoon spring onion oil (page 37)

1 tablespoon fried red Asian shallots
   (page 38)
1 tablespoon chopped roasted peanuts
   (page 38)
1 bird's eye chilli, finely sliced

Brush the skin of the eggplants with the vegetable oil and place on a chargrill pan. Cook until the skin firms and cracks and the flesh is tender. Allow to cool slightly, then remove and discard the skin. Place the eggplant on a plate and spoon over the dipping fish sauce and spring onion oil. Garnish with fried shallots, peanuts and sliced chilli.

SERVES 2

LUKE NGUYEN: *Tofu is a dietary staple throughout Vietnam — it is made fresh daily in thousands of tofu stands throughout the country, and sold on the streets. Tofu acts like a sponge to soak up and carry the flavours that are added to it. It is made by compressing the curds of hot soy milk into blocks.*

In this recipe silken tofu is used for its soft and creamy texture. It is low in fat with no cholesterol, high in protein and easy to digest. Mum always made me this soup whenever I was feeling a little under the weather.

Leftover tofu should be rinsed in cold water and refrigerated. Change the water daily and use within 3 days.

CANH ĐẬU HỦ HẸ

silken tofu and garlic chive soup

1.5 litres (52 fl oz/6 cups) chicken
   stock (page 36)
350 g (12 oz) silken tofu, cut into
   bite-sized cubes
1 bunch garlic chives, cut into 4 cm
   (1¹/₂ in) pieces

4 spring onions (scallions), finely sliced
1 handful coriander (cilantro) leaves,
   roughly chopped
pinch of cracked black pepper

Pour the chicken stock into a saucepan and bring it to the boil. Add the tofu and garlic chives and simmer for 1 minute. Carefully transfer the soup into serving bowls, garnish with spring onions, coriander and cracked black pepper.

SERVES 4

CÀ RI CHAY

turmeric and lemon grass vegetarian curry

CURRY PASTE
4 long dried chillies, soaked in hot
    water for 5 minutes, finely chopped
1 lemon grass stem, white part only,
    finely chopped
6 coriander roots, scraped clean
6 garlic cloves, finely chopped
1 tablespoon ground galangal
1 tablespoon ground turmeric
1¹/2 tablespoons red curry powder
    ('Ayam' brand)

4 tablespoons vegetable oil
50 g (1³/4 oz) palm sugar (jaggery)
1 tablespoon tamarind paste
1 white onion, cut in half and sliced
200 g (7 oz) potatoes, cut into
    1 cm (¹/2 in) cubes
2 x 540 ml (19 fl oz) tins
    coconut cream

2 teaspoons salt
200 g (7 oz) Japanese pumpkin
    (winter squash), peeled and
    cut into 1 cm (¹/2 in) pieces
200 g (7 oz) button mushrooms,
    quartered
100 g (3¹/2 oz) baby corn
1 bunch bok choy (pak choy), quartered
100 g (3¹/2 oz) snow peas (mangetout)
100 g (3¹/2 oz) long, purple (Japanese)
    eggplants (aubergines), quartered
    lengthways, cut into 4 cm (1¹/2 in)
    lengths, then fried until crisp
100 g (3¹/2 oz) chopped roasted
    peanuts (page 38)
100 g (3¹/2 oz) fried red Asian shallots
    (page 38)
100 g (3¹/2 oz) bean sprouts

To make the curry paste, pound the chilli, lemon grass, coriander and garlic in a mortar, then stir through the galangal, turmeric and curry powder. Heat the oil in a large saucepan over medium heat, then add the curry paste, palm sugar and tamarind paste and fry for 2 minutes. Add the sliced onion and potato, stir to combine, then continue to fry for another 2 minutes. Add the coconut cream, 250 ml (9 fl oz/1 cup) water and salt, bring to the boil, then reduce and simmer for 5 minutes. Add the pumpkin and simmer for another 5 minutes, then add the mushrooms, corn, bok choy and snow peas and simmer for a further 5 minutes. Add the eggplant and stir through.

Ladle the curry into a large serving dish and garnish with the peanuts, shallots and bean sprouts. Serve with steamed jasmine rice.

SERVES 6

ĐẬU ĐŨA XÀO
wok-tossed snake beans in oyster sauce

275 g (9³/4 oz) snake (yard-long) beans,
    cut into 5 cm (2 in) lengths
1 tablespoon oil
1 garlic clove, crushed
¹/4 onion, cut into 5 mm (¹/4 in) strips

1 tablespoon oyster sauce
2 teaspoons fish sauce
2 teaspoons sugar
salt, to taste
sesame seeds (optional), for garnish

Blanch the snake beans for 1 minute, strain and set aside. Place a wok over high heat and add the oil, garlic and onion. Stir-fry until the garlic starts to change colour, then add the snake beans, oyster sauce, fish sauce and sugar. Stir-fry for a further 2 minutes, season with salt, then turn out onto a plate and garnish with sesame seeds (if using).

SERVES 4 AS PART OF A SHARED FEAST

LUKE NGUYEN: *I enjoy the simplicity and texture of this dish — it's like a vegetarian's version of salt and pepper squid.*

ĐẬU HỦ RANG MUỐI
salt and pepper tofu

250 g (9 oz) tofu pillows (Chinese-style
    pressed firm tofu)
oil, for deep-frying
2 spring onions (scallions), sliced

1 bird's eye chilli, sliced
1 teaspoon minced garlic
salt and pepper seasoning mix
    (page 335)

Cut the tofu into 4 x 2 cm (1½ x ¾ in) pieces and place on a cloth to dry. Put enough oil in a wok to deep-fry the tofu and heat to 180°C (350°F), or until a cube of bread dropped in the oil browns in 15 seconds. Deep-fry the tofu for about 5 minutes, or until it is golden and very crisp. Once all of the tofu is cooked, remove the oil from the wok and reserve for later use.

Add 2 teaspoons of oil back to the wok and place over high heat. Add the spring onions, chilli and garlic, stir-fry for 30 seconds, then add the tofu back to the wok. Toss to combine the flavours and season with the salt and pepper seasoning mix. Serve with salt, pepper and lemon dipping sauce (page 302) or vegetarian dipping sauce (page 243).

SERVES 2

LUKE NGUYEN: *Water spinach (ong choy) grows abundantly on the banks of ponds and streams throughout Southeast Asia and it is a much-loved vegetable in the Nguyen household. It is the main leafy green in my diet and is a great source of iron. Other sauces matched for water spinach are X.O. sauce, spicy satay sauce, tamarind and plum sauce or simply wok-tossed with fresh garlic. A good trick when preparing it, is to tear the water spinach instead of using a knife — parts of the stems that are too tough to tear will be too tough to eat, so discard.*

RAU MUỐNG XÀO CHAO

wok-tossed water spinach with fermented bean curd sauce

1 tablespoon oil
1 tablespoon julienned ginger
1 garlic clove, crushed
200 g (7 oz) water spinach (ong choy),
    torn into 5 cm (2 in) lengths

1 tablespoon fermented bean curd
2 teaspoons sugar
pinch of salt
sesame seeds, to garnish

Add the oil to a wok over high heat, then add the ginger and garlic and stir-fry until the garlic starts to colour. Add the water spinach and, using a wooden spoon or charn, work the spinach around in the wok until it starts to wilt. Add the bean curd, sugar and salt and continue to stir-fry the spinach for 3–5 minutes, or until all of the flavours have combined and the spinach has wilted. Turn out onto a plate and garnish with sesame seeds.

SERVES 4 AS PART OF A SHARED FEAST

LUKE NGUYEN: *Bamboo shoots are canes harvested to eat before they are 2 weeks old. Crisp and tender in character, bamboo shoots work wonders in vegetable stir-fries.*

Commercially tinned shoots are common; however, fresh bamboo has superior flavour and texture. Always cook your shoots in boiling water, uncovered, for 15 minutes, as this eliminates the bamboo's bitter aftertaste. I also like to add a cheeky tablespoon of sugar to the boiling water.

MĂNG XÀO NẤM ĐÔNG CÔ
wok-tossed bok choy with bamboo shoots and shiitake mushrooms

1 tablespoon oil
1 garlic clove, crushed
250 g (9 oz) bok choy (pak choy), quartered
50 g (1¾ oz) fresh bamboo shoots
4 dried shiitake mushrooms, reconstituted, stems removed, cut in half
1 tablespoon oyster sauce
½ teaspoon dark soy sauce
2 teaspoons sugar

125 ml (4 fl oz/½ cup) water, vegetable stock or chicken stock (page 36)
1 teaspoon potato starch, mixed with 1 tablespoon water
salt, to taste
1 tablespoon fried red Asian shallots (page 38)
1 small handful coriander (cilantro) leaves

Add the oil to a wok over high heat and add the garlic. Stir-fry until the garlic starts to colour, then add the bok choy, bamboo shoots and shiitake mushrooms and continue to stir-fry for 1 minute. Add the oyster sauce, dark soy sauce and sugar, then toss the wok to combine the flavours and then add the water or stock. Bring to the boil, then reduce the heat and add the potato starch mixture and season with salt. To serve, turn out onto a plate and garnish with fried shallots and coriander.

SERVES 4 AS PART OF A SHARED FEAST

LUKE NGUYEN: *This is the vegetarian equivalent to dipping fish sauce (page 33). This sauce is quick and easy to make, and if you want to liven it up, add some pickled vegetables (page 34) and chilli.*

NƯỚC CHẤM CHAY
vegetarian dipping sauce

55 g (2 oz/^{1}/4 cup) caster
   (superfine) sugar
185 ml (6 fl oz/^{3}/4 cup) boiling water

3 tablespoons lemon juice
3 tablespoons light soy sauce

Dissolve the sugar in the boiling water, then allow to cool. Once cooled add the lemon juice and soy sauce and mix well to combine.

MAKES 375 ML (13 FL OZ/1^1/2 CUPS)

red is for
reconciliation

My sigh of relief could have blown out twenty candles at once.

I was so pleased to have finished another shift at that depressing cafe. My first paid job — I had not planned to stay long but it covered the rent for now. Spoken to like an idiot most days, the staff wore the assumption that the colour of my skin and the non-Anglo features of my face meant that I was not only fresh off the boat with a repertoire of caveman English, but also that I suffered from a chronic case of deafness. 'You got orda table two!' They would shout at me in their mock Asian accents and patronizing grins, 'They won vienna extra cream an ham cheese pineapple mel *okay*? Extra two dollar for pineapple *okay*? Two dollar. You got orda?' Nobody there seemed the type who would appreciate a coffee-break lesson in grammar and articulation. Nor did they seem the type who would take too kindly to a few tips on culinary enhancement and appreciation. Tinned asparagus and cheese melts, bacon and cheese melts, tomato and cheese melts, cinnamon toast, raisin toast, cheese on toast, baked beans on toast. I was up to my eyeballs in melted cheese and soggy bread. Like a child starved of affection, I craved desperately the food of home.

Saturday mid-morning and Town Hall station was dead. The quiet was almost eerie. Cabramatta would have been pumping at this time of day. It baffled me why the cafe bothered to open on the weekend. Standing at attention, waiting for someone to come through the front door was like watching sand dry in the sun. Pho Cay Du would be full of customers without a doubt. The Pavilion on George echoed empty.

Left: My parents with Joe, their cooking instructor, 1995.

247

Every store had its shutters down and grill doors padlocked. The only muffled sounds were the sporadic trains moving deep underground.

As I fumbled in my backpack for a TravelTen, hoping I had a trip left to make it home to Glebe, I was careful to stay alert for suspicious characters of the bag-snatching kind — a habit spawned from growing up during Cabramatta's 'tough times'. Except for three male figures in the distance, there was no-one about as I entered the thoroughfare to my bus stop. The three sat at the only occupied table in the otherwise deserted food court. I usually avoided this kind of scenario, steering clear of the possibility for any unpleasant confrontation. But my legs worked independently of my head that day — my mind still hazy from the morning of uninspiring work. I could see vaguely that one of the taller males was wiping the smaller one's face with a paper towel. If I strained my eyes, I could see that he was holding an ice cream cone with ice cream smeared from ear to ear. My heart stopped. Leroy is that you?

'Leroy is that you?' I shouted at the top of my lungs. Picking up speed then breaking into a run, I screamed with joy, 'Leroy!' Three heads turned my way looking as surprised as I did. What are the chances? The entire Pavilion, empty, with just the four of us. Had it been a weekday, when Town Hall station hummed like a beehive of determined commuters, I would have missed them in the crowd. More than two years had passed since I last saw my brothers. Lewis and Luke had not changed much; they looked as overworked as I remembered them. Leroy, on the other hand, what a beautiful boy he had become — much chubbier around the cheeks and belly but still beautiful. I didn't mind that he was standoffish — who could blame him. To smother him with kisses was all that I could do.

'Leroy, do you remember me?'
'Yes.'
'Do you miss me?'
'Yes.'
'Have you been a good boy?
'Yes.'

They had snuck out of the house to see a movie in the city — my parents believed they were at maths school.

'We had to get out to save our sanity,' said Lewis. 'Mum's in a really bad way, I seriously think you should see her.'

Luke pursed his lips and nodded his head in quiet confirmation, 'Yeah, she's really skinny and still doesn't eat much … She still cries every day.'

'What about Dad?' I asked, trying hard to steady the tremble in my voice.

'The same.' They both answered in unison.

I swallowed hard, 'What do you think I should do?'

Lewis replied candidly. He had already given it much thought, 'I reckon you should give her a call.

We'll let you know when Dad's not home. Mum cleaned out your room the other day — Grandma's moving in there. She found your diary and some of the poems you used to write. She read the one that goes, "… there comes a time when every girl must leave her family home, as every bird must leave its nest and learn to fly alone …" etcetera, etcetera, etcetera. You know the one.' I certainly remembered my state of mind when I wrote it.

'Well, she broke down and sobbed for hours after reading it. She's really hurting you know. You should give her a call and meet — make her promise not to let Dad know where you are. Tell her she'll lose you again for good if she does.' He looked at his watch and motioned to Luke and Leroy that it was time to leave. 'Our movie starts soon, we better go.'

'Oh no, so soon? I haven't smothered Leroy with enough kisses yet!' As I covered Leroy with more kisses, he giggled with childish delight. I wanted us to stay together longer but I couldn't be sad, I could only be grateful for this surreal moment of chance. Leroy leaned closer into my chest when he realized our time was up. Sighing, he wrapped his arms tight around my waste and nuzzled his face into the hollow of my neck. We savoured our last moment of closeness.

'What movie are you seeing?' I asked, trying to sound chirpy.

With more enthusiasm than the others Lewis replied, '*Hellraiser 3* … hell on earth! Oooh yes.'

Acting more like the Leroy I use to know, he struck a pose, placed both hands on his hips, rolled his eyes and quipped in his most serious seven-year-old voice, 'I keep telling them that I'm way too young to be watching this film, but they won't listen. I hope I don't come out of it more psychologically damaged than I already am.'

Leroy is an old soul. He has, for as long as I have known him, displayed intelligence beyond his years. He was clever even in the womb. He must have known that if he did not enter this world with a brain big enough to please my father, he would have found himself in a lot of trouble. As it happens, Leroy was born a child genius, utterly gifted and incredibly special. Since a young age, he had the great fortune of obtaining sponsorship to attend the exclusive programs of Gerric and Scientia. Programs that are held twice a year at the University of New South Wales enabling gifted children across Sydney to meet and compete with peers of the same intellectual calibre. At the age of five, Leroy liked to memorize a favourite song from a Video Hits film clip. After hearing it only once, he would have it memorized complete with animated dance steps and dramatic facial expressions. Each night he would perform for me as if his life depended on it.

With a bounce in my step, but an ache in my heart, I followed my three brothers across George Street to the cinemas where we stood for what seemed like an eternity just holding each other, making up for lost time and thinking about the hopeful possibilities of our future.

Meeting with my mother would be tough. I had decided against the initial phone call, leaving Lewis to set up the meeting instead — what does a daughter say to her mother, to whom she has caused so much pain? It was Thursday night, late night shopping, so the cafe stayed open until seven — it baffled me why they bothered, seeing there were no nearby shops open at that hour to go shopping in. Thursday night also meant chewing gum night. An incomprehensible but true phenomenon — there are some people in this world who like to dispose of their chewed up chewing gum by sticking it under a table or chair. Even more incomprehensible is why the proprietors of the cafe put the staff through the weekly ordeal of removing the mess. Okay — once or twice a year maybe, but weekly?

I didn't want my mother to see where I worked. My brothers agreed that they would keep her waiting at the steps of Town Hall until I had finished — still half an hour to go. I felt sick with nerves. The sight of putrid chewing gum didn't help my state of nausea. The hard-as-rock wads were the easiest to remove. The stubborn strains of the sticky stretchable variety caused me the most grief. With vacuum cleaner in one hand and a ruler in the other, I got down on all fours determined to get the job done in half the time. Half way through the last table and wrestling with the vacuum cleaner entanglement, I felt my scalp shiver

and the hairs on the back of my neck stand on end. That's when I turned around and saw my mother; staring at me through the glass, a flood of tears streaming down her sad, white face. It surprised me that she could see through all the tears in her eyes. This was not the first image I wanted my mother to have of me after all this time — on my hands and knees, arse in the air, scraping chewing gum from under a table.

'All uni students have crappy jobs.' I tried to tell my mother, clearly making matters worse. The pain and confusion she carried was virtually tangible; any minor remark would shatter her like brittle honeycomb. She must have cried for at least three hours. Our reunion was difficult enough without having to explain to her all the reasons I had to leave. It didn't surprise me that she refused to accept my words. She kept shaking her head, telling me that I had broken my father's heart. This revelation didn't hurt me as much as her tears did. I tried to convince her that there was a way out for her as well — hoping that she could see just how brave, resourceful and independent a Vietnamese woman can be. Only now, in my early thirties, am I able to look beyond my unrelenting fervour of self-importance, to ask myself, just who the braver really is?

It is my mother, who has stood firm on her cultural beliefs in the face of displacement and adversity. It is my mother, who has unconditionally upheld her duty as a loyal Vietnamese wife. It is my mother, who has endured my father all these years. She is the one who has borne the most suffering.

On occasions such as this, she looked beyond her own resentment and self-pity, instead displaying her usual compassion and selflessness. Reluctantly she promised not to tell my father that we had met. When I told her how painful it was for me to be without her cooking, she made it her mission to ease my pain. At home, when she cooked for the family, she made sure to cook a little extra, hiding the food in the back of the freezer until the next time that she saw me. We didn't meet often, as it was difficult for her to sneak out of the house and catch a train into the city without my father knowing. Still, she always managed to find a way. My brothers told me that she started to smile again and even laughed at the occasional joke. She began eating meat and looked less pale as her weight returned. At night, when everyone else was sleeping, she snuck into the dining room where she would quietly sit, and in secret, write down all the recipes of the dishes she thought would remind me of home.

When happiness returned to my mother's life, inspiration followed suit. As with every culinary expression, she continued to tinker with the recipes, adjusting the quantities, replacing certain ingredients, changing the portions — as though she were asking, 'Would Pauline like it better with more chilli and less lemon grass? Or would she like it with less meat and more bones? Will she prefer the firmness of the thigh to the density of the breast? Or would the anchovy stink out her apartment too much? As with every manifestation, she put another before herself. In every mouthful of my mother's cooking, I could taste the heart she poured into marinades, I could smell the soul she stirred into the sauces, I could sense her patience in the fine quality of the ingredients, I captured her care in the combination of flavours that filled my mouth and made me cry with appreciation. Her sentiments oozed from her food, quenching my hunger and filling me with a sense of comfort and security that radiated the words she could never speak, 'I am here if you need me. I will do anything for you.'

My father could not help but notice the about face in my mother's demeanour. He appreciated that the clouds of sadness had finally lifted from her being. He too began to cook again. Their passion for food and flavour reignited with the intensity of a sudden fever, greedily possessing them. With hunger, they welcomed the change as it dragged them out of the mire that had trapped them for the past two years. They spent their days reading cookbooks and reviving old recipes that had lay dormant. Each morning, they would catch the same train as Luke to attend their cooking classes in the city. 'This was very embarrassing for me,' says Luke. 'It made it harder to jig school.' My parents continued learning and thrived on the new knowledge of all things culinary. They received diploma after diploma and wore their chef's uniforms with pride.

When they were not cooking, they spent their time in quiet reflection, looking back on their past behaviour and state of mind. Not working permitted them both to take a belated step back and allow for self-discovery and internal advancement. Going on fifty, they decided to take the first holiday of their lives. 'I couldn't believe it,' says Luke. 'I thought they'd never leave.'

My parents finally 'saw the world' and visited extended family in Paris and Marseille. My mother went to Lourdes and brought back holy water for her children. They visited Aunty Ten in Minnesota and met up with long lost relatives spread across the United States — relatives they had not seen since escaping Vietnam. They learned how to relax on the beaches of Hawaii and even went to Thailand to revisit the Dinh Dieng refugee camp for old times sake. No matter how far they were from home, my father did not neglect to remind the boys to 'keep up their studies and not run amuck'. He sent regular postcards — 'Keep working hard at school', 'Do not forget your homework', 'Do not go around too much', 'It is all for your HSC'. But it was not these words that made my brothers look at each other in astonishment. It was other parts of the correspondence expressing words unfamiliar — words they had never heard before. 'We miss you', 'We love you', 'Please look after each other'. All signed with the words, 'With love from Mum and Dad.'

My mother wanted to see me as soon as she returned. If we feared the consequences of my father finding out about our secret meetings, my mother was not too afraid to act. She arrived at my flat determined to get her family back together. She wasted no time pleading with me to see my father again. Four years had passed since I saw him last.

'He has changed.' She tried to convince me. 'He is not the man he was before.'

It didn't matter how much she begged, my answer remained 'No'. Even when she told me how he had broken down and cried at a formal dinner in front of his hardened friends, my answer remained 'No'.

'She has ripped out my heart and crushed it,' he had apparently sobbed to them. 'How can I go on?' To be honest, it amazed me at the time, that my father had it in him.

My mother's unrelenting compassion for my father still amazes me to this day. Forever the mediator, she persisted. 'Your father and I are proud of all of you. We love you very much … it is just that … we don't know how to show it … it has never been our way.'

'But anger does not belong to love.' I tried to tell my mother. 'Nor does violence nurture.'

Nothing she said that day could persuade me to see my father again. How could I face the man I had spent my whole life fearing? The man who had caused us all such misery? I had banished the memories from my consciousness — the pain buried long ago. Four years is not long enough for wounds like that to heal. Healing requires forgiveness — such grace I did not

Postcard 1

PARIS
La Cathédrale Notre-Dame - La Rosace sud
The Notre-Dame Cathedral - The "Rosace Sud"
Die Kathedrale Notre-Dame - Südrosette

My Son! keep working
hard at school -
you'll deserve it.
All for your HSE - OK.

Love From
Mom & Dad -

²⁷/₅ 94 L. Nguyen

Mr. Luke

ABEILLE-CARTES - Editions "LYNA" - PARIS
8/10, Rue Saint Marc - 75002 PARIS
Tél. (1) 39.35.90.70 - (1) 42.36.41.28
Reproduction interdite

N° 1626

Lyna

Postcard 2

HSC107 Hawaii
'Waikiki'

Hi Son !
Do not forget your
Home Work - We love
you - We Bought Some
Very Nice T shirts for
you - OK -
    Love from Dad & Mum.

LEROY NGUYEN

©CITY SIGHTS Postcards
Printed in USA

CITY SIGHTS Box 8, Bond Head, Ont. LOG 1BO Tel. (416) 775-4828

William T. Piper
Aviation Pioneer
USAirmail
40

Postcard 3

1794 - PARIS LA DEFENSE
La Grande Arche
©1991 Johan Otto Von Spreckelsen

Please, look after
your family - be not
go around too much!

Love from
Mom & Dad.

²⁷/₅ 94 L. Nguyen

Mr. Lev

ABEILLE-CARTES - Editions "LYNA" - PARIS
8/10, Rue Saint Marc - 75002 PARIS
Tél. (1) 39.35.90.70 - (1) 42.36.41.28
Reproduction interdite

Photo Pierre DENEUFCHATEL

Lyna

Above: My parents on the River Seine, Paris 1994, and the postcards they sent home to the boys.

possess. Healing requires acknowledgement from both the victim and the perpetrator — acknowledgement of the harm inflicted. This simply would not happen. My father could never confront any of it with his children — to whom he is yet to offer a single word of apology. In Asia, parents do not say that they are sorry and admit to the wrongs that they have done.

As for me, I wanted my fears forgotten, not faced up to. I resented my mother for asking me to do this. No way was I ready to see my father again. Anxiety overwhelmed me as it always did. It came in waves, at times more bearable than others — paranoia, irritability, insomnia, nausea, apprehension. The years of living with fear and oppression had programmed me to internalize all my problems, keeping my pain and frustrations in the pit of my gut. I misled everyone, including myself, by projecting an exterior of strength, confidence and determination. But anger was the real culprit that fuelled me. Anger fooled me into thinking that I could cope, that I was a tough nut — nothing could break me. On the outside was all hardness. On the inside was red raw vulnerability rubbing away at nerves damaged long ago. The emotional ulcer that grew within began to fester. The persistent fumes of bitterness suffocated me. What a mess I had grown up to be. Parents do not realise that the unhealed injuries they carry themselves, inevitably pass down to their children. Unresolved trauma has a way of transmitting across many generations. So much remains unresolved.

For my brothers, it was a waiting game — counting down the days, months and years they had left living in that house. When Lewis made it into university, he found as many excuses as possible to stay away from home. It was hardest for Luke, who did not like school or particularly care for educational institutions of any kind. My father demoralized him because of this, crushing his spirit until it was crippled, telling him year after year that he was 'stupid' and a 'no hoper', that he 'would never amount to anything worthy of respect'. Looking back, I think that we all felt ripped off — robbed sensationally of a childhood of peace, happiness and most of all, respect: something every child deserves. Our opinions did not count, nor did our thoughts ever matter — our personalities were of little consequence.

My parents knew little about their children. They had built a wall of indifference so high it never occurred to them to ask 'How are you?' 'How was your day?' 'Is something troubling you?' 'Can I help?' If someone had asked them what our favourite colour was, which subjects we liked at school, which sports we excelled at, what the names of our friends were, they couldn't have answered. As long as we brought home outstanding results and performed our duties, they didn't need to know more. As it happens, when they did finally want to know more, it was too late — we had all left home.

Parents should realize the profound effect of their repression. They should always nurture their children's voices and hear carefully what they have to say — give them the tools to realize their highest potential.

I carried my pathetic sense of self-worth well into my early adult years. People with little self worth always end up with the wrong people. Inflated value and misguided trust, poured into quick-fix friendships based on dancefloor smiles and nightclub solidarity. I have had more than my fair share of abnormal intimacies with the unstable and losers of this world — the foundations of a bad habit that almost killed me.

Parents should realize the damage that silencing a child can cause. My father had so successfully demoralized us that when I entered the 'real' world, I truly believed that my opinion did not matter — no-one wanted to hear what I had to say. Any original thoughts I had were surely childish and insignificant. That is, until someone else verbalized my thoughts and got the credit for it. I would keep my true opinions and feelings to myself, locking them away internally, communicating little about my wants and needs, paranoid that others would reprimand, make fun or simply not care. This was the only mode of communication I had ever known.

Self-awareness had passed me by. Self-respect, I didn't know about. The assault on my spirituality occurred years ago, leaving behind an overwhelming sense of helplessness. I was never in control. As a result, the rot ate away at my insides, slowly permeating outwards for all to see. Bosses accused me of being 'unapproachable'. Friends admitted to being scared of me. Colleagues would complain that I was withdrawn, aggressive and hard to please. How could I possibly respect another when in my heart, I could not respect myself. Inevitably, I was always misunderstood. People are afraid of what they do not understand.

My mother did not hear me when I said I was not ready. As much as she could play the submissive wife, she could also play the stubborn mother. She consistently begged me to see my father, each time leaving my apartment surrendering to a kind of temporary resignation. Temporary, as she was not without hope. Trust in her own emotional stamina sustained her.

After six months of persistent badgering, she successfully harassed me into submission. Did I want to see my father again? No way. Why was I doing it? For my mother of course — the first thing I had ever done in my life solely for the happiness of my mother. Typically, she had had it all planned. The occasion would be on neutral ground; at the cooking school in the Queen Victoria Building — a graduation ceremony for yet another diploma. In the weeks leading up to the event, I prepared myself mentally and emotionally. I even prepared myself physically in the event that I should meet the swift backhand of my previous tormentor.

I paced around Queen Victoria's statue until I could gather my nerves. Looking up at her face, I hoped that she could anoint me with courage and strength, but I saw only sorrow in her sad droopy eyes. I broke away from her solemn stare and, with the help of my brothers, headed toward the lifts. Inside, the heavy air smelled of cardboard and sweat. I held my breath and felt faint for it. If the near panic I felt had had physical substance, it would have filled the lift with quicksand.

'Is it just me, or is it really hard to breathe in here?'

'It's just you,' said Lewis.

'I don't know if I can do this. I think I need to get out … I'm gonna get out.'

'No you're not,' said Leroy, in his assertive deadpan voice. 'You're going to be okay. We're here, right beside you.'

'Can we just get this over and done with please?' concluded Luke.

My brothers were my support team that day — they were also my bodyguards. As the small lift climbed higher and higher, my breathing got shallower and shallower. I focused on the wad of chewing gum some thoughtful person had stuck on the red 'Stop' button and remembered the night I was reunited with my mother. Yet another sticky situation to overcome.

I tried taking deep breaths, tracing the tips of my fingers around the tops of my ears, squeezing the lobes to confirm that they were really burning. Yep, they were really burning. When the doors dinged open at level three, Leroy took my hand so that he didn't leave the lift without me. As we turned the corner, the celebratory smells of fresh baked pastries, sliced watermelon and alcohol filled my nostrils and instantly calmed my nerves. The low buzz of muted conversations and clinking glassware reminded me that I was not alone. I scanned the room for Asians. I found a group of familiar faces that I hadn't seen for some time — relatives on my father's side. They hovered around the buffet table juggling paper plates, lamb skewers and cups of orange juice. When their heads turned my way, I wondered if I looked as nervous as they all did.

I had already prepared myself for the worst. Two things could happen that day. One, my father would abuse me and humiliate us all in public. Two, he would break down and cry and humiliate us all in public. Then I saw them — both of them, wearing crisp white chef's jackets, starched white aprons, tall chef's hats and black and white chequered pants. My mother looked so happy to see me, I thought she would burst. She beamed and bounced around the entire event. My father greeted me without expression. He gave a single throaty 'Ello,' and then let me be. We didn't speak for the rest of the time.

The room quietened for the commencement of ceremonies. Lewis took photos while the rest of us watched. My father had aged. He looked heavier, moved slower and seemed smaller than before. It is always difficult to guess what he is thinking. We clapped as each student shook the head chef's hand and walked away with their diploma. When it came to my father's turn, he did not walk away like everyone else, he held centre stage and paused for effect. In a voice soft and serious, he asked the master of ceremonies if he could say a few words. The Asians in the room instantly became nervous. We looked at each other and I wondered if I should make a quick exit. My father began by thanking Joe, the cooking instructor, for his knowledge and his patience, and then, without any eye contact or emotional disclosure, acknowledged his family for being there for him on this special day.

Deep down I felt grateful to everyone present that day, my father's relatives included. They had all contributed to making the occasion as easy for me as possible. There were no probing questions or unpleasant confrontations. They had given me room to breathe and get a grip on myself. I had, after all, achieved the ultimate — I had overcome my fear by looking at it in the face. And in the face of fear I had discovered a new courage. The following weeks allowed me the time to reflect. It dawned on me that, without knowing, I had already forgiven my father. How else could I have moved on with my life? The key to it all, I realized, was forgiveness. My own capacity to do so surprised no one more than I. Forgiveness helped me open the door to compassion. It gave me a chance to look forward with hope. I had my mother to thank for that.

The road to healing has been a long one — one on which I am still travelling. But I had taken the first small step. To be truly free, I would have to learn how to forgive myself. This I did not discover until almost a decade later.

Typically, my mother's persistence did not stop there. Like a cunning tactician, she would lure us home with the dishes that we liked best. She called every couple of months to secure a visit by strategically mentioning the amount of time and energy they would both put into making our favourite foods. 'Your father has gone through great lengths to cook this one. He has painstakingly spent all day standing at the stove for you.' How can anyone turn down an offer like that? At times, the visits were forced and uncomfortable but I knew they just enjoyed having us there. They made such an effort and so did we. They would fuss about for hours, sometimes days, planning and preparing the food for our arrival — making sure to have secured only the freshest and finest ingredients. Sometimes, they would plan close to ten courses in the hope that we stayed with them longer. There were times when I even enjoyed myself, sitting back and joking with my brothers throughout lunch and into dinner. We never spoke of the bad things, only of what we all knew most and had in common … the love of food and family.

It is easiest for my parents to speak through their food. For them, food is language. Food allows them to express the words they can never say — the perfect medium to transcend the communication barrier that has always existed between us. My father's greatest enjoyment comes from the cooking of noodle soups. We all know what it means. For him, it is a special ritual, requiring constant care and patience. I can see him now, standing seriously in front of the pot that is almost as big as he is, his legs shoulder width apart, his right hand holding a ladle like a magician holds his wand. His left arm, folded behind his back, fingers naturally curled. His breathing is meditative and his eyes look half closed as he focuses only on stroking the liquid in front of him, skimming it of impurities. His lips move quietly as he coaxes his broth to 'open up'. Sometimes if I listen hard enough, I can just make out what it is that he is saying. 'Help me to make the best soup that I can. Help me to make my children happy with the enjoyment of this creation.'

Noodle soups are my favourite food. Nowhere else in Asia embraces the noodle soup as strongly as in Vietnam. They are a complete meal in themselves, containing all the elements to nourish and satisfy in one convenient bowl. The combinations are endless. We each have our favourites. While Luke prefers a bowl of *pho* to any other, Lewis loves *banh canh cua gio heo* (crab and pork hock soup with tapioca noodles). He enjoys the gelatinous firmness of the noodles and the simplicity of the broth. Leroy is addicted to *bun mam* (prawn, pork and anchovy soup with rice noodles). It is the pungent aroma of fermented anchovies

that he likes best. My father enjoys a simple bowl of *mi* (egg noodles). He appreciates that there is a fine art to cooking the noodles to perfection. My personal favourite is *bun bo Hue* (spicy beef and pork leg soup). Like my mother, I love that this dish is not simple at all. The broth is a ferocious full-bodied combination of beef and pork laced with lemon grass, Vietnamese mint, shrimp paste and chilli. The thick rice vermicelli are firm, yet soft and silken. It comes with all the trimmings: pork hock, sliced beef, pork terrine and blood jelly — a welcome assault on all my senses. My mouth waters without fail.

Bun bo Hue is a dish close to my heart. For me, it represents a deep sense of renewal and reconciliation, and at times, even regret. Amid the enchanting years of living in Europe, surrounded constantly by extended family and friends, loneliness remained my closest companion. What it was that I longed for I could never pinpoint, but I knew that I could find the remedy, however temporary, in a bowl of *bun bo Hue*.

In London, a decent bowl is impossible to find. I would count the days until I could save up enough for a Eurostar ticket back to Paris, back to Treizieme, *au quartier Chinois* and back to the comfort of a bowl of *bun bo Hue*. As I bowed my head in reverence to the divine aroma, the first slow inhalation would bring back memories of my parents back home. I could see them cooking in their kitchen, fussing about, bickering over whose *bun bo Hue* is really 'Number One'.

'I like yours the best.' I would whisper in my mother's ear and she would lean over and whisper quietly back.

'Don't tell your father that, he'll just get upset.'

As I sat alone, slowly savouring every mouthful, my mind would wonder back to the very last time my parents cooked *bun bo Hue* for us. My mother had spent a whole day running around Cabramatta, eagerly trying to find the freshest possible ingredients while my father had spent two whole days nurturing his beloved broth. They were so excited that all their children would be together at home with them again. My parents truly enjoy the complexities of preparing for our arrival. Like fools, we fell to peer-pressure and let a forgettable dance party take precedence over their efforts. I will never forget my father's disappointed voice of resignation when I called to cancel at the very last minute. An offer of peace thwarted by an act of carelessness. How was I to know, that home, the place I ran away from in my youth, would be the place that I would yearn for years later.

Right: Enjoying a bowl of bun bo Hue *in Saigon, 2003. Above: Reunion Day at the Queen Victoria Building as my parents recieve yet another cooking diploma, 1995.*

LUKE NGUYEN: *I particularly enjoy this soup for the texture of the tapioca noodles. Made from tapioca starch, the noodles are deliciously chewy and sticky, and translucent in appearance — another noodle cannot substitute. Dried tapioca sticks are also available, but always go for fresh tapioca noodles.*

Eating your way around the pork hock can be something of an art — don't try to use your chopsticks with this one, get your hands into it!

BÁNH CANH CUA GIÒ HEO
crab and pork hock soup with tapioca noodles

800 g (1 lb 12 oz) tapioca noodles
1.5 litres (52 fl oz/6 cups) pork hock
   broth (next page)
12 pieces of cooked pork leg, finely
   sliced (reserved from the pork hock
   broth, next page)
4 chunks of the cooked pork hock
   (reserved from the pork hock broth,
   next page)

cooked crab claw meat (reserved from
   the pork hock broth, next page)
3 tablespoons fried red Asian shallots
   (page 38)
2 spring onions (scallions), green part
   only, sliced
1 bunch coriander (cilantro) leaves
lemon wedges, to serve
pure fish sauce, to serve
2 red bird's eye chillies, sliced, to serve

Blanch the tapioca noodles in boiling water, then divide them evenly into 4 bowls. Bring the broth to the boil, divide the pork leg, pork hock, crab meat, shallots, spring onions and coriander into the bowls and pour over the boiling broth. Serve with lemon wedges and pure fish sauce with fresh sliced chilli on the side.

SERVES 4

NƯỚC LÈO CUA GIÒ HEO

crab and pork hock stock base for banh canh cua gio heo

1 pork hock
1 kg (2 lb 4 oz) pork leg, skin on
140 g (5 oz/½ cup) salt, plus
   3 teaspoons extra
200 g (7 oz) crab claw meat
2 tablespoons sugar
2 tablespoons fish sauce
1 tablespoon vegetable oil
3 garlic cloves, crushed

2 teaspoons crab paste with bean oil
   (from Asian supermarkets)
10 spring onions (scallions)
2 white onions, cut in half
50 g (1¾ oz) dried shrimp (washed
   and strained)
1 teaspoon black peppercorns
5 litres (175 fl oz/20 cups) chicken
   stock (page 36)

Chop the pork hock in half lengthways with a large cleaver. Soak the pork leg and hock in 4 litres (140 fl oz/16 cups) cold water with the salt for 20 minutes. Rinse under cold water, then place in a colander to drain. Combine the crab claw meat with ½ teaspoon of the extra salt, ½ teaspoon of the sugar and 1 teaspoon of the fish sauce. Allow to marinate for 10 minutes.

Place a saucepan over medium heat, add the vegetable oil, 1 crushed garlic clove, the marinated crab claw meat and the crab paste. Reduce the heat and fry for 5 minutes, or until fragrant, keeping the claw meat intact. Set aside to add to the soup later.

Bruise the white part of the spring onions with the back of a cleaver and tie them up in a piece of muslin (cheesecloth) along with the white onions, remaining crushed garlic, dried shrimp and black peppercorns. Put the chicken stock in a large saucepan over high heat. Add the pork leg, pork hock, muslin bag, remaining sugar, fish sauce and remaining salt and bring to the boil. Reduce the heat to a simmer and cook for 1 hour, skimming constantly.

Remove the meat from the broth and set aside, strain the broth through a piece of muslin into another pan and allow to cool. The broth will keep in the fridge for 3 days or freeze for up to 3 months.

MAKES 5 LITRES (175 FL OZ/20 CUPS)

BÚN BÒ HUẾ

spicy beef and pork leg soup

4 tablespoons shrimp paste
500 ml (17 fl oz/2 cups) hot water
2 kg (4 lb 8 oz) pork leg meat, skin on
2 kg (4 lb 8 oz) gravy (shin) beef
500 ml (17 fl oz/2 cups) fish sauce
3 white onions, sliced into rings
4 garlic cloves, bruised
250 ml (9 fl oz/1 cup) vegetable oil
1 cinnamon stick, lightly pounded
4 cloves
2 tablespoons cracked black pepper
4 tablespoons rock salt
2 kg (4 lb 8 oz) oxtail

2 lemon grass stems, bruised
1 bunch spring onions (scallions),
    white stems lightly bashed, green
    part finely sliced
2 small bunches Vietnamese mint
2 tablespoons sugar
2 lemons, quartered
500 g (1 lb 2 oz) bean sprouts
500 g (1 lb 2 oz) thick rice vermicelli,
    cooked as per packet instructions
shrimp paste and chilli sauce
    (page 266), to serve

Dissolve the shrimp paste in the hot water and leave to steep for 2 hours, strain the liquid and reserve, discarding the sediment. Marinate the pork leg and gravy beef in 250 ml (9 fl oz/1 cup) of the fish sauce for 1 hour.

Stir-fry 2 of the sliced onions and the garlic in 2 tablespoons of the oil until soft and translucent. Wrap it up in a piece of muslin (cheesecloth) along with the cinnamon, cloves and black pepper and set aside. Add 12 litres (420 fl oz/48 cups) water to a very large saucepan or stockpot with the remaining fish sauce, rock salt and oxtail, and bring to the boil. Skim the impurities from the stock as they rise to the surface. Once boiled, reduce to a simmer and skim constantly for 30 minutes.

Put the gravy beef, pork leg, lemon grass, the white part of the spring onions, half the Vietnamese mint and the muslin bag in the saucepan and return to the boil. Reduce the heat to a slow simmer and continue to cook for 1½ hours, skimming regularly. Carefully remove all of the meat from the stock and set aside.

Add the shrimp paste liquid and sugar and continue to cook at a slow simmer for 1 hour, or until reduced by half. Strain the soup through a fine sieve layered with muslin into another saucepan and allow to cool. The broth can be stored for 3 days in the fridge or frozen for up to 3 months.

To serve the *bun bo Hue*, allow 400 ml (14 fl oz) of stock per person and bring that amount of stock to the boil. Slice the gravy beef and pork leg into 3 mm (⅛ in) thick slices. Place a handful of vermicelli noodles into individual

continued over

spicy beef and pork leg soup cont...

serving bowls and layer 3 slices beef, 3 slices pork and 1 oxtail in each bowl over the noodles. Put 2 teaspoons of the shrimp paste and chilli sauce on top of the meats and pour over the boiling stock. Garnish each bowl with some onion rings and slices from the green part of the spring onions. Serve with lemon wedges, Vietnamese mint and bean sprouts on the side, fresh sliced chilli, pure fish sauce and extra shrimp paste and chilli sauce to dip.

MAKES 6 LITRES (210 FL OZ/24 CUPS)

SA-TẾ BÚN BÒ HUẾ
shrimp paste and chilli sauce

125 ml (4 fl oz/¹/₂ cup) vegetable oil
100 g (3¹/₂ oz/¹/₂ cup) minced garlic
2 lemon grass stems, finely chopped
25 g (1 oz/¹/₄ cup) chilli flakes

125 ml (4 fl oz/¹/₂ cup) chilli oil
    ('Lee Kum Kee' brand)
2 tablespoons shrimp paste

Place a saucepan over medium heat, add the vegetable oil and fry the garlic until light brown. Remove the garlic from the oil and set aside. Add the lemon grass and chilli flakes to the oil and fry for 2 minutes until lightly browned. Remove the saucepan from the heat and add the chilli oil to stop the cooking process. Add the fried garlic back to the oil along with the shrimp paste and mix well to combine.

MAKES 250 ML (9 FL OZ/1 CUP). THIS IS A COMPONENT OF BUN BO HUE (PAGE 265).

LUKE NGUYEN: *There are many variations of this soup — some add quail eggs, fish or squid. One ingredient that cannot be substituted, however, is Asian celery (also known as Chinese celery). Grown wild in Vietnam, Asian celery resembles an elongated bunch of common celery, but can easily be mistaken for flat-leaf (Italian) parsley, as the stalks are slim and leafy. Dark green in colour, Asian celery is aromatic, earthy, clean in flavour and plays a perfect role in Vietnamese soups.*

HỦ TIẾU MỸ THO
prawn and pork soup with rice noodles

500 g (1 lb 2 oz) lean pork loin
2 tablespoons fish sauce
1 tablespoon caster (superfine) sugar
1 garlic clove, crushed
2 cm (3/4 in) piece of ginger, finely grated
800 g (1 lb 12 oz) wide-cut fresh rice noodles
2 litres (70 fl oz/8 cups) stock base (page 275)
16 cooked king prawns (shrimp), peeled and deveined
2 Asian celery stalks, finely sliced
1/2 bunch watercress

1/2 bunch coriander (cilantro) leaves
1 bunch garlic chives, cut into 4 cm (1 1/2 in) lengths
6 spring onions (scallions), sliced
2 bird's eye chillies, sliced, plus extra to serve
2 tablespoons fried red Asian shallots (page 38)
1 tablespoon oil
2 teaspoons fried garlic (page 39)
lemon wedges, to serve
2 large handfuls bean sprouts, to serve
pure fish sauce, to serve

Place the pork loin, fish sauce, sugar, garlic and ginger in a saucepan and fill with enough water to cover the pork by 4 cm (1 1/2 in). Bring to the boil, skim and reduce the heat to a simmer, then cook for 30 minutes. Remove the pork from the saucepan and allow it to cool, then cut it into 3 mm (1/8 in) wide slices.

Bring a saucepan of water to the boil and blanch the rice noodles for 20 seconds, then divide them into 4 bowls. Bring the *mi* stock to the boil. Distribute the pork slices, prawns, celery, watercress, coriander, garlic chives, spring onions, chillies, shallots, oil and fried garlic into the four bowls, pour over the *mi* stock and serve. Serve with lemon wedges, bean sprouts, extra sliced chilli and pure fish sauce on the side.

SERVES 4

BÚN MẮM

prawn, pork and anchovy soup

25 g (1 oz) dried krachai (from
    Asian supermarkets)
500 g (1 lb 2 oz) pork belly
4 litres (140 fl oz/16 cups) chicken stock
    (page 36)
450 g (1 lb) jar pickled gourami fish,
    drained (from Asian supermarkets)
500 ml (17 fl oz/2 cups) coconut juice
125 ml (4 fl oz/$^1/_2$ cup) fermented
    anchovy sauce ('Mam Nem Phu
    Quoc' brand)
500 g (1 lb 2 oz) thick rice vermicelli,
    cooked as per packet instructions

16 cooked prawns (shrimp), peeled
    and deveined
500 g (1 lb 2 oz) ling fillets, cut into
    3 cm (1$^1/_4$ in) pieces
1 small handful garlic chives, cut into
    5 cm (2 in) lengths
shrimp paste and chilli sauce
    (page 266), to serve
2 lemons, quartered
5 red bird's eye chillies, sliced
500 g (1 lb 2 oz) cabbage, sliced
1 bunch mint
200 g (7 oz) bean sprouts

Soak the dried krachai in hot water for 1 hour. Place the pork belly in a saucepan and cover with 1 litre (35 fl oz/4 cups) of the chicken stock. Bring it to the boil, skim, reduce the heat to a simmer, cover the saucepan with a lid and cook for 30 minutes. Remove the pork from the pan and allow to cool. Once cooled, slice the pork into 2 mm ($^1/_{16}$ in) wide slices and set aside for later use.

Strain the krachai, then add it to another saucepan with 1 litre (35 fl oz/ 4 cups) water and the pickled gourami fish, and bring to the boil. Reduce the heat to a simmer and cook for 5 minutes, or until the fish dissolves. Strain through a fine sieve into another saucepan and add the remaining chicken stock, coconut juice and fermented anchovy sauce. Bring to the boil, then turn off the heat. Once cooled, the soup can be stored in the fridge for 3 days or frozen for up to 1 month.

To serve the soup, divide the vermicelli, pork and prawns into 8 bowls. Add the slices of ling fillet to the *mam* broth and bring to the boil, simmer for 1 minute, then pour into the bowls. Garnish with garlic chives and 2 teaspoons of the *mam* sauce on top for aroma. Extra *mam* sauce can be served on the side. Serve with lemon wedges, sliced chilli, cabbage, mint and bean sprouts on the side.

When finished, a Mint is recommended.

SERVES 8

LUKE NGUYEN: *This soup is a delicacy for me — my family, like many Vietnamese families, only cook this broth on special occasions. Its rarity is evident throughout the streets of Saigon. My brother Lewis and I once walked for hours in search of a* bun rieu *vendor. After walking around in circles, getting lost and almost getting hit by four different scooters, we finally found her. The steaming broth smelled and looked divine, and we ended up having five bowls between us.*

I like to add an extra teaspoon of shrimp paste to my bowl for added punch. Preparation and patience is needed for this recipe, but your dedicated work will be well rewarded.

BÚN RIÊU

crab and tomato soup with

vermicelli noodles

RIEU SAUCE
1¹/₂ tablespoons vegetable oil
¹/₂ large onion, finely diced
3 bulb spring onions (scallions),
    finely sliced
3 garlic cloves, finely sliced
200 g (7 oz) blue swimmer crabmeat
200 g (7 oz) crabmeat paste with
    soya bean oil ('Pork Wan' brand)
2 teaspoons shrimp paste, plus extra
    to dip
500 g (1 lb 2 oz) very ripe tomatoes,
    peeled and puréed
2 large eggs

1 whole blue swimmer crab
4 litres (140 fl oz/16 cups) chicken stock
    (page 36)

1¹/₂ tablespoons fish sauce
1¹/₂ tablespoons sugar
1 teaspoon salt
200 g (7 oz) thin rice vermicelli,
    cooked as per packet instructions
6 spring onions (scallions), sliced
2 lemons, quartered, to serve
200 g (7 oz) bean sprouts, to serve
¹/₂ bunch mint, to serve
¹/₂ bunch rau kinh gioi (ask your
    Asian grocer), to serve
¹/₂ bunch perilla leaf, to serve
pure fish sauce, to serve
fresh chilli, sliced, or pickled chilli,
    to serve

To make the *rieu* sauce, place a saucepan over medium heat, then add the vegetable oil, onion, spring onion and garlic. Gently fry until the onion is soft but not coloured. Add the crabmeat, crabmeat paste with soya bean oil and the shrimp paste, and continue to fry for 2 minutes to release the flavour. Add the tomato purée and simmer slowly for 10 minutes. Pour into a bowl and allow to cool. Once cooled, whisk the eggs in a separate bowl, then fold it through the crab and tomato purée and set aside.

Remove and discard the body shell and gills from the blue swimmer crab. Rinse it under cold water, then pat dry and place on a chopping board. Using a cleaver or large knife, remove the legs and claws from the body. Crack the shell and remove the meat from the legs and claws, roughly chop the crab body with the cleaver and place all of the meat and soft shell in a food processor with 500 ml (17 fl oz/2 cups) water and process for 2 minutes.

Put the chicken stock, fish sauce, sugar and salt in a large saucepan over medium heat and bring to a slow simmer. As the stock starts to simmer, add the processed crabmeat and shells to the pan. Do not allow the mixture to boil. Scoop up 1 ladle of the prepared *rieu* sauce and hold it in the stock until it starts to set, then gently release it into the stock. Repeat this process with the remaining sauce.

To serve, divide the noodles into the bowls, then pour over the soup. Garnish with spring onions and serve with lemon wedges, bean sprouts, fresh herbs, chilli, extra shrimp paste and pure fish sauce with fresh sliced chilli to dip.

SERVES 8

MÌ HOÀNH THÁNH
egg noodle soup with pork won tons

250 g (9 oz) minced (ground) pork
$^1/_2$ teaspoon sugar
$^1/_2$ teaspoon garlic oil (page 39)
$^1/_2$ teaspoon sesame oil
pinch of salt
$^1/_4$ teaspoon white pepper
$^1/_4$ egg white
16 sheets of 7 cm (2$^3/_4$ in) square fresh
    won ton wrappers
1 litre (35 fl oz/4 cups) pork stock base
    (page 275)

400 g (14 oz) thin egg noodles
$^1/_2$ bunch watercress
$^1/_2$ bunch coriander (cilantro) leaves
6 spring onions (scallions), sliced
$^1/_2$ bunch garlic chives, sliced into
    4 cm (1$^1/_2$ in) lengths
1 lemon, quartered
100 g (3$^1/_2$ oz) bean sprouts
2 red bird's eye chillies, sliced
pure fish sauce, to serve

Put the pork, sugar, garlic oil, sesame oil, salt, pepper and egg white in a bowl and mix well to combine. Lay the won ton wrappers out on a bench with one corner of each wrapper facing you. Place a teaspoon of the pork filling in the centre of the won ton, brush the top two edges with water and fold the bottom up to create a triangle; push down on the edges to seal them. Brush the two bottom corners with water, bring them together and press to seal. Fold the remaining corner backwards and press to secure against the back of the won ton. Repeat this process, placing each completed won ton under a damp cloth to keep them moist. Bring a large saucepan of water to the boil. Add the won tons and cook for 2 minutes, then remove and refresh them in iced water. Place the won tons in a colander and set aside.

To serve *mi hoanh thanh*, put the *mi* stock in a saucepan and bring to the boil. Meanwhile, divide the egg noodles into 4 portions and blanch them separately for 20 seconds, then refresh in iced water. This allows the noodles to develop a nice firmness. Return them to the boiling water for 10 seconds, then place them in the serving bowls. Place the won tons back in the boiling water to heat through, then place them in the bowls. Pour the boiling broth over the noodles and garnish with the watercress, coriander, spring onions and garlic chives. Serve with lemon wedges and bean sprouts on the side, along with sliced chilli and pure fish sauce to dip.

SERVES 4

MÌ SỦI CẢO

egg noodle soup with prawn won tons

8 raw king prawns (shrimp)
1/4 teaspoon salt
1/2 teaspoon white pepper
16 sheets of 7 cm (2³/4 in) square
    won ton wrappers
2 litres (70 fl oz/8 cups) stock base
    (opposite)
800 g (1 lb 12 oz) thin egg noodles
1/2 bunch watercress

1/2 bunch coriander (cilantro) leaves
6 spring onions, sliced
1/2 bunch garlic chives, sliced into
    4 cm (1¹/2 in) lengths
1 lemon, quartered
100 g (3¹/2 oz) bean sprouts
2 red bird's eye chillies, sliced
pure fish sauce, to serve

Peel and cut the prawns into small pieces, season with salt and pepper and set aside. Lay the won ton wrappers out on a bench with one corner of each wrapper facing you. Place a teaspoon of the prawn filling in the centre of the won ton, brush the top two edges with water and fold the bottom up to create a triangle; push down on the edges to seal them. Brush the two bottom corners with water, bring them together and press to seal. Fold the remaining corner backwards and press to secure against the back of the won ton. Repeat this process, placing each completed won ton under a damp cloth to keep them moist. Bring a large saucepan of water to the boil. Add the won tons and cook for 2 minutes, then remove and refresh them in iced water. Place the won tons in a colander and set aside.

   To serve the *mi sui cao*, put the *mi* stock in a saucepan and bring to the boil. Meanwhile, divide the egg noodles into 4 portions and blanch them separately for 20 seconds, then refresh in iced water. Return them to the boiling water for 10 seconds, then place them in the serving bowls. Place the won tons back in the boiling water to heat through, then place them in the bowls. Pour the boiling broth over the noodles and garnish with the watercress, coriander, spring onions and garlic chives. Serve with the lemon wedges and bean sprouts on the side, along with fresh sliced chilli and pure fish sauce to dip.

SERVES 4

LUKE NGUYEN: *The use of dried flounder and dried squid in this recipe is essential — their concentrated pungent flavour serves to lift the broth. Both are pale in colour with strong, fishy aromas, are tough and chewy and have a powerful taste. They're both found in any Asian supermarket.*

A small bowl of this broth can accompany a meat or poultry dish, served with rice — dishes such as ga xao xa ot (page 276), suon nuong (page 281) or bo luc lac (page 301). The broth is sipped throughout the meal to refresh and restore the palate, as well as aid digestion. The pork in this broth gives it body and strength. A much cleaner broth than others, it can substitute the basic chicken stock.

NƯỚC LÈO MÌ VÀ HỦ TIẾU

pork stock base for mi and hu tieu

2 whole chickens, quartered
8 hip pork bones
140 g (5 oz/1/2 cup) salt
1 dried flounder

2 dried squid
125 ml (4 fl oz/1/2 cup) fish sauce
220 g (7³/4 oz/1 cup) sugar

Soak the chickens and pork bones in cold water with 2 tablespoons of the salt for 2 hours. Discard the water, then wash the chickens and bones under cold water and set aside. Chargrill the dried fish and squid over low heat until browned. Remove and scrape off any burnt bits with a knife. Wrap the fish and squid up in muslin (cheesecloth).

Add the chickens and pork bones to a large saucepan and cover with 10 litres (350 fl oz/40 cups) cold water. Place over high heat and bring to the boil, skimming constantly. Once boiled, reduce the heat, continue to cook and occasionally skim for 1 hour. Add the muslin bag and reduce the heat further, until the water is barely rolling over. Cover with a lid and cook for 4 hours.

Once cooked, pass the stock through a double muslin sieve into another saucepan. Add the fish sauce, remaining salt and sugar, and return to a simmer, skim off any impurities, then allow to cool. Transfer the soup into smaller containers and refrigerate or freeze until required.

MAKES APPROXIMATELY 8 LITRES (280 FL OZ/32 CUPS)

LUKE NGUYEN: *This is a classic, and very popular, Southern Vietnamese chicken dish. The thigh fillet of the chicken is commonly used in Vietnamese cooking, as it is inexpensive and perfect for grilling or frying — it absorbs flavour and remains tender and succulent throughout the cooking process.*

This is a quick and easy dish to prepare, with loads of flavour and fragrance. Be sure to drizzle the sauce over your steamed jasmine rice.

GÀ XÀO XẢ ỚT
lemon grass and chilli chicken

500 g (1 lb 2 oz) boneless, skinless
    chicken thighs
2 tablespoons fish sauce
1 tablespoon caster (superfine) sugar
1 lemon grass stem, white part only,
    finely chopped
1 teaspoon pickled chilli
2 garlic cloves, crushed

2 tablespoons vegetable oil
1 bird's eye chilli, sliced
1/2 small white onion, cut into wedges
125 ml (4 fl oz/1/2 cup) chicken stock
    (page 36)
1 small handful coriander
    (cilantro) leaves

Discard the fat and cut the chicken thigh fillets into bite-sized pieces. Combine the fish sauce, sugar, half the lemon grass, pickled chilli and garlic in a bowl. Mix well to dissolve the sugar, then fold the chicken pieces through the marinade and refrigerate for 4 hours, or overnight.

Place a large saucepan over medium heat, add the oil, remaining lemon grass and sliced chilli. Fry until the lemon grass starts to brown, then add the chicken to the saucepan. Stir and seal on all sides, add the onion and continue to fry for 2 minutes, stirring occasionally. Add the chicken stock and cover the pan with a lid, reduce the heat slightly and cook for 5 minutes. Remove the lid, increase the heat, stir and reduce the liquid slightly, then turn out into a serving bowl. Garnish with the coriander and serve with jasmine rice.

SERVES 4 AS PART OF SHARED FEAST

GÀ KHO GỪNG
caramelized ginger chicken

500 g (1 lb 2 oz) chicken thighs,
  bone in with skin on
2 tablespoons fish sauce
2 tablespoons minced ginger
2 teaspoons minced garlic
1 red chilli, sliced
4 tablespoons sugar
1 tablespoon oil

½ small onion, cut into wedges
500 ml (17 fl oz/2 cups) chicken stock
  (page 36)
1 spring onion (scallion), finely sliced
  on the diagonal
1 small handful coriander
  (cilantro) leaves

Remove the fat and excess skin from the chicken thighs, then cut them in half across the bone. Combine the fish sauce, ginger, garlic, chilli and 1 tablespoon of the sugar in a bowl. Add the thigh pieces to the bowl and mix well. Marinate in the fridge for at least 4 hours. For the best result, marinate the chicken overnight.

Place a large saucepan over medium heat and add the oil, then fry the chicken pieces, skin side down, for 3–5 minutes, or until golden brown. Turn the chicken over and seal the other side, then remove from the saucepan and drain off any excess oil from the chicken. Add the remaining sugar to the saucepan and cook until it is a light caramel colour. Add the chicken back to the pan with the onion and marinade. Pour over the chicken stock and bring it to the boil. Then reduce the heat to a simmer and cook the chicken, uncovered, for 15–20 minutes, or until cooked through. Turn out into a serving dish and garnish with the spring onions and coriander and serve with jasmine rice.

SERVES 4

LUKE NGUYEN: *This is such a simple meal. All I need is my delicious fish terrine and I balance its saltiness with crisp cucumber, raw cabbage and fresh mint — which I then match with a cold beer.*

MẮM CHƯNG CÁ LÓC
steamed egg and fish terrine

450 g (1 lb) jar fermented mullet
    or mud fish, bones removed
300 g (10$\frac{1}{2}$ oz) pork belly, cut into
    small pieces
100 g (3$\frac{1}{2}$ oz) red Asian shallots
4 garlic cloves, crushed
1 teaspoon cracked black pepper
1 teaspoon caster (superfine) sugar

3 eggs, plus 1 egg yolk
2 bird's eye chillies, sliced
$\frac{1}{4}$ cabbage, sliced into 1 cm ($\frac{1}{2}$ in)
    wide strips
1 Lebanese (short) cucumber, sliced
    into 1 cm ($\frac{1}{2}$ in) wide strips
$\frac{1}{2}$ bunch mint

Put the fermented fish, pork belly, shallots, garlic, pepper, sugar and the 3 whole eggs into a food processor and process to form a paste. Line a 1 litre (35 fl oz/ 4 cup) terrine mould with plastic wrap, leaving a 5 cm (2 in) excess hanging over the sides. Transfer the paste into the terrine mould and arrange the sliced chilli over the top, then bring the excess plastic wrap up and over to seal tightly.

Bring a steamer, large enough to hold the terrine, to the boil over medium heat. Place the terrine on the steamer tray, cover and steam for 1 hour.

Lightly whisk the egg yolk. Uncover the terrine and pour the yolk evenly over the top and steam, uncovered, over high heat for 15 minutes. Remove from the steamer, then carefully remove the terrine from the mould and place on a cutting board. Slice the terrine into 2 cm ($\frac{3}{4}$ in) wide pieces and serve with raw cabbage, cucumber, mint and steamed rice.

SERVES 6

MARK JENSEN: *This recipe works best when the pork chops are cut thinly with minimal bone and left to marinate overnight in the fridge. Ask your butcher to cut the loin chops 1 cm (¹/₂ in) thick and to cut most of the bone off the bottom T-section.*

SƯỜN NƯỚNG
chargrilled pork cutlets marinated with honey and spring onions

1 kg (2 lb 4 oz) thin pork loin chops
   (about 1 cm/¹/₂ in thick)
4 tablespoons oyster sauce
4 tablespoons fish sauce
1 tablespoon honey
1 tablespoon sugar
1 lemon grass stem, white part
   only, chopped
12 spring onions (scallions), white
   part only, bashed

1 garlic clove, crushed
125 ml (4 fl oz/¹/₂ cup) vegetable oil
4 tablespoons dipping fish sauce
   (page 33), plus extra to serve
1 tablespoon spring onion oil (page 37)
1 red bird's eye chilli, sliced
1 small handful coriander
   (cilantro) leaves

Bash the pork loin chops, one at a time, with a meat mallet and set aside. Combine the oyster sauce, fish sauce, honey, sugar, lemon grass, spring onions, garlic and vegetable oil in a bowl and mix well. Add the loin chops to the bowl and cover thoroughly with the marinade and refrigerate overnight.

Place the chops on a preheated chargrill pan. Cook for 2 minutes, then turn the chops 90 degrees (on the same side) and cook for another 2 minutes. This should create a crisscross pattern on the meat. Turn the chops over and repeat this process on the other side. Once cooked, place on a cutting board and cut into 1 cm (¹/₂ in) wide pieces with a heavy cleaver. Arrange the pieces of pork loin on a serving platter and spoon over the spring onion oil, sliced chilli and coriander. Serve with jasmine rice and dipping fish sauce.

SERVES 4

red is for
renewal

It was one of those rare moments that grabbed me, shook me up and let me know that I was alive.

The Parisian daylight had yet to become night, even at the late hour of half past eleven in the evening. An unnatural stillness filled the air as the city waited for darkness to truly fall before the night-owl activities commenced. The sun, in its mysterious glory, had cast a warm majestic hue over the city's beige limestone walls, setting her aglow in magical pink-orange luminosity. Like the millions before me, I too fell under the spell of Paris. Many enchanted moments, such as this, lay embedded in my memory. The years spent living under her beautiful, lascivious skies will forever remain some of the happiest of my life. Paris' warm embrace reminded me, time and time again, that life is full of the most wonderful surprises — moments of astonishing clarity that sneak up when you least expect it.

On this particular summer's night, everyone's spirit glowed. All the usual suspects gathered together to celebrate my friend Minh's return from a holiday to Sydney. A round-faced and unfoolish man, Minh had a habit of extracting individual pieces of stubble from his face using the tips of his fingers while in conversation. He also liked to break into unrequested renditions of the most heartfelt Vietnamese opera. Like so many of my Parisian friends, Minh was a good man. He had paid my parents a special visit so he could report back to me on his return.

'What news of my folks?' I asked.

'They look well …' Minh assured me. 'They plan to open another restaurant.'

My father preparing at Café Cay Du Kitchen;
photo taken by Leroy Nguyen, 2005.

My heart sank; sadness instinctively took over. Uneasiness settled in my stomach at the thought of the two of them working like dogs once again.

Later, when I picked up the phone to call home, I prayed the grim information could not be true. Why on earth would they want to put themselves through that again? My parents are the hardest working people I know — more often than not, unnecessarily so. I spoke briefly to both of them. As always, our conversation finished just as stifled as it had begun. My mother admitted that she didn't want anything to do with my father's new business venture.

'He can do what he likes. I don't care. I won't be out there working like a slave for him again.' I did not believe her indignation for a single moment. My father's answer, however, threw me.

'This is my livelihood,' he said, '… if I don't do this now, I will stale and die.'

I hung up the phone feeling nervous. I knew that the time had come for me to collect my things and head for home.

As I watched the city disappear below, gratitude overwhelmed me. Paris had opened my eyes to the abundant possibilities that my life could hold. I blew her a kiss, bid her farewell and thanked her for everything. Paris had allowed me, for the first time in my life, to have fun — a magical, crazy, beautiful kind of fun. I thought of my parents waiting for me on the other side of the world and wondered if they would ever approve of some of the adventures I had embarked upon. The answer to that one, I knew with certainty.

Sunday morning 6am, the whole family stood waiting at the gates. My flight had been delayed half an hour. Typically, my father wore his 'I am very annoyed now' crease in his brow. In the five or so years spent abroad, it appeared that little had changed. Everyone looked heavier though — food clearly playing just as integral a part of their lives as it always had. The greeting with my parents felt forced and uncomfortable. This did not surprise me in the slightest. Our first point of call was to the new restaurant, where my mother fussed over us, and my father, with brooding care and patience, cooked for me a most 'welcome home' bowl of *pho*.

When my father opened his new restaurant, my mother was there to help. It was part of the pattern. She would always help, but only after threatening to never help again. Luke also had a vested interest in my father's activities. He carefully watched my father's every move for other reasons — he had bigger plans on the horizon. 'I have learned from the past …' my father assured us, 'I won't make the same mistakes again.' He called his new restaurant Café Cay Du. Unlike Pho Cay Du, Café Cay Du does not sit showily in the middle of the busiest street in Cabramatta. It is tucked away in a small alley, clear from the view of pedestrians on the main street. The restaurant is a quarter of the size of the first, so too is its kitchen. Outdoor seating still features, as do his signature umbrellas. He brewed the same blend of coffee and the same regulars returned. 'I recognize them from fifteen years ago,' says Luke. 'I still remember what coffee they drink.' My biggest surprise came when my father showed me his menu. I counted the dishes on one hand — *pho, mi, bo luc lac, bo kho* and *cari de*.

My father explained it: 'These are the five dishes I cook best. I have spent my whole life refining and perfecting these dishes. If people want the best they can come here. If they want to eat something else, they can go somewhere else.' My father can get worked up when he talks about his food. 'I tried to do too much before — I wanted to be good at everything. Too much passion — no real focus. We even made our own ice cream cones for heaven's sake. Do you remember?' He looks at my mother who is clearly not impressed. She clicks her tongue, rolls her eyes, then looks the other way. My father continued. 'I am Vietnamese, I must cook Vietnamese food.' He pauses before admitting to us solemnly, his voice tinged with regret. 'If I knew then, what I know now, I would have saved myself over half a million dollars over the years. All that hard work, for what? I was forever signing debt papers.' He takes a deep breath before continuing, 'I should have known I was always meant to cook.' He waves a pointed finger at Luke to make sure his point is understood. 'Do what you know best. Keep it simple … keep – it – simple.'

It came as no surprise to any of us when Luke told of his plans for Red Lantern. For as long as I can remember, he has always dreamed of opening his own establishment. While Lewis and I pursued other careers, the art of hospitality is all that Luke has ever known. It is in his blood. Merely to watch Luke work is to die a little. At the age of four he was already dashing around like an efficient midget, cleaning ashtrays, wiping tables and taking orders. While Lewis and I worked for my parents simply because we had no choice, Luke performed all his duties with genuine enthusiasm and an unceasing 'can do' attitude. I can still picture him, carefully carrying individual cups of coffee to the customers with both hands, taking tiny steps with the focus of a tightrope walker, making sure not to spill a single drop. When the bowls of noodle soup went out, he would remind the customers in his authoritative little man voice to '... eat slowly, and be careful, don't burn your tongue.' Of course, all the regulars loved him. He was their little star and he knew it. All around the restaurant, Luke liked to think of himself as a speed demon.

'Bread …' he would coach me, '… should arrive to the customer as quick as Flash Gordon.'

'Oh yeah? Why's that?' I humoured him.

'So that it's still as hot and crusty as possible.'

'Oh really? Why's that?'

With great annoyance he would sigh, 'It is the only way.'

'Oh really? The only way to where?'

'Oh my gawwwd, don't you know anything? The only way to eat *cari de* and *bo kho*!'

To ensure the success of his son's future restaurant, my father wanted to teach Luke everything. Luke in turn wanted to learn it all. He spent day after day alongside my father in the Cay Du kitchen, honing his cooking skills, watching, tasting, copying. Although he didn't always agree with my parent's style of service, it amused him that no matter how inefficient he thought their systems were, it always worked out in the end.

My mother would secretly complain to me about how hard my father made her work. 'He treats the staff better than he treats me,' she would say. But I knew that deep down she thrived on the hustle and bustle of restaurant life. She enjoyed being a part of the community. For a time, my parents appeared happy. Just like the old days, my father loved cooking for his friends. Each dish he would make with the same slowness of good omen and the fine concentration of an artist. Luke sometimes grew impatient at the amount of time it took for my father to cook each dish ordered. But the customers never complained — they all knew the reason for it. It was the same reason that drew them back time and time again.

'Just a hole in the wall,' is how Luke liked to imagine his first business venture, '… somewhere I can just sell *goi cuon* and *bi cuon* … maybe a salad bar for *goi du du*, and *bo tai chanh* and definitely some kick-

arse Vietnamese coffee.' So when he first showed me the future Red Lantern site, to say that I was extremely surprised is a serious understatement. There was nothing 'hole in the wall' about it. A charming converted terrace house, it had the potential to seat just over fifty customers in one sitting. It had a split-level outdoor terrace area at the front of the restaurant, a spacious, yet intimate interior, as well as a slimline 10 metre (30 foot) walkway and work area, leading to a large backyard. The moderately-sized kitchen even had an adjoining scullery.

Forever the big sister, I made the decision then to take a break from my at times slow and never really steady career in film production, to help my little brother. Besides, Luke's enthusiasm is contagious. He has enough motivation and drive to gee up an entire football team on the brink of losing the biggest grand final of their lives. Luke's entire life's savings went into securing that site. 'Make or break. Do or die,' were the words he used. How could I not be there to help? When I first laid eyes on the location, it was a quiet Persian cafe in desperate need of a good clean and a serious injection of customers. It was clear that we would all have to put in an enormous amount of work before the place resembled anything like the Vietnamese restaurant we had envisaged. First up on the agenda, we would need a head chef who knew what he was doing.

We first met Mark at The Olympic Hotel, opposite the Sydney Football Stadium. An Australian with Danish and Welsh ancestry, it was here that Mark was head chef, and where Luke and I both took on second jobs as waiters. While Luke saved up the extra cash to help fund his future restaurant, I needed the extra money to help fund yet another ineffective short film — the typical sob story for a struggling filmmaker. Mark instantly impressed both of us. Watching him work was like watching an industrious choreographer performing a complicated dance piece within the confines of a tiny cubicle. Luke and I, having both worked in some very fine restaurants (and, for myself, some very poor establishments), have seen and can appreciate the amazing quality that can come out of a fully equipped kitchen with a brigade of chefs ten strong. But to witness the feats Mark achieved within a matchbox of a kitchen, was something we immediately admired and respected.

With the help of only two apprentices, Mark dished out an impressive three course *à la carte* dinner, including sides, for a pre-football crowd of over a hundred within just one hour. This, he would then repeat for the post-football diners. This meant service for over two hundred customers in little over two hours.

It is said that the high level of stress and adrenaline of a chef during the peak intensity of service is second only to that of an air traffic controller during complicated manoeuvring. We watched Mark do all of this, not without a joke up his sleeve and 'Love Song Dedications' blaring in the background.

What most attracted me to Mark was the fact that he never seemed to take himself too seriously — a most alluring trait in my books. Luke and I both agreed that Mark was a breath of fresh air to work with — a head chef who did not possess an inflated ego to handicap him — a phenomenon rarely found in any professional kitchen. As well as being organized, focused and extremely efficient, Mark is articulate, incredibly cool headed and devilishly self-deprecating. When Mark agreed to join the Red Lantern team, we were faced with just one tiny hurdle. He had never cooked Vietnamese food before.

Mark's training is in traditional French and Mediterranean styles of cooking. He was eager to become acquainted with his new best friends: the cleaver and the wok — two items he had never handled before. He looked forward to the mammoth challenge of learning the art of Vietnamese cooking from scratch. What better teachers for Mark than my food obsessed parents? Mark also had the honour and privilege of receiving guidance from a Master Chef whom we call Sifu. Sifu, meaning 'master' in Chinese, is a strikingly handsome square-jawed, chisel-featured seventy-five-year-old gentleman. With a full head of luscious white-pepper hair, dashing attire and the physique of a gymnast, he could make most men half his age shrink with envy. At home, he leads a solitary life tending to over eighty perfectly manicured bonsai trees and his tranquil pond full of shimmering koy fish. At work, he is a machine. His work ethic exceeds even that of my parents. Sifu does not believe in coffee breaks or sick days — he is a Trojan who works non-stop until his day is done. His body is a temple which he pays full respect to every day — nothing but fine food and jasmine tea passes his wizened lips. He is a softly spoken and patient man who at times likes to flex his bulging pecs for all the waitresses to swoon over.

Sifu handed down to Mark a lifetime of Asian cooking techniques. From my parents, he earned a treasure chest of secret family recipes. The strength with which my parents have embraced Mark has surprised no-one more than me. Never before have they accepted any partner of mine let alone trust enough to pass down their precious recipes. Their doing so meant that they love Mark like their own son and, for the first time in my life, respected me as a woman.

Mark and I fell in love long before the opening of Red Lantern, but not until a few years after we first met. At that time, he did not belong to me, nor I to him. Our relationship remained strictly professional, until I returned from a short holiday to Europe. A quick, post-vacation catch up saw me enquiring into everyone else's personal life, except Mark's.

'You haven't asked Chef how his relationship is going,' contributed one of the apprentices, a wry smile appearing at the side of his mouth.

I looked at Mark apologetically. 'Sorry Chef, but you're married, I didn't think to ask.'

Mark put on a brave face. 'She's left me for someone else.'

'Oh, I'm so sorry to hear that.' I was genuinely surprised. 'Does that mean you're available now?'

His face lit up, 'Yep, I'm on the market.'

Two months later, Mark and I shared our first meal and we have achieved much together ever since. His easy going nature, well developed sense of humour, strong mental discipline and sharp awareness for the presence of others are just a few of the many things that I love about him. It was not long before my family fell in love with him as well. To see us work together, one would not guess that we are partners. Mark likes to put me in my place, and I often like to return the gesture. 'She is my biggest critic,' he would say. This passionate, combative edge is one of the things that make us click. In private, we laugh. Mark chips away my hard veneer. With him, I can let down my guard and together we bask in glory of perpetual silliness.

My parents' trust in my judgement revealed to me just how far we have come as a family and how much we have evolved as people. It is nothing short of a miracle that we can be at the place we are at today. To feel free enough to approach them for help is a revelation in itself. To be able to sit with them over a meal and share a genuine laugh is priceless. Sometimes, without knowing it, my parents let their guard down

Clockwise from top: Luke, Mark, Leroy, my mother and father, and Sifu, celebrating Leroy's birthday at Teppanyaki in the city, 2002; Luke is invited to Manila by the Asia Society Philippines and the Embassy of Australia; Luke and his brigade of twenty chefs preparing a plate for the ten-course degustation menu for 200 hungry guests.

and can actually speak with us as grown ups. Sometimes, if we are lucky, they even speak with us as friends.

For many months, my mother and Sifu commuted into the city to teach Mark all that they knew. Under instructions from my father, they had an itinerary of the things they wished for Mark to achieve. Back at Cay Du, my father struggled to hold the fort while my mother was away. In Cabramatta, finding staff who did more than just carry food to a table was a challenge in itself. Either that or they were simply too scared to work under my father. After a time, my father eventually stopped making *pho* at Cay Du. Much to the dismay of his customers, the work had become increasingly difficult for him. The chronic affliction of acute sciatica pained him more each year. Some days he struggled to get out of bed, let alone run a busy restaurant. On these days, my mother would do the running around while my father did his best to stand in one spot and arrange the kitchen so that he didn't have to move too much.

As much as we were all used to seeing our father fight the pain through gritted teeth and a face as ailed as a scrunched up paper bag, it still shocked us when he finally conceded to defeat and gave up cooking his beloved broth. For my father, cooking *pho* his way, is a time consuming and physically draining labour of love. Continuing to keep the recipe a secret meant that he would have to continue cooking *pho* without the help of others. My father no longer possessed the strength or stamina to carry, cook and clean the enormous amount of beef bones required everyday. My mother was not much help when it came to lifting the giant stock pot on and off the stove. During this time, what sight remained in my father's left eye had completely abandoned him. It had been another stubborn reminder of an ill fortunate war, which finally defeated him in the end. At times, he would grow faint and unstable standing on his feet for hours skimming his broth. It impressed me that my father could make the conscious decision to ease his own workload, in turn, making my mother's life easier as well. But the reality did not escape me. My parents continued to look sicker, weaker and more tired. It pained me to see how voraciously old age and ill health could devour them.

My father supplemented the exclusion of *pho* from his menu by creating more specialty dishes which were just as delicious to eat, but much kinder on his body to make. The word spread and the customers soon flocked for his new signature dishes of *mi vit tiem* (braised duck and shitake mushroom in broth with egg noodles), *chim cut chien don* (crisp spiced quail), *ga sot me* (tamarind chicken) and *ga xao xa ot* (lemon grass and chilli chicken). As much as my father boasted of change, some things clearly could not. The sad routine of the past somehow found its way back into my parents' work obsessed lives, wedging itself firmly between the two of them. They worked like dogs once more — fourteen hour days, seven days a week, no break, no time off. Luke finally convinced them to at least take one day off per week. They did this for only three weeks before returning to the familiar trap they had created for themselves.

Around this time, we found out that my mother required surgery to remove some internal cancers. We also discovered that she had developed a menacing heart condition that would require two more surgical procedures and a perpetual plan of medication to contain it. Both afflictions she tried to keep from her children. My parents' inability to communicate these sorts of things to us has a habit of successfully morphing from an act of selflessness on their part, to a stranglehold of guilt and frustration on our part.

Although the health of my parents continued to decline, their determination to help did not. Each night, after a long, hard day at Cay Du they would pick up Sifu and drive the hour-long journey to Surry Hills, to teach Luke and Mark more that they knew. My father looked terrible. Sometimes he could hardly move, he was in so much pain. But without the drama of complaint or the slightest suggestion of martyrdom, they would stay until one or two in the morning if need be, to guide Luke through the careful making of his stocks. Afterwards, they would make the quiet journey back to Bonnyrigg, have a quick shower, take a short sleep and be back at Cay Du at 6.30 sharp the next morning. This routine they kept up for more than six

months, until my father could no longer withstand the physical ordeal. Instead, he arranged special days for us to visit him. My father looked forward to our visits with much excitement and anticipation. Like a schoolboy before show-and-tell, he would jump out of his skin as he was so eager to share his new 'secrets' with Luke and Mark. My father liked the idea that he had another 'son' to cook for and show off newer and better versions of his creations to — creations he would continually tweak, improve and perfect. My father tries to explain it, 'If I give my children money, they just spend it. Gone. If I give them my recipes they last forever.'

Opening night at Red Lantern was indeed a family affair. My parents closed Cay Du early and rushed to Surry Hills for the event. My mother immediately donned an apron and posted herself at the salad section with Leroy as her gofer. My father armed himself at the grills while Sifu prepared his woks. I couldn't help but notice that Mark looked a little anxious peering over the pass. Having previously worked in three-hatted restaurants, he had never before seen such a mismatched bunch of kitchen aficionados. The night was a complete unknown. At the front of house ran Luke and me, with Luke's long-time partner Suzanna. A lithe and intriguing creature, Suzanna is frank, generous and occasionally internal. An art teacher by day, with a gift for detecting untypical beauty, the patience and kindness she shows to others is matched only by her love and loyalty for my brother.

Red Lantern opened without fanfare. We could ill afford advertising or publicity of any kind. Truth be known, it never occurred to us that we might not have any customers on our first night. We would worry about that later. The sheer relief of opening to schedule was enough to get us by — for the first few hours at least. For months, we had sleeplessly thrown ourselves into the task with near fanatical enthusiasm. We could never have opened on time had it not also been for Suzanna's parents Don and Charlene Boyd who helped us saw, sand, paint and polish. By opening night, we were happy, as we had already achieved our greatest objective — to build something of which we could all be proud.

Minutes before opening our doors, it suddenly occurred to us that among all the mayhem we had failed to research the alignment of the stars. No-one checked to see if the date we had chosen was in fact an auspicious one. The momentous blunder drew a cloud of silence over the entire team. My father quickly interjected, 'The thirteenth of June, yes, no worries, it's good.' On hearing those words, we sighed with relief and carried on. I doubt if my father really knew the answer to our superstitions, but his fast convincing words saved the spirit of the night. Within the first hour, the customers poured in and the restaurant filled to the brim. We had people sitting in every corner of the restaurant. We did 82 covers on our first night with just the three of us on the floor. The kitchen didn't know what had hit them. My poor mother — it is always difficult to see her in such a state of distress. My father and Sifu on the other hand, kept chuckling among themselves as they watched the dockets roll in. The stars had aligned well for us after all.

Within twelve weeks, we had won our first award. Red Lantern was always a unique concept: innercity hip with honest food, smart service, an intelligent wine list, but still very Vietnamese — no fusion, no tricks. When the Asian Society Philippines and the Embassy of Australia invited Red Lantern to host a fundraising dinner for 200 diplomats and their VIPs in Makati, Manila, it was with the knowledge of what Red Lantern was about. They had invited Luke especially, because he 'embodied the Asia Society's mission to building a bridge of understanding between the West and Asia'.

Welcoming some 100 guests each night, the Australian ambassador to the Philippines, Tony Hely presented 'Dine at the Red Lantern'. In his address, he said that, 'The event represents many things about Australia. Our country's diversity and multiculturalism, our active involvement and commitment to understanding and building partnerships between Australia and Asia, and our fondness for good food and good company.' With the help of Philippines' top chef Jessie Sincioco and her kitchen brigade at Le Soufflé, Luke hosted the sold-out ten-course degustation menu featuring the dishes that my parents passed down to him. Naturally, well-matched wines from Australia accompanied the food. The event took place as Australia celebrated its 30th Anniversary of dialogue partnership with the Association of South East Asian Nations (ASEAN). Each night saw Luke praised by a standing ovation — he had received the recognition he so well deserved. My parents could not be prouder. He had proved them wrong — he didn't need a university degree to make a reality of his dreams. His success just goes to show that a little street wisdom and a whole lot of clout can also take you a long way in this world.

Suzanna, Luke, Mark and I on opening night at Red Lantern, 13 June 2002.

MARK JENSEN: *The fact that we have Mr and Mrs Nguyen's blessing to reveal some of their fervently guarded recipes is a miracle. This recipe for* bo kho *was entrusted to me from the very opening of Red Lantern. My knowledge of slow-braising secondary cuts of meat had impressed the in-laws, even if I had never before cooked in a wok large enough to braise 15 kilograms (33 lb) of meat.*

Several weeks into operating Red Lantern, with my confidence in the cuisine growing, I made a huge mistake — it was a mistake that made me acutely aware of how intense Mr Nguyen's look of disapproval could be. I had always marinated the bo kho *early in the morning, before anyone else arrived for work. On this particular day, however, we had had an extremely busy day and had sold out. Exhausted and delirious, I collected all of the marinade ingredients and proceeded to marinate the brisket that night, in front of 'none family' staff members. At that precise moment, Mr Nguyen walked into the kitchen to find his secret ingredients spread out for all to see. For a man who stands a little over 5 feet in stature, he gave me a look that could raise me from my sleep in a cold sweat. Thankfully, with their permission, I can now share this long guarded recipe.*

LUKE NGUYEN: Bo kho *is definitely comfort food for me — perfect for a cold winter's day. The Vietnamese usually eat this dish for breakfast, but it is also served for dinner, either on top of soft rice noodles, steamed jasmine rice or, as they do in Saigon, with a hot crispy French baguette.*

Brisket is the cut of beef taken from the breast or lower chest section beneath the front ribs. It is inexpensive and boneless, perfect for this slow-cooked dish.

Until now, Mark and I have kept this recipe a secret from all the staff at Red Lantern. Many have queried the presence of sarsaparilla and Laughing Cow cheese in our pantry. 'Figure it out for yourselves,' I would tell them. No-one ever guessed it was for bo kho.

BÒ KHO
beef brisket stewed in aromatic spices

MARINADE
6 hop bap (from Asian supermarkets)
3 star anise
1 cassia bark
2 cloves
1/2 teaspoon five-spice
2 teaspoons rice wine
1/2 box 'Laughing Cow' cheese
1 tablespoon hoisin sauce
170 ml (5 1/2 fl oz/2/3 cup) sarsaparilla
   or cola

1.25 kg (2 lb 12 oz) beef brisket, cut
   into 5 x 2 cm (2 x 3/4 in) pieces
2 tablespoons oil
1 onion, diced
1 tablespoon minced garlic
4 tablespoons tomato paste
   (concentrated purée)
3 litres (105 fl oz/12 cups) beef stock
   base for pho (page 210)
2 teaspoons salt
250 g (9 oz) carrots, sliced
1 small onion, cut into thin rings
1 handful Vietnamese basil

In a small frying pan, separately roast the hop bap, star anise, cassia bark and cloves until fragrant and slightly coloured, then grind them in a mortar. Combine the spices and the remaining marinade ingredients in a large bowl, add the beef brisket and mix well. Refrigerate and marinate overnight.

Place a wok over medium heat and add the oil, diced onion and garlic. Stir-fry until the onion becomes translucent, then add the beef brisket and increase the heat. Continue to fry until the meat is sealed on all sides. Add the tomato paste and combine it with the beef and stir-fry for 1 minute. Add the *pho* stock and salt and bring it all to the boil. Skim the impurities from the surface, then lower the heat to a slow simmer. Cook the beef for about 2 hours, or until it is very tender. Once cooked, add the carrots and cook for a further 5 minutes. To serve, divide between 6 bowls and garnish with sliced onion rings and Vietnamese basil.

SERVES 6

LUKE NGUYEN: *This is one of Red Lantern's most popular dishes. We use Black Angus for this dish — Angus being the area in Scotland where this cattle breed originated. It has a high degree of marbling, which makes this beef so succulent. Hence, you must not overcook this great meat; we only wok-char the sides of the cubes and wok-toss for no more than 5 minutes. The wok should be flaming, literally — you need intense heat to capture the beef's flavour.*

BÒ LÚC LẮC
*black angus rump wok-tossed
with soy and sesame*

500 g (1 lb 2 oz) Black Angus beef
    rump or eye fillet
3 tablespoons lucky sauce (page 302)
1 tablespoon oil
1 garlic clove, crushed
1/2 small onion, cut into large dice
50 g (1³/4 oz) butter

pinch of salt
pinch of cracked black pepper
red rice (page 306)
1 tomato, sliced
1 Lebanese (short) cucumber, sliced
2–3 tablespoons dipping fish sauce
    (page 33)

It's best to cook this dish in small batches to maintain the highest possible heat in the wok. Cut the beef into 1.5 cm (⁵/8 in) cubes, then marinate it by massaging the lucky sauce into the beef and letting it stand for 5 minutes. Drain the excess marinade from the meat before cooking.

Heat the wok over the highest heat until smoking hot. Drizzle the oil around the top of the wok, allowing it to run down the side and into the middle. This should be done quickly and the oil should ignite into flames. Add the beef in batches and seal it on all sides, shake and toss the beef in the wok. The beef should be charred and the wok flaming. Add the garlic, onion and butter to the wok and continue to stir-fry, moving the ingredients around with a wooden spoon or wok ladle. Cook the beef to your liking (ensuring you don't overcook the meat) — medium–rare should take 3–5 minutes. Add a pinch of salt and cracked black pepper and turn out onto a serving plate. Serve with red rice and a salad of tomato and cucumber dressed with dipping fish sauce.

SERVES 4

SỐT LÚC LẮC
lucky sauce

125 ml (4 fl oz/¹/2 cup) oyster sauce
3 tablespoons hot water
2 teaspoons sesame oil
2 teaspoons caster (superfine) sugar

Combine all the ingredients and mix well.

MAKES 185 ML (6 FL OZ/³/4 CUP)

MUỐI TIÊU CHANH
salt, pepper and lemon dipping sauce

2 tablespoons lemon juice
¹/2 teaspoon salt
1 teaspoon fine white pepper

Combine all the ingredients and mix well.

MAKES 2 TABLESPOONS

LUKE NGUYEN: *A favourite customer of mine, Mr Michael Sideris, once said to me, 'Luke, this crispy skin chicken is the best in Sydney!' Of course, I have to agree! The chicken is juicy and tender and its skin so agreeably crisp.*

GÀ CHIÊN DÒN
crispy skin master stock chicken

6 litres (210 fl oz/24 cups) master stock
   (page 35)
1.6 kg (3 lb 8 oz) whole chicken
125 ml (4 fl oz/¹/₂ cup) white vinegar
1 tablespoon maltose
2 litres (70 fl oz/8 cups) oil,
   for deep-frying

red rice (page 306)
1 tomato, sliced
1 Lebanese (short) cucumber, sliced
¹/₂ bunch watercress
1 tablespoon dipping fish sauce
   (page 33), plus extra to serve

Bring the master stock to the boil in a large saucepan. Meanwhile, wash the chicken well under cold water to remove any viscera. When the stock boils, add the chicken, bring the stock back to the boil and turn off the heat. Allow the chicken to steep for 45 minutes, then remove it from the stock and place it, breast side up, in a colander. Bring the vinegar to the boil in a small saucepan, then stir through the maltose until it dissolves. Place the colander containing the chicken into a large bowl and spoon the vinegar over the chicken, making sure to cover all of it. Transfer the vinegar that has collected in the bowl under the chicken to the saucepan and spoon it back over the chicken, then repeat the process two more times. Place the chicken in a cool, airy position for 2 hours to allow the skin to dry.

Put the oil in a wok and heat to 180°C (350°F), or until a cube of bread dropped in the oil browns in 15 seconds. Cut the chicken in half along the breast bone, place, skin side up, in the oil and fry, carefully ladling the hot oil over the top of the chicken, for 3–5 minutes, or until crisp and golden. Once cooked, place on a cutting board, skin side up, separate the leg from the breast, chop the breast into 5 pieces with a heavy cleaver, then chop the leg into 5 pieces.

Place on a serving platter and serve with red rice and a salad of tomato, cucumber and watercress, dressed with dipping fish sauce and with extra dipping fish sauce to dip the chicken into.

SERVES 6

LUKE NGUYEN: *This is a delicious and aromatic way to season quail. If you prefer, the quail can be chargrilled, roasted in the oven, cooked under the grill (broiler) or simply thrown on the barbecue.*

On a recent visit to Hanoi, my friend Samson and I discovered a quail and pigeon stand. After demolishing six serves, I received a phone call from my Mum telling me to stay clear of all birds because something called 'bird flu' had hit Vietnam. I freaked out, but as it was too late and the quail too good, we continued to order a few more serves.

CHIM CÚT CHIÊN DÒN

crispy spiced quail

MARINADE
1 teaspoon dark soy sauce
1 tablespoon soy sauce
1½ teaspoons salt
2 teaspoons sugar
½ teaspoon five-spice
½ teaspoon ground ginger
2 star anise, crushed
1½ teaspoons shaoxing (Chinese rice wine)
125 ml (4 fl oz/½ cup) chicken stock (page 36) or water

6 quails
2 litres (70 fl oz/8 cups) oil, for deep-frying
1 tomato, sliced
1 Lebanese (short) cucumber, sliced
½ bunch watercress
1 tablespoon dipping fish sauce (page 33)
salt, pepper and lemon dipping sauce, to serve (page 302)

Combine the marinade ingredients together in a bowl and mix well. Cut off the neck and cut the quails along the breastbone to open out flat. Wash away any remaining viscera under cold water, then pat dry with paper towel. Add the quails to the marinade and leave to marinate for 2 hours in the fridge.

Put the oil in a wok or large saucepan over high heat and heat to 180°C (350°F), or until a cube of bread dropped in the oil browns in 15 seconds. Meanwhile, remove the quails from the marinade and pat dry with paper towel. When the oil reaches the correct temperature, fry the quails for 5 minutes, or until crisp and golden, then remove from the oil and cut into quarters.

Serve with a tomato, cucumber and watercress salad dressed with dipping fish sauce, with salt, pepper and lemon dipping sauce to dip the quail into.

SERVES 6

CƠM ĐỎ
red rice

150 g (5^1/$_2$ oz/^{3}/$_4$ cup) jasmine rice,
    cooked, left in the fridge overnight
50 g (1^3/$_4$ oz) butter
1 teaspoon minced garlic

2 tablespoons tomato paste
    (concentrated purée)
salt, to season

Put the cooked rice into a large bowl. Wet your hands slightly so the rice doesn't stick to them, or don a pair of plastic gloves, and break up the rice.

Place a wok over medium heat, add half the butter and the garlic and stir-fry until the garlic is fragrant, then add the rice. Increase the heat and, using a wooden spoon, stir and toss the rice. Add the tomato paste and continue to stir-fry, working the tomato through the rice until it is evenly coloured. Add the remaining butter and fry until it is incorporated. Season with salt and serve.

SERVES 4

GÀ XÀO ME

chicken thighs with tamarind and sesame

500 g (1 lb 2 oz) boneless, skinless
   chicken thighs
1 garlic clove, crushed
3 tablespoons fish sauce
1 tablespoon caster (superfine) sugar
1 tablespoon oil
1/2 small onion, cut into wedges
125 ml (4 fl oz/1/2 cup) tamarind and
   plum sauce (page 207)

2 teaspoons toasted sesame seeds
1 tomato, sliced
1 Lebanese (short) cucumber, sliced
1/2 bunch watercress
1 tablespoon dipping fish sauce
   (page 33)

Cut the chicken into bite-sized pieces and marinate with the garlic, fish sauce and sugar for 1 hour. Place a wok over medium heat, add the oil, then the chicken and its marinade and stir-fry for 2 minutes. Add the onion and the tamarind and plum sauce and continue to stir-fry for 5 minutes, or until the sauce has totally reduced and has absorbed into the chicken.

Sprinkle the chicken with the sesame seeds and serve with steamed jasmine rice and a salad of tomato, cucumber and watercress dressed with a little dipping fish sauce.

SERVES 4 AS PART OF A SHARED FEAST

MÌ VỊT TIỀM

*braised duck and shiitake mushroom broth
with egg noodles*

8 duck leg quarters (marylands)
125 ml (4 fl oz/½ cup) dark soy sauce
1 litre (35 fl oz/4 cups) vegetable oil
16 dried shiitake mushrooms
1 bunch spring onions (scallions),
   white part bashed, green part
   finely sliced
1 garlic bulb, sliced horizontally in half
6 cm (2½ in) piece of ginger
250 ml (9 fl oz/1 cup) fish sauce
2 star anise

1 cinnamon stick
1 tablespoon sugar
2 teaspoons fine white pepper
1 kg (2 lb 4 oz) thin egg noodles
1 bunch watercress
1 bunch garlic chives, cut into
   4 cm (1½ in) lengths
2 lemons, quartered
2 red bird's eye chillies, sliced
2 large handfuls bean sprouts

Wash the duck under cold water, then pat dry with paper towel. Place the duck into a bowl and thoroughly coat it with the dark soy sauce and refrigerate for 1 hour.

Put the oil in a wok over high heat and fry the duck pieces, a couple at a time, until the skin is a rich golden-brown colour. Remove the duck from the oil and place it in a colander to drain. Once drained of excess oil, put the duck and shiitake mushrooms in a large saucepan and cover with 6 litres (210 fl oz/24 cups) water. Bring to the boil over high heat, skimming off the fat and impurities that float to the surface. Add the white part of the spring onions, garlic, ginger, fish sauce, star anise and cinnamon, reduce the heat and simmer slowly for 1½ hours.

Remove the duck and shiitake from the pan and set aside. Skim the remaining fat from the surface of the soup, then pass it through a strainer into another saucepan, season with the sugar and white pepper. You should have about 4 litres (140 fl oz/16 cups) of soup.

To serve, cook the egg noodles and divide them evenly into 8 bowls. Place 1 duck leg and 2 shiitake mushrooms on top of the noodles in each bowl, then pour over the boiling soup. Garnish with sliced spring onion greens, watercress and garlic chives. Serve with the lemon wedges, sliced chilli and bean sprouts on the side.

SERVES 8

red is for life

To raise a red lantern outside your home is a symbol of honouring good company.

The art of hospitality has remained the livelihood of my family for generations. For us, the bringing of people together is the most important role that food plays. Food is the binding force that has saved my family time and time again. Never in my wildest dreams did I think Red Lantern would be the ultimate salvation of my first family, and the catalyst for the creation of my future family.

Since the age of thirteen, I knew that I would one day have a child. I had even picked the names. In the melancholy of my youth, I often escaped into the land of the idyllic. While other kids my age wished for fancy shoes and shiny bicycles, I prayed for only one thing — my freedom. To be free was all that mattered — free to live a happy life with a loving family of my own. I never did ask for much.

My father did not flinch when he heard. Luke played messenger, casually breaking the news of Mark's and my intentions to have a child. My mother literally jumped for joy. Like a young girl about to receive her biggest present, she skipped around the restaurant, clapped her hands and giggled with absolute delight. My father, on the other hand, remained expressionless. In the months leading up to the pregnancy, he did not once approach the subject with me. Even when I started to show, he uttered not a single word. I do not know if his silence was, in fact, concern for my wellbeing, or perhaps the indignation of not having sought his permission on the matter. Whatever the case, the absurdity of the situation was not new to me.

Previous page: My paternal grandmother, Thi Than Nguyen, with my father (age 2) and his Aunty, Saigon 1949. Left: Mark and I; photo taken by Leroy Nguyen, 2004.

313

I wanted desperately to have a child. A little person I could nurture and protect with every ounce of my being; to whom I could pour all my love, kindness, patience and understanding. Someone I could grow with, never lay a finger on, and equip with all the tools that they would ever need to overcome the challenges that life can carry. When I made the decision to have a baby, I knew that things would have to change.

My spirit was still a mess. I didn't want to be the person I had always been. At the expense of my own healing, like my parents, I too threw myself into obsessive work. If I didn't work hard enough, I felt as if the whole world would collapse around me and life as I knew it would end. Every day became an emotional struggle as my internal time bomb stood ready to explode at the most insignificant problem. My constant drive for perfection left me highly strung, intensely frustrated and sorely unfulfilled. Angry people are skilled at noticing what is wrong.

I tired of being angry all the time and began to wonder if it was possible for anyone in my situation to ever fully recover from years of such abuse. Whatever the case, I was determined to do all I could to end the sense of drowning. I simply had no other choice. I approached every avenue with an open mind and the desperate desire to be the best person that I could be. I sought individual counselling, group therapy, spiritual healing. I even underwent months of acupuncture to put out the fire in my heart. It was not that I was so much unhappy as I was incredibly frightened — frightened of history repeating; frightened of treating my own child the way I had been treated.

In the sixth month of my pregnancy, it happened that I was left alone with my parents — a much-avoided scenario. Usually, I am supported by the company of my brothers who are all expert at deflecting unwanted subjects and softening the blow of the usual confrontations. It was meant to be a family dinner but the boys cancelled at the last minute. With dread, I accompanied my parents to a restaurant in Canley Vale specializing in *ca bay mon* (fish seven ways). My mother did most of the talking and funnily enough, avoided the subject of my bulging stomach in the presence of my father. It was just as well that the fish came seven ways. It gave us seven different opportunities of conversation to drag out in as much detail as possible. My father hardly said a thing. He responded only in short grunts and half nods as if to underline his nonchalance at the present scenario. I wanted to eat quickly and get the hell out of there. I didn't need his blessing. I even had my speech prepared should he blast me with his malice. I wanted to tell him that if he so chose to disapprove of this baby, then the loss would be his, not mine.

To keep the silence at bay, my mother did not stop talking. She spoke of how she thought the dill complimented the ling. She liked that the chargrilled snapper wrapped in betel leaves imparted such a fragrant aroma. She complained that the congee was too bland and needed seasoning. I knew that she would approve of the fish cakes; they were firm and full of flavour. The chargrilled barramundi she liked best. We wrapped pieces of the juicy flesh in rice paper and fresh herbs.

'This anchovy dipping sauce could do with a little more anchovy.' Just as she was about to continue, my father interjected.

'You walk too heavy.' It was the closest thing he had said all night that resembled a full sentence.

'Sorry Dad, did you say something?'

'You – walk – too – heavy.' I had no idea what he was talking about. My mother finally stopped rambling and let my father speak.

'You walk too heavy. You are carrying a baby now, it can hear everything. You need to be gentler. You move around too much. Your baby needs to be comfortable. Peaceful. You need to walk softer.'

I hid the wonderful surprise of his words behind a gesture of obedience. 'Yes Dad.'

My father did not stop there.

'You must also remember to be happy. Don't ever be depressed. A happy mother gives birth to a happy baby. A depressed mother gives birth to a depressed baby. Try always to be happy. The most important thing is your happiness. Do you understand?'

'Yes Dad.'

A little girl grew inside of me and I named her Mia Angel — my angel, who came to save me in the nick of time. The counsel of others had indeed led me onto the right path, but it was Mia who helped me figure it out. The secret, I discovered, was compassion — compassion for myself. Never before had I thought of myself in that way. By wanting to be the best person that I could be for my baby, I slowed down, cut myself some slack and offered kindness to my soul. I had at last understood what it really means to forgive oneself. I had forgiven my parents years ago, although it was conditionally, I forgave them nevertheless. By trying to understand the sorrow of their own wounds, I had shown them mercy. The time had come to show mercy to myself. We are, after all, only human. As I learned to possess true compassion, I felt myself being healed. Mia helped to free me of my greatest burden; anger and bitterness. With the lifting of the crippling weight, I finally discovered what it means to really love.

Mia Angel arrived on Wednesday, 9 March 2005, at 11.56pm. The labour lasted twenty-one long, agonizing hours and was worth every second of it. In all the literature that I had ever read and the numerous birth classes that I had attended, not once had anyone told me about the immense force of emotion that would hit me in the gut and leave me gasping for air. I was simply not prepared for the powerful nature of this intense and overwhelming love. It is a profound love that resides in an entirely new realm of emotion and I feel absolutely privileged to have discovered it.

When my parents first laid eyes on Mia, I saw a side of them I never knew existed. They flapped over her like two proud mother hens bewildered by such fragility. My father wanted to teach me the 'four steps to properly swaddle a baby'. He spoke in a whisper as he gently demonstrated the folds. He discussed in great detail the medicinal relief of placing cold cabbage leaves on my engorged breasts. As he continued to tell me that I 'walk too heavy,' my mother berated me for walking at all.

'In Vietnam …' she said, '… women lie horizontal for three months after giving birth. They do not get out of bed. Hot coals are placed around them the entire time.'

'But why the hot coals?' I asked my mother.

'How am I supposed to know?' she replied.

My parents have never known how to give the conventional gifts of clothing, bibs or toys. Instead, they spent several days carefully brewing a whole month's supply of a medicinal pork hock and paw paw soup. It is an ancient recipe proven to bring on rich, abundant mother's milk to help baby grow big and strong.

There is no doubt in my mind that Mia played an instrumental part in my parents' decision to finally stop working. Mia had made them stop to think about the wheel of life and question their own mortality. They put Cay Du up for sale and in no time at all, received an offer too good to refuse. At last they wanted to enjoy the rest of their lives. Mia is their first grandchild and they didn't want to miss out. 'There are more important things,' says my father. 'I know that now.'

In December 2005, more than 30 years after the fall of Saigon, my parents boarded a plane and headed for home. Unlike many of their friends, they had not once returned to the motherland. My father, the eldest and most prodigal son, would return from exile to face the victimizer of his own youth — his father, who lay sick and dying. To both his parents, all those years ago, he had vowed for 'lightning to strike him dead' if he were to ever lay eyes on them again. It was in my own mother's honour that he had done this.

It happened a few months after my parents had wed, when my father was called to war. It is tradition that the wife is left with the husband's side of the family while he is gone. My mother was pregnant with me at time. Upon returning from battle, my father discovered that his own parents had not at all treated his beloved bride with the respect and kindness they had promised to her parents. In my father's absence, they had used my mother as a common slave. In the day, she cooked for them, cleaned for them, scrubbed and scraped for them. They thanked her with cruelty and loathing. Perhaps it was out of resentment for her privileged background that they did this, or perhaps it was just in their nature. In the night, they forced her to hand-make candy for them and churn toffee so tough her arms would burn

316

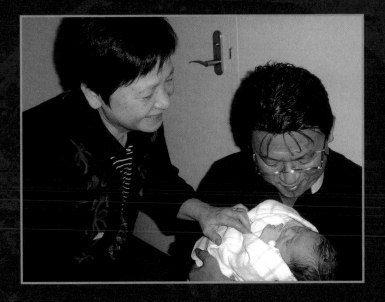

Clockwise from bottom left: Mia Angel is born 9 March 2005; my parents meet their first grandchild, 10 March 2005; Mia's first birthday, Nielsen Park, March 2006.

with pain. At the crack of dawn, they sent her out onto the street to sell the sweets to anyone who was interested. My mother's greatest fear at this time was that her own family would find out. Her heart stopped one morning when her mother passed her on the street. She thanked the heavens that her mother had not noticed her. As long as her family did not find out, she could endure the humiliation alone.

My mother had never wanted to marry my father. Her own father had promised her to him. She was an irreversible agreement between both my grandparents. My father loved my mother but she did not return his love. When she first refused to marry him, her own father shaved his head. When she refused a second time, he threatened to join the monastery. Either my mother obeyed or he would disappear rather than bring his family shame. He had given his word and could not be dishonoured. So with her own father's urging, my mother married someone she did not love. In time, she did grow to love my father and has spent the rest of her life married to him. For her, the difficult times have far outweighed the good. But in all the years, she has not once left my father or raised a hand against him, either to defend herself or protect her children. She still stands by his side and willingly supports any decisions that he makes, with little regard to her own opinions. It is for the sanctity of marriage that she does this — her filial duty unfailing. It is also for the belief that, in this life, she must reap what she has sown in her past. She must accept her karma with gracious resignation. I confess that I do not share my mother's way of thinking, but her strength of will I must respect. Her endurance I cannot match. She had made a promise; a promise she will never break.

My father made it back to Saigon just in time to properly farewell his father. Video footage of this time allowed me the privilege to witness what was for my father an important and life changing experience. Upon arriving, my father took charge of a situation he ultimately had no control over. He needed to buy some time and arranged for my grandfather's immediate transfer into a hospice, where he paid for the best of care. Prior to my parents' arrival, the old man lay dying at home; his family unable to afford the hospital fees. I watched as my father stood over my grandfather, his face expressionless as usual. It is always difficult to guess what my father is thinking. The man in the hospital bed did not seem scared. Curious eyes and neatly combed white hair gave the impression that he still cared what other people thought of him. He knew that he did not have long. His rusted face had sunk into its skull. The skin on his cheeks drooped lifelessly onto the bones that had once held them high. His lips which had always pleased his women well, now disappeared into the chasm of his gaping mouth.

My father insisted that he be the one to administer my grandfather's medicine. 'You don't need to inhale too heavily,' my father told him. 'This ventilator is designed for sick people. The doctors know that sick people can't inhale heavily. Save your strength.' Whether or not the old man understood, he nodded rhythmically. The next lot of medicine, my father refused to give. 'This medicine has expired,' he said, as he instructed the nurse to dispose of it.

'But there is still so much left,' argued the dying man, unaccustomed to the waste of such a valuable commodity.

'It doesn't matter, it has passed its use by date, you cannot have it.'

The shock of my grandfather's dramatic decline just one day later filled me with the deepest sorrow. My sorrow pained for both men — if only they had more time. I tried to imagine the tremendous regret that plagued their hearts in these desperate hours and it frightened me. I never want to face the force of such regret. I watched as my grandfather's chest rose and fell furiously, hopelessly out of sync with each random breath that escaped his quivering lips. The family had brought a tape recorder to tape the dying man's last words. In vain, my father held the tape recorder to my grandfather's mouth and instructed everyone in the room to be quiet. 'He can still hear you,' he said, '… he might become frightened and forget his thoughts.' It was clear to everyone else that the old man could no longer talk. They doubted he could still hear them. But my father continued regardless. In great detail, he explained to my grandfather the intricate procedures of his funeral. 'Tomorrow we will take you to the temple,' he said. 'There you will die with dignity.' As they held each other's hand and spoke only with their eyes, they made peace with one another and made up for lost time.

As my grandfather lay in the temple surrounded by all his children and grandchildren, his eldest son sat solemnly at his side. They prayed as he breathed his last breath and watched as his milk-clouded eyes finally retired to the back of his head. My father gave instructions and everyone obeyed. 'Wrap this scarf under his chin and around his head,' he told them, 'it will help keep his mouth closed.' When the people around him began their wailing, my father raised his hand and politely requested that they leave the room. 'Just say goodbye,' he told them, 'Don't cry. Allow him to leave as easily and comfortably as possible.' The procession of monks soon arrived and the air filled with the vibrations of their meditative chanting. My mother prayed from afar, allowing my father the space to grieve. Beside her sat her mother-in-law, the woman who had once treated her with such cruelty and disrespect. My mother rested her arm around the old woman's shoulders and at the sound of each monk's gong, prompted her to bow at the appropriate moment. The funeral was an elaborate one — the best that money could buy. My father took care of everything and was honoured that he had been given the chance to do so. Everyone came to pay their last respects and say farewell to a once outspoken and charismatic man.

As my father knelt beside my grandfather, his head bowed low, his hands cupped neatly in his lap, three questions churned in his mind. It was the three questions he reserved especially for moments of deep despair.

'Who am I? Where am I? What am I?'

Thirty years they had not spoken. Thirty years he had held onto bitterness and resentment. And for what? Anger is a selfish bastard that robbed him of precious time. The answers to his own questions came clearly to him.

'I am no-one. I am nowhere. I am nobody. Everything must change. This is my redemption.'

The capacity to forgive exists, even in the most hardened of us. Forgiveness, long overdue, had finally freed my father. He had made peace with the victimizer of his youth and had at last made peace with himself.

The pilgrimage back to Vietnam was a life changing experience for my parents. It had occurred to me, how easy it would have been for them to readopt the overly strict and emotionally distant values of the typical Vietnamese parent, but it is in their old age that my parents continue to surprise. Upon returning to Sydney, I saw a look in their eyes I could hardly describe as deficient. They treated one another with a new softness and spoke to their children with deliberate respect. 'I was wrong.' My father admitted to me unexpectedly.

The sound of those three foreign words — 'I was wrong' — made me sit up and pay attention.

'Do you know why Buddha sits on a lotus flower?' my father asked me. 'Nothing is as beautiful as a lotus flower. Out of watery chaos it grows, emerging from the depths of a muddy swamp and yet remains pure and unpolluted. So pure you can eat it — all of it, the flowers, the seeds, the leaves, the roots. But the lotus has another characteristic. Its stalk you can bend in two, but it cannot easily break. It has strong, tenacious fibres that holds the plant together … My children are lotus flowers.' His words left me speechless. My silence enabled him to carry on. 'Like the lotus flower, all of you have grown out of the mud of your origins. You grew out of the aftermath of war, you grew out of Cabramatta during its murkiest time — and you grew out of me. I was mud. Our family was mud. I was shit. I am very lucky to have you all.'

Had it been a dream? Had my father really given me the moment I had waited twenty years for? He had caught me by surprise — he had indeed given me that and so much more. Acknowledgement was all that I had ever needed, not an apology, acknowledgement of the harm he had inflicted. That night as I lay awake, still reeling from the events of the evening, I thought about my father and the courage it took to admit his wrongs. I realized the enormity of what had just occurred. I understood how hard it would have been for him to face his demons and I felt proud of his determination to relinquish them. I turned out the light and let a blanket of calm cover me. In the dark, I closed my eyes; I had finally found my peace.

Motivated by the will to change, my parents searched their spirituality. They had always considered themselves Buddhists; celebrating the holy days and traditions. But for the first time, they actually studied Buddha's words and endeavoured to practise what he preached. My parents chose to *Tu*. I had always thought that to *Tu* was to shave your head, join the monastery and spend your days sitting in meditation. My father corrected my ignorance. *Tu*, he says, 'means to fix, to rectify, to make amends. The word "Buddha" literally means "awakened one" — to experience the truth for oneself. Buddha teaches that the greatest of conquests is not the subjugation of others but of the self … I understand that now.' My father spoke slowly and firmly, as assured in his humility as he is a human being. 'Even though a man conquers ten thousand men in battle, he who conquers himself is the greatest of conquerors.'

Buddha teaches that true greatness springs of love, forgiveness and compassion, not hatred, resentment and cruelty. I must pay the utmost reverence to the one belief spread not by weapons or political power, but by love and compassion for humanity. Not a drop of blood stains its pure path. My father no longer preaches about the natural instinct of breaking someone's arm should they do him wrong. These days it is talk of kindness to one another and of love for your fellow man. 'The practical nature of Buddha's teaching,' says my father, 'is revealed in the fact that not everyone is expected to attain the same goals in one lifetime. Some are spiritually more advanced than others and can proceed to the greater heights according to their state of development — our mental impurities are deeply rooted. But every single human being has the ultimate potential to attain the supreme goal if he has the determination and will to do so … My will is strong. I have long suffered the consequences of my ignorance and my anger … I do not want to suffer anymore.'

Following the death of my grandfather, my parents rented a three-storey house in the centre of Saigon and hosted all the family and friends they had long ago missed. For three months, they also ate their way across Vietnam, rekindled by the desire to recapture the flavours and memories of their youth.

When Mark and I journeyed through the homeland three years prior to my parents, I realized that things may have been very different for the Nguyen family had my father not smuggled us out on that small boat thirty years ago. My heart ached at the poverty and desperation before me. With what little they had, the Vietnamese people met us with warmth, thoughtfulness and kind-heartedness. The fact that I was Vietnamese indeed opened doors that might have otherwise remained closed. Once we had scratched the surface, we discovered an openness and generosity driven by a ferocious sense of pride in their heritage.

But in their eyes I saw the same look time and time again. 'You are over there and I am still here. We are not the same.'

Upon returning from their culinary travels, my parents concluded that, 'Vietnamese food is better in Australia than Vietnamese food in Vietnam.' They had confirmed an observation made by many (including ourselves) who returned from Vietnam on holiday. 'The reason is simple,' says my father with great conviction.

'There is no doubt that the cooks in Vietnam cook for pure pleasure and love of food, but few are formally trained. It is essentially the same method employed but much of it is passed down or imitated. The professionalism of cooks in Australia ensures that the preparation and execution of the dish carries a higher-level of technique and understanding. Food just tastes better in Australia because the quality of produce is better. Meat and seafood is far superior. Fruit and vegetables are fresher and have more flavour. There is a greater knowledge and respect for the raw ingredient.'

My mother has another explanation. She believes that Vietnam lost the majority of top Vietnamese master chefs in the mass exodus following the war, taking their skills, talents and secret recipes with them. The spread of Vietnamese Diaspora has seen my parents eat better Vietnamese food in Australia, the United States and France. Authentic recipes are preserved and executed by the great cooks of immigrant families all around the world. It is no wonder that Vietnamese cooks outside Vietnam strive to hold onto the tradition of these dishes more so than in Vietnam itself. My mother also believes that before communism, history's most destructive ideology, abundance existed in mind, in attitude and in practice. 'Communism equates to scarcity,' explains my mother. 'There are some areas of the Vietnamese countryside not yet recovered from the ravages of the war. Most of the country is still suffering from a chronic food shortage. How can you cook good food when you must skimp on the quality and quantity of ingredients?'

Both formally trained chefs, my parents have a deeper understanding and appreciation for the application of both Eastern and Western techniques to Vietnamese cuisine. This does not mean fused or hybrid versions of authentic recipes to suit a contemporary palate. It means to raise the bar higher in technique for the preparation and execution of these dishes. My father prefers the food of peasant origins. 'Food that maintains its naiveté. Food that has a simple authenticity of flavour and presentation, perhaps leaving an odour on the breath and has enough heat to cause a certain degree of perspiration; resilient food that has sustained the masses since the earliest of time.' Like my father, my mother enjoys the immediate addictive appeal of spicier, bolder flavours, of assertive contrasting textures. She prefers the front of mouth and tongue experience of nibbling on skin, bones and cartilage — savouring crunch and texture. That sensory bombardment is something the whole family enjoys but the rest of us can also appreciate the deliberate subtlety of some Vietnamese dishes where richer flavours and softer textures are experienced in the back palate. But we do agree on one thing — we are all obsessed with the raw ingredient. The less you do to it, the more natural it tastes, the more we like it.

This appreciation of our dual cultures is the secret of Red Lantern. To share with others the food that we have grown with and to remain true to our parents' recipes, is to acknowledge the culture and history of our family's personal journey — as individuals and combined. To allow Mark the application of his skills and experience to the dishes that mean so much to us, is to respect the Western appreciation of fine technique and professionalism that he brings. With open arms, we have embraced the Australian way without relinquishing our own culture. We must always hold onto our origins. We cannot forget where we came from.

Six years on and Red Lantern is still going strong. We are full to capacity every night and the wait list is long. We are truly blessed to have received such success. Every day we strive to please our guests, but in business as with everything in life, it is impossible to please everyone. Food lovers and food critics alike have honoured us with many favourable reviews, and for this, we are grateful. Red Lantern belongs to my family. It is the food that we have grown with, the food we like to eat: fresh, simple, honest, nothing fancy, nothing pretentious. We accept that our food may not please everyone, but we invest in it with pride. True passion and creativity in cooking happens only when one is truly happy. It is the same when we are eating. Our taste is heightened when we feel good or are at peace. When we are upset or angry, everything is sour. These family dishes will always remain loyal to our menu and like our parents, we will continue to refine and perfect.

They say that successful migration is the result of work ethic, intermarriage and strong family values. As the children of refugees, we are no strangers to hard work. Naturally, for some who like to work less and live well, it is a shock to see us work so tirelessly. As we have inherited our parent's work ethic, we strive not to make the same mistakes they have made. Sometimes when I look at my parents, I think back of how it used to be. How many years we wasted running away from each other and ourselves, hiding behind work and emotional distance. Time, dialogue and tolerance have enabled us to look forward with hope. We are no longer just survivors: victims of war, trauma and abuse. We are resilient people trying to be the best we can be. We too want to 'take it easy' — to be kinder to one another and kinder to ourselves, to live more, work less, take time to get to know one another and enjoy our achievements. Now when I look at my parents, I see two small, soft and sometimes nervous people finally at peace with one another, at peace with their children and at peace with themselves. I just never presumed for one moment that we would one day become friends. ■

red lantern
authentic v
545 crown street surry hills
t/f. 0
AUSTRALIA POST

Above: Mark, Luke and I, 2007. Left: Outside Red Lantern, 2007.

VỊT TIỀM GỪNG HÀNH
braised duck with ginger and spring onions

6 duck leg quarters (marylands)
6 spring onions (scallions), white part
    bashed, green part finely sliced
3 garlic cloves, crushed
3 tablespoons minced ginger
125 ml (4 fl oz/¹/₂ cup) fish sauce

2 tablespoons light soy sauce
2 tablespoons caster (superfine) sugar
1 litre (35 fl oz/4 cups) vegetable oil
2 litres (70 fl oz/8 cups) chicken stock
    (page 36)

Wash the duck leg quarters under cold water, pat dry with paper towel, then place on a cutting board. Trim and discard the excess fat. Add the white part of the spring onion, garlic, ginger, fish sauce, soy sauce and sugar to a large bowl and mix well to dissolve the sugar. Cut the duck leg quarters in half through the knee joint and place the pieces into the bowl. Mix well and marinate for 2 hours.

Remove the duck from the marinade (reserving it for later use) and dry the excess marinade off the duck with paper towel. Put the oil into a wok over medium heat and fry the duck pieces for 3–5 minutes, or until golden, then remove from the oil and place in a single layer in a large saucepan. Add the reserved marinade and cover the duck with the chicken stock by 2 cm (³/₄ in). Bring to the boil, skim off excess oil and impurities, then reduce the heat to a slow simmer. Cook for 1 hour, or until the duck pierces easily with a skewer.

Once cooked, place on a serving platter, garnish with the sliced spring onion greens and serve with steamed jasmine rice.

SERVES 6

BẮP BÒ NẤU NẤM

braised veal shanks with asian mushrooms and taro

1 garlic bulb
100 g (3¹/2 oz) red Asian shallots
20 g (³/4 oz) butter
6 veal shanks
3 tablespoons vegetable oil
6 dried shiitake mushrooms
approximately 2 litres (70 fl oz/8 cups)
    beef stock base for pho (page 210)

300 g (10¹/2 oz) taro, cut into 1 cm
    (¹/2 in) cubes
100 g (3¹/2 oz) oyster mushrooms
100 g (3¹/2 oz) shimeji mushrooms
100 g (3¹/2 oz) chestnut mushrooms
salt, to taste
white pepper, to taste

Break the garlic bulb into individual cloves, peel and place them in a piece of foil with the red Asian shallots and butter. Fold the foil into a parcel and roast in a preheated oven at 220°C (425°F/Gas 7) for 20 minutes. Remove from the oven and reserve for later use.

Seal the veal shanks in the oil in a frying pan, then transfer to a large saucepan or wok. Add the shiitake mushrooms and enough *pho* stock to cover the shanks by three-quarters, and bring to the boil. Reduce the heat and skim the surface. Cover with a lid and simmer for 1¹/2 hours. Add the taro and continue cooking, covered, for 15–20 minutes, or until the veal is succulent and the taro is tender. Once cooked, add the remaining ingredients, season with salt and pepper and return to the boil.

Serve with steamed jasmine rice and wok-tossed snake beans in oyster sauce (page 238).

SERVES 6

BÒ NƯỚNG TỎI GỪNG

chargrilled sirloin with chilli, garlic and ginger

2 x 250 g (9 oz) sirloin steaks
2 handfuls shredded green papaya
1 small handful mixed herbs (perilla,
    Vietnamese mint and basil)
1 tablespoon fried red Asian shallots
    (page 38)
1 tablespoon dried shrimp, soaked in
    hot water for 5 minutes and drained
3 tablespoons dipping fish sauce
    (page 33)

MARINADE
2 teaspoons pickled chilli (from Asian
    supermarkets)
2 garlic cloves, crushed
2 cm (3/4 in) piece of ginger, minced
2 tablespoons fish sauce
1 tablespoon caster (superfine) sugar
2 teaspoons vegetable oil
pinch of salt

Mix all the marinade ingredients together until the sugar dissolves. Add the steaks and marinate for 2 hours in the fridge. Chargrill the steaks over medium–high heat, to your preference (6 minutes for rare, 10 minutes for medium), then rest the steaks for 5 minutes. Reheat the steaks on the chargrill, then cut into thin slices.

Serve with a salad of green papaya, mixed herbs, fried red Asian shallots and dried shrimp, dressed with dipping fish sauce.

SERVES 4

GÀ NƯỚNG THIÊN HƯƠNG

chargrilled spatchcock with garlic, lemon grass and five-spice

4 spatchcocks (poussins)
1/2 lemon grass stem, finely sliced
6 spring onions (scallions), white part
    bashed, green part finely sliced
6 garlic cloves, crushed
5 cm (2 in) piece of ginger, minced
125 ml (4 fl oz/1/2 cup) fish sauce

3 tablespoons soy sauce
juice of 1 lemon
2 tablespoons honey
2 teaspoons five-spice
125 ml (4 fl oz/1/2 cup) vegetable oil
1 lemon, quartered

Place the spatchcocks on a cutting board, breast side up. Using a large knife, cut through the breastbone and open the spatchcock out flat. Wash the spatchcock under cold water and pat dry with paper towel.

Combine the remaining ingredients, except the green part of the spring onion and lemon quarters, in a large bowl and stir until the sugar dissolves. Add the spatchcock to the bowl and toss through the marinade. Refrigerate for at least 4 hours, or for the best result, overnight.

Place the spatchcock, skin side down, on a chargrill pan over medium–high heat. Cook for 3–5 minutes, or until the skin lifts easily off the pan, then rotate it 90 degrees on the same side and put it back on the chargrill for 3–5 minutes, to form a crisscross pattern. Turn the bird over and cook for 5–7 minutes, until done. Remove to a plate and garnish with the reserved spring onions and serve with steamed jasmine rice and lemon quarters.

SERVES 4

GỎI CÁ SỐNG

cured ocean trout with fresh herb and bean sprout salad

2 tablespoons sugar
1 tablespoon sea salt
1 tablespoon chopped coriander
    (cilantro) roots and stems
300 g (10¹/₂ oz) ocean trout fillet,
    skin on, bones removed
2 teaspoons Cognac
100 g (3¹/₂ oz) bean sprouts

1 large handful mixed herbs (basil,
    mint, Vietnamese mint and perilla),
    finely sliced
2 tablespoons fried red Asian shallots
    (page 38)
3 tablespoons dipping fish sauce
    (page 33)
1 lemon, quartered

Combine the sugar, salt and coriander in a bowl. Sprinkle a quarter of the mixture onto a plate and lay the trout on top, skin side down. Pour the Cognac over the top of the fillet and cover with the remaining sugar, salt and coriander mixture. Cover with plastic wrap and refrigerate for 12 hours.

Wipe the fillet well with a damp cloth, removing the remainder of the curing mixture. Place on a cutting board, skin side down. Finely slice the cured trout off the skin and arrange on a serving platter. Mix the bean sprouts, mixed herbs and shallots with the dipping fish sauce and place on top of the trout. Serve with lemon wedges on the side.

SERVES 4

LUKE NGUYEN: *This recipe was passed down to me by my mentor, Master Chef Sifu Ling — a 70-year-old man built like Bruce Lee. This guy can work a wok like no other and I hope that one day I will be as skilful and graceful as he ...*

MỰC RANG MUỐI
salt and pepper squid

200 g (7 oz) squid tubes
2 litres (70 fl oz/8 cups) vegetable oil,
    for frying
1 egg white
200 g (7 oz/1 cup) potato starch
1 spring onion (scallion), finely sliced

1 bird's eye chilli, finely sliced
½ garlic clove, crushed
½–1 teaspoon salt and pepper
    seasoning mix (next page)
2 tablespoons salt, pepper and lemon
    dipping sauce (page 302)

Lay the cleaned squid out on a cutting board, insert your knife into the top edge of the body and run your knife down to the bottom of the squid. Fold the tube open as you would a book. Working from the top right of the squid to the bottom left, make diagonal slices in the flesh, making sure not to penetrate through. Then work from the top left to the bottom right of the squid so you now have a crisscross pattern. Cut the squid in half from top to bottom, turn it horizontally and slice through to make 5 mm (¼ in) wide pieces, then place them in a bowl.

In a wok over high heat, heat the oil to 180°C (350°F), or until a cube of bread dropped in the oil browns in 15 seconds. Meanwhile, whisk the egg white and pour half of it into the bowl with the squid. Work the egg white into the squid with your fingers, then start adding the potato starch, a little at a time. Keep adding the potato starch to the squid until the squid is well covered and feels quite dry.

Shake off any excess flour then start adding the squid to the oil, a few pieces at a time, but in quick succession to maintain the heat of the oil. Lift out the starch that floats free of the squid with a metal strainer and discard. Cook for 3–5 minutes, or until the batter on the squid feels quite firm when tapped with a wooden spoon.

Carefully pour the squid into a colander to drain the oil. Drain all but 2 teaspoons of oil from the wok, then return it to the heat. Add the spring onion, chilli and garlic, toss to combine then add the squid. Continue to toss while shaking over the seasoning mix. Remove and serve with salt, pepper and lemon dipping sauce to dip.

SERVES 2

TÔM RANG MUỐI
salt and pepper king prawns

8 raw king prawns (shrimp)
2 litres (70 fl oz/8 cups) vegetable oil,
   for frying
50 g (1³/4 oz/¹/4 cup) potato starch
1 spring onion (scallion), finely sliced
1 bird's eye chilli, finely sliced

¹/2 garlic clove, crushed
¹/2–1 teaspoon salt and pepper
   seasoning mix (below)
2 tablespoons salt, pepper and lemon
   dipping sauce (page 302)

Remove the beak from the prawns by cutting behind the eyes with a pair of scissors. Then cut off the legs and place the prawns in a bowl and set aside. In a wok over high heat, heat the oil to 180°C (350°F), or until a cube of bread dropped in the oil browns in 15 seconds.

Dust the prawns with the potato starch, shake off excess starch, then add them, one at a time in quick succession, to the oil. Fry for 3 minutes, then carefully remove to a colander to drain the oil. Drain all but 2 teaspoons of oil from the wok, then return it to the heat. Add the spring onion, chilli and garlic, toss to combine then add the prawns. Continue to toss while shaking over the seasoning mix. Remove and serve with salt, pepper and lemon dipping sauce to dip.

SERVES 2

MUỐI THIÊN HƯƠNG
salt and pepper seasoning mix

1 tablespoon salt
1 teaspoon sugar
1 teaspoon fine white pepper

1 teaspoon ground ginger
¹/2 teaspoon five-spice

Put all of the ingredients in a bowl and mix together well.

MAKES 2 TABLESPOONS

CHẢ CÁ SÀI-GÒN
southern vietnamese fish cakes

500 g (1 lb 2 oz) Spanish mackerel,
   taylor fillet or red fish fillet
2 spring onions (scallions), white part
   only, finely sliced
1/4 teaspoon salt

1/2 teaspoon fine white pepper
1 garlic clove, crushed
3 tablespoons fish sauce
1/4 bunch dill, chopped
vegetable oil, for deep-frying

Blend the fish, spring onion, salt, pepper and garlic in a food processor until it forms a smooth paste. Scrape the fish paste out into a mortar, dip the pestle into the fish sauce, then pound the fish. Keep dipping the pestle into the fish sauce, then continue pounding and dipping until you have used all of the fish sauce and the fish doesn't stick to the pestle. When the fish no longer sticks, you have achieved the right texture for the fish cakes. Place the fish paste into a bowl and, using wet hands, fold the dill through the mixture. This process takes a while and gives your arm quite a workout, but the result is worth it. Alternatively, you can add the fish sauce to the food processor with the fish and then add the dill at the last minute and pulse it through the mixture.

Form the fish paste into 5 x 2 cm (2 x 3/4 in) patties and fry in oil over medium heat for 3–5 minutes, or until golden. Serve wrapped in lettuce, with Vietnamese herbs and vermicelli, with dipping fish sauce (page 33) to dip, or serve in a salad of snake (yard-long) beans and Vietnamese herbs.

SERVES 6

FURTHER READING

Australian Bureau of Statistics Census 1991

Patricia Blake, 'World: Safe Ashore at Last', *Time Magazine*, 19 January 1981

Rodney Birrell and Siew Ean Khoo, *The Second Generation in Australia: Educational and Occupational Characteristics*, Bureau of Immigration and Multicultural Research (BIMPR), Australian Government Publishing Service (AGPS), Canberra, 1995

William Branigin, 'Australia Questions Open Door Policy to Asiatic Migrants', *Guardian Weekly*, 11 April 1993

Guy Burgess and Heidi Burgess, 'Trauma Healing': *Beyond Intractability*, Conflict Research Consortium, University of Colorado, Boulder, Posted: January 2004 <http://www.beyondintractability. org/essay/trauma_healing/>

Bernard Cohen, 'Asian Immigration Reawakens Old Anxieties', *Refugees — From the Media: Liberation*, August 1985

Jock Collins, 'John Chinaman and John Newman: Challenging Asian stereotyping', *Advising Quarterly*, Summer 1994

Mary Cook, *Protection or Punishment: The Detention of Asylum Seekers in Australia*, Federation Press, 1994

James Coughlan and Deborah McNamara, *Asians in Australia: Patterns of Migration and Settlement*, Macmillan, Melbourne, 1997

Mark Day, 'Being a Tourist in Your Own City', *Telegraph Mirror*, 2 March 1993, quoting a speech by John Newman

Amber De Nandi and Thang Luong, 'Down But Not Out in Wounded Cabramatta', *Champion*, 21 September 1994

Stan Denham, 'Cabramatta East Moves West: Asian Refugees Find New Life and Hope', *Sunday Telegraph*, 27 November 1983

Emily Dunn, 'Vibrant Community Beats its Gang Rap', *Sydney Morning Herald*, 7–8 October 2006

Mason Florence and Robert Storey, *Vietnam Lonely Planet*, 6 ed, Lonely Planet, Melbourne, 2001

Kong Foong Ling, *The Food of Asia — Fabulous Recipes from Every Corner of Asia*, Periplus, Hong Kong, 2002

Vance George, Fairfield: *A History of the District*, 2 ed, Fairfield City Council, Fairfield, 1991

Philip Grenard, 'Australia's Little Indo: China Immigration', *Bulletin*, 17 February 1981

I ♥ Pho: Casula Powerhouse Arts Centre Project Curator: Cuong Phu Le Artist: Mai Long

Gavin W Jones, 'Australian Identity: Racism and Recent Responses to Immigration in Australia', *Working Papers in Demography*, no. 71, 1997

Stanley Karnow, *Vietnam: A History*, Penguin Books, London, 1997

Frances Letters, *The Surprising Asians: A Hitch-hike Through Malaya, Thailand, Laos, Cambodia and South Vietnam*, Angus and Robertson, Sydney, 1968

David Lo & Sylvie Huynh, *Cabramatta: The New Image*, Fairfield Community Arts Network & Young Christian Workers, Fairfield, 1994

Pyong Gap Min and Rose Kim, 'Formation of Ethnic and Racial Identities: Narratives by Young Asian-American

Professionals', *Ethnic and Racial Studies*, Routledge, vol. 23, no. 4, 1 July 2000, pp 735–760

Mike Morris, 'Shopping Centre is a Rival for Sydney's Dixon St, *Champion*, 31 July 1985

Lance Morrow: 'Viet Nam, A Bloody Rite of Passage: Viet Nam Cost America its Innocence and Still Haunts its Conscience', *Time Magazine*, 15 April 1985

Damian Murphy, 'The Mighty Migrants: Vietnam's Gift to Australia — Refugees', *Bulletin*, 30 April 1996

Anne Musgrave, 'Getting to Know the Women of Vietnam: Extending the Hand of Friendship', *ITA*, June 1990

Duy Long Nguyen and James Knight, *The Dragon's Journey*, HarperCollins, Pymble, 2004

Laurie Anne Pearlman PhD and Ervin Staub PhD, *Creating Paths to Healing*, Trauma, Research, Education, and Training Institute, Inc. <http://www.heal-reconcile-rwanda.org/lec_path.htm>

Karen Pyke, '"The Normal American Family" as an Interpretive Structure of Family Life Among Grown Children of Korean and Vietnamese Immigrants', *Journal of Marriage and Family*, vol. 62, February 2000, p 240

Sogyal Rinpoche, *The Tibetan Book of Living and Dying*, Harper, San Fransisco, 1992

Nina Simonds, *A Spoonful of Ginger: Irresistible, Health Giving Recipes from Asian Kitchens*, Alfred A. Knopf, New York, 1999

Jill Smolowe, 'After the Euphoria, a Letdown for Troops Returning from the Gulf and for Their Loved Ones Battles Loom in Resuming Normal Family Life', *Time Magazine*, 25 March 1991

Charmaine Solomon, *Charmaine Solomon's Encyclopedia of Asian Food*, William Heinemann, Port Melbourne, 1996

Alison Soltau, 'Tourism Hit After Newman's Death', *Advance*, 16 May 1995

K Sri Dhammananda Message, *Vietnamese Buddhist Phuoc Hue Monastery Publication*, no. 33, May 2006

Kylie Steven, 'Locals Tell the Real Cabramatta Story', *Advance*, 20 March 2002

Phillip Taylor, *Fragments of the Present: Searching for Modernity in Vietnam's South*, Allen & Unwin, Crows Nest, 2001

Corinne Trang, *Essentials of Asian Cuisine: Fundamentals and Favourite Recipes*, Simon & Schuster, New York, 2003

Nancy Viviani, *The Indochinese in Australia 1975 to 1995: From Burnt Boats to Barbecues*, Oxford University Press, Melbourne, 1996

Alan Watt, *Vietnam: An Australian Analysis*, F.W Cheshire Publishing, Melbourne, 1968

Peter White, 'How Prosperity Saved Little Asia', *Sydney Morning Herald*, 16 August 1996

Paul A Witteman: 'Vietnam: 15 Years Later Guilt and Recrimination Still Shroud America's Perceptions of the Only War it Ever Lost', *Time Magazine*, 30 April 1990

Paul A. Witteman, 'Captain Cook, Lost in America: For Vietnam Vets Hunkered Down in the Jungles of Hawaii, the War Never Came to an End', *Time Magazine*, 11 February 1991

Published in 2007 by Murdoch Books Pty Limited

Murdoch Books Australia
Pier 8/9, 23 Hickson Road,
Millers Point NSW 2000
Phone: +61 (0) 2 8220 2000
Fax: +61 (0) 2 8220 2558
www.murdochbooks.com.au

Murdoch Books UK Limited
Erico House, 6th Floor,
93–99 Upper Richmond Road
Putney, London SW15 2TG
Phone: + 44 (0) 20 8785 5995
Fax: + 44 (0) 20 8785 5985
www.murdochbooks.co.uk

National Library of Australia Cataloguing-in-Publication Data

Nguyen, Pauline.
Secrets of the Red Lantern : stories and Vietnamese recipes from the heart.

Includes index.
ISBN 978 1 74045 904 4 (hbk.).

1. Nguyen family. 2. Red Lantern (Restaurant).
3. Ethnic restaurants - New South Wales - Surry Hills. 4. Cookery, Vietnamese - Social aspects.
5. Food - Social aspects. 6. Vietnamese - Australia - Economics conditions. 7. Vietnamese - Australia - Social life and customs.
I. Nguyen, Luke. II. Jensen, Mark, 1967- . III. Title.

647.9594

Printed by 1010 Printing International Limited.
PRINTED IN CHINA.

Chief Executive: Juliet Rogers
Publishing Director: Kay Scarlett

Editor: Paul McNally
Concept and design: Sarah Odgers
Food photographer: Alan Benson
Background pattern, floral pattern and photograph page 82: Melanie Ngapo
Stylist: Michelle Noerianto
Food preparation: Andrew de Sousa
Production: Maiya Levitch
Vietnamese translation and typesetting: All Language Typesetters and Printers Pty Ltd
Colour reproduction: Splitting Image Colour Studio, Melbourne, Australia

IMPORTANT
Those who might be at risk from the effects of salmonella poisoning (the elderly, pregnant women, young children and those suffering from immune deficiency diseases) should consult their doctor with any concerns about eating raw eggs.

CONVERSION GUIDE
You may find cooking times vary depending on the oven you are using. For fan-forced ovens, as a general rule, set the oven temperature to 20°C (35°F) lower than indicated in the recipe. We have used 20 ml (4 teaspoon) tablespoon measures. If you are using a 15 ml (3 teaspoon) tablespoon, for most recipes the difference will not be noticeable. However, for recipes using baking powder, gelatine, bicarbonate of soda (baking soda), small amounts of flour and cornflour (cornstarch), add an extra teaspoon for each tablespoon specified.

ACKNOWLEDGEMENTS
Cambodia House for Asian ceramics, furniture and artefacts; Orient House for antique asian furniture and artefacts; The Ceramic Shed for original handmade ceramics; Major & Tom — for antique finds; all other items were secondhand finds